THE HISTORY OF AL-ṬABARĪ

AN ANNOTATED TRANSLATION

VOLUME XXXVII

The ʿAbbāsid Recovery

THE WAR AGAINST THE ZANJ ENDS

A.D. 879–893/A.H. 266–279

The History of al-Ṭabarī

Editorial Board

Ihsan Abbas, University of Jordan, Amman

C. E. Bosworth, The University of Manchester

Jacob Lassner, Wayne State University, Detroit

Franz Rosenthal, Yale University

Ehsan Yar-Shater, Columbia University (*General Editor*)

SUNY

SERIES IN NEAR EASTERN STUDIES

Said Amir Arjomand, Editor

Bibliotheca Persica
Edited by Ehsan Yar-Shater

The History of al-Ṭabarī

(Ta'rīkh al-rusul wa'l-mulūk)

VOLUME XXXVII

The ʿAbbāsid Recovery

translated by

Philip M. Fields

annotated by

Jacob Lassner

State University of New York Press

The preparation of this volume was made possible by a grant from the Program for Research Tools and Reference Works of the National Endowment for the Humanities, an independent federal agency; and in part by the Persian Heritage Foundation.

Published by
State University of New York Press, Albany

Printed in the United States of America

For information, address State University of New York Press, State University Plaza, Albany, N.Y. 12246

Library of Congress Cataloging in Publication Data

Ṭabarī, 823?–923.
The war against the Zanj ends.

(SUNY series in Near Eastern studies) (The History of Al-Tabari; v. 27)
Bibliography: p.
1. Islamic Empire—History—750–1258. 2. Iraq—History—634–1534. 3. Slaves—Iraq—Early works to 1800. I. Fields, Phillip. II. Title. III. Series.
IV. Series: Ṭabarī, 838?–923. Tārīkh al-rusul wa-al-mulūk. English; v. 27.
DS38.6.T38 1985 909'.097671 84—16312
ISBN 0–88706–054–4
ISBN 0–88706–053–6 (pbk.)

10 9 8 7 6 5 4 3 2 1

Acknowledgement

In 1971 the General Editor proposed to the UNESCO to include a translation of al-Ṭabarī's *History* in its Collection of Representative Works. UNESCO agreed, but the Commission in charge of Arabic works favored other priorities. Deeming the project worthy, the Iranian Institute of Translation and Publication, which collaborated with UNESCO, agreed to undertake the task. After the upheavals of 1979, assistance was sought from the National Endowment for the Humanities. The invaluable encouragement and support of the Endowment is here gratefully acknowledged.

The General Editor wishes to thank sincerely also the participating scholars, who have made the realization of this project possible; the Board of Editors for their selfless assistance; Professor Franz Rosenthal for his many helpful suggestions in the formulation and application of the editorial policy; Professor Jacob Lassner for his painstaking and meticulous editing; and Dr. Susan Mango of the National Endowment for the Humanities for her genuine interest in the project and her advocacy of it.

Preface

THE HISTORY OF PROPHETS AND KINGS (*Ta'rīkh al-rusul wa'l-mulūk*) by Ab Ja^{c}far Muhammad b. Jarr al-Ṭabarī (839-923), here rendered as the *History of al-Ṭabarī,* is by common consent the most important universal history produced in the world of Islam. It has been translated here in its entirety for the first time for the benefit of non-Arabists, with historical and philological notes for those interested in the particulars of the text.

Ṭabarī's monumental work explores the history of the ancient nations, with special emphasis on biblical peoples and prophets, the legendary and factual history of ancient Iran, and, in great detail, the rise of Islam, the life of the Prophet Muhammad, and the history of the Islamic world down to the year 915. The first volume of this translation will contain a biography of al-Ṭabarī and a discussion of the method, scope, and value of his work. It will also provide information on some of the technical considerations that have guided the work of the translators.

The *History* has been divided here into 38 volumes, each of which covers about two hundred pages of the original Arabic text in the Leiden edition. An attempt has been made to draw the dividing lines between the individual volumes in such a way that each is to some degree independent and can be read as such. The page numbers of the original in the Leiden edition appear on the margins of the translated volumes.

Al-Ṭabarī very often quotes his sources verbatim and traces the chain of transmission (*isnād*) to an original source. The chains of transmitters are, for the sake of brevity, rendered by only a dash (—) between the individual links in the chain. Thus, according to Ibn Ḥumayd—Salamah—Ibn Isḥāq means that al-Ṭabarī received the report from Ibn Ḥumayd who said that he was told by Salamah, who said that he was told by Ibn Isḥāq, and so on. The numerous subtle and important differences in the original Arabic wording have been disregarded.

The table of contents at the beginning of each volume gives a brief survey of the topics dealt with in that particular volume. It also includes the headings and subheadings as they appear in al-Ṭabarī's text, as well as those occasionally introduced by the translator.

Well-known place-names, such as, for instance, Mecca, Baghdad, Jerusalem, Damascus, and the Yemen, are given in their English spellings. Less common place-names, which are the vast majority, are transliterated. Biblical figures appear in the accepted English spelling, Iranian names are usually transcribed according to their Arabic forms, and the presumed Iranian forms are often discussed in the footnotes.

Technical terms have been translated wherever possible, but some, such as dirham and imām, have been retained in Arabic forms. Others that cannot be translated with sufficient precision have been retained and italicized as well as footnoted.

The annotation aims chiefly at clarifying difficult passages, identifying individuals and place-names, and discussing textual difficulties. Much leeway has been left to the translators to include in the footnotes whatever they consider necessary and helpful.

The bibliographies list all the sources mentioned in the annotation.

The index in each volume contains all the names of persons and places referred to in the text, as well as those mentioned in the notes as far as they refer to the medieval period. It does not include the names of modern scholars. A general index, it is hoped, will appear after all the volumes have been published.

Ehsan Yar-Shater

Contents

Acknowledgements / v
Preface / vii
Translator's Foreword / xiii

The Events of the Year 266 (879/880) / 1

Provincial Appointments / 1
The Cause of the Hostilities between Jaʿfarids and ʿAlids at al-Madīnah / 6
Why the Zanj Journied to Rāmhurmuz / 8
The Battle between the Zanj and the Kurds / 9

The Events of the Year 267 (880/881) / 12

The Victory of Abū al-ʿAbbās and His Activity against the Zanj in This Area / 13
The Strategy of the Zanj / 16
The Battle for Sūq al-Khāmis / 20
How Abū Aḥmad and His Troops Occupied Ṭahīthā and How al-Jubbāʾī Was Killed / 30
Siege of the Profligate's Camp / 43
The Reason for the Requests of Safe Conduct / 51
The Zanj Attack / 51
The Reason for This Engagement / 54
The Reason Why al-Muwaffaq Crossed over to the Profligate / 57

The Events of the Year 268 (881/882) / 65

The Battle against the Tribesmen / 68
How Bahbūdh Was Slain / 75

The Events of the Year 269 (882/883) / 80

Abū Aḥmad Enters the Profligate's City / 86
How Abū Aḥmad's Troops Plundered the City / 91
How Nuṣayr Drowned / 96
The Reason for the Battle between Abū Aḥmad and the Zanj and What Transpired / 98
The Rebel's Situation and That of His Men When He Transferred from the West / 101
How Abū Aḥmad Came to Succeed in the Battle for the Abū Khāṣīb Canal / 107
The Account of This Battle / 118

The Events of the Year 270 (883/884) / 128

The Two Battles / 128
The Profligate Flees / 131
The Death of the Abominable / 139

The Events of the Year 271 (884/885) / 146

Pilgrims from Khurāsān at Baghdad / 147
The Battle Between Abū Aḥmad and Khumarawayh / 148

The Events of the Year 272 (885/886) / 149

Abū al-ʿAbbās Ousted from Ṭarsūs / 149
An Escape from the Maṭbaq Prison / 150
High Prices Cause Riots in Baghdad / 151

The Events of the Year 273 (886/887) / 153

Ibn Abī Dulaf Battles the Ṣaffārid / 153
Ibn Kundāj Routed / 154

The Events of the Year 274 (887/888) / 155

Abū Aḥmad Goes to Kirmān / 155

The Events of the Year 275 (888/889) / 156

A Military Force is Sent to Sāmarrā / 156
The Brigand al-ʿAbdī at Sāmarrā / 157
Abū Aḥmad Imprisons al-Ṭāʾī / 157

The Events of the Year 276 (889/890) / 159

ʾAmr b. al-Layth Encharged with Baghdad's Security / 159
A Burial Place Discovered / 160

The Events of the Year 277 (890/891) / 162

Yāzamān Calls for Allegiance to Khumarawayh / 162
Fighting in Baghdad / 162
An Appointment to the Court of Appeals (*maẓālim*) / 163

The Events of the Year 278 (891/892) / 164

A Three-Sided Battle / 164
Abū Aḥmad Returns from al-Jabal / 165
The Origins of the Qarmaṭians / 169

The Events of the Year 279 (892/893) / 176

Controversial Books Banned / 176
Al-Mufawwaḍ Stripped of His Right to Rule / 176
Battle between Muḥammad b. Mūsā and Maknūn in Ṭarsūs / 177

Bibliography of Cited Works / 179
Index / 183

Translator's Foreword

This work comprises the second part of the reign of the caliph al-Muʿtamid (r. 256–79/870–92). It centers on the struggle against the Zanj revolt which had been ravaging the south of Iraq since 255/868. The revolt was fomented by black slaves working in the saline areas of lower Mesopotamia to remove the salt sands and brine (*sibākh*) and open the area up to cultivation. The slaves were led by one ʿAlī b. Muḥammad, who is termed al-Khabīth (the Abominable), al-Khā'in (the Traitor), and "enemy of God" in the chronicles. After the Zanj pillaged and looted Baṣra, Ahwāz, Ubullah, Wāṣiṭ, and disrupted the economies of the approaches to the capital, Muʿtamid summoned his brother al-Muwaffaq from Mecca to conduct the campaign against the rebellion. With various signs of discontent and secessionist sentiment growing in the area, al-Muwaffaq's mission was an important one indeed; the preservation of the caliphate was at stake.

The battle between the Zanj rebels and the forces of the caliph was fought on a riverain area below Baṣra composed of mud flats, rivers, canals, and swamps many of which are no longer in evidence. The terrain was affected by the ebb and flow of sea water and mud. Al-Muwaffaq, assisted by his son (who later became the caliph al-Muʿtaḍid), studied the terrain carefully and applied a policy aimed at dividing the rebel forces. He offered generous conditions to those who agreed to give up the rebellion: such concessions as amnesty, safe conduct, security, robes of honor, stipends, and integration into caliphal government forces and operations. These offers were advertised, and those who accepted them were paraded before the remaining enemy forces. The Abominable was even approached but the message remained unanswered. Both sides demonstrated great valor and ingenuity in the river battles in erecting and destroying earthen dams, bridges, and walls among the canals and on the adjacent land.

The Zanj had their own strongholds and villages, e.g., al-Manīʿah (the Impregnable), Manṣūrah, Mukhtārah, Zanj headquarters, and, during the course of their operations, the forces of the caliph established their own city al-Muwaffaqiyah. al-Muwaffaq's forces blocked sea approaches to the rebel towns. When government peace offers failed to dislodge the rebels, the struggle became more brutal as heads and limbs were paraded before the enemy. The Abominable's vizier was bent on surrender, but he failed to convince his master of the inevitability of their end.

The final assault on the rebels was signaled by a black banner and a trumpet. Al-Muqaffaq besieged Mukhtārah which fell in 269/882. The final battles featured chemical warfare (naphtha) that ignited fires in the enemy's wooden structures, bridges, and ships. Reputedly fifty thousand imperial troops with 400 vessels opposed forces six times as numerous (these figures may be subject to the customary exaggeration). After the brutal suppression of the revolt, much was made of the propaganda value of the thousands of women prisoners (among them ʿAlid matrons) who were liberated by caliphal forces, which included both blacks and whites, Turks, Khazars, Greeks, and peoples from northern Iran (Daylam and Ṭabaristān) and from Africa. The struggle between al-Muwaffaq and the Abominable became the subject of many poems that Ṭabarī has recorded in this volume. One aftermath of the struggle that demonstrates just how sensitive the government was to any remaining pro-Zanj sentiment among the populace was that imprisoned Zanj leaders in Wāsiṭ paid with their lives, when serenading of a political nature was heard.

In this volume, the general trends and currents in ʿAbbāsid history, midway in its course, are seen. The caliph lived at Samarrā, which had served as the capital for half a century (since 224/838), while the imperial governmental machine was split between Samarrā and Baghdad. Both, however, evinced an atmosphere redolent of endless intrigues, plots, and secessions.

The eastern empire in Iran was shaken by local dynasts (the Ṭahirids and Ṣaffarids); in the west, Syria and Egypt were ever more bent on self-rule (under Ibn Ṭūlūn and his son Khumārahayh). Frictions among officials and petty revolts instigated by tribes and pretenders were also rife. These kept officials in the central administration very busy. Ṭabarī specifically mentions that Ibn Ṭūlūn formed a plot to abduct the caliph and bring him to Egypt (273/886). Signs of unrest were also evidenced by the caliph's public cursing of the various disturbers of law and order.

In Mecca, clashes and bloodshed occurred when supporters of the sundry factions converged during pilgrimage season. In other cities, revolts broke out and mobs attacked monasteries. A kind of censorship on preachers and booksellers was implemented to prevent provocative theological debates and fermentation in Baghdad.

Ṭabarī also chronicles the corruption that characterized the mid-ʿAbbāsid period. With all the demands made on it by corrupt officials and the needs of the military, the treasury was often empty. To remedy the poor fiscal situation, the government would often levy punitive taxes on grandees.

This volume also foreshadows events to come by tracing the origins of the powerful Ismāʿīlī movement. Regrettably, Ṭabarī does not offer data about the aspirations, plans, and ideology of the rebellion.

The Events of the Year

266

(August, 23, 879–August 11, 880)

In Ṣafar (September 22–October 20, 879), ʿAmr b. al-Layth appointed ʿUbaydallāh b.ʿAbdallāh b. Ṭāhir as his deputy in charge of security (*shurṭah*) at Baghdad and Sāmarrā, and invested him with robes of honor. ʿUbaydallāh b. ʿAbdallāh then returned to his residence, where ʿAmr b. al-Layth invested him with robes of honor and had a bar of gold consigned to him.

In Ṣafar, (September 22–October 20, 879), Asātakīn seized al-Rayy and ousted Ṭalmajūr the governor of the city. Then he and his son Adhkūtakīn went to Qazwīn, whose governor was Abrūn, the brother of Kayghalagh. After negotiating peace with Abrūn, the two entered the city, seized Muḥammad b. al-Faḍl b. Sinān al-ʿIjlī, his clients and his estates. Asātakīn killed him and then returned to al-Rayy. Its inhabitants fought against him, but he overcame them and entered the city.

A detachment of Byzantines arrived in the Tall Basmā of [1937]
Diyār Rabīʿah,[1] killing or capturing about two hundred fifty

1. Not to be confused with the place of that name situated in the region of Shabakhtān. See Yāqūt, *Muʿjam*, I, 864.

Muslims. The people of Naṣībīn[2] and Mosul fled, and the Byzantines withdrew.

In Rabiʿ II (July 4–August 2, 879), while in Jundīsābūr, on his way back to Baghdad from the camp of ʿAmr b. al-Layth, Abū al-Sāj died. Sulaymān b. ʿAbdallāh b. Ṭāhir[3] died before him in the month of al-Muḥarram (August 23–September 21, 879).

ʿAmr b. al-Layth appointed Aḥmad b. ʿAbd al-ʿAzīz b. Abī Dulaf governor of Iṣbahān. Muḥammad, the son of Abū al-Sāj, was appointed governor of the Ḥaramayn[4] and the road to Mecca.

Aghartmish was appointed governor for the districts of al-Ahwāz which had been under Takīn al-Bukhārī. He arrived there in the month of Ramaḍān (April 15–May 14, 880).

Muḥammad b. al-Ḥasan reported that Masrūr ordered Aghartmish, Abbā and Maṭar b. Jāmiʿ to fight ʿAlī b. Abān. They marched until they reached Tustar, where they halted and seized those men who had been in Takīn's prison, among them Jaʿfarawayh and a group of followers of the leader of the Zanj. All of them were killed; it was Maṭar b. Jāmiʿ who was responsible. They marched on and arrived in ʿAskar Mukram.[5]

Meanwhile, ʿAlī b. Abān set out against them sending forward his brother al-Khalīl with the vanguard of his troops. Al-Khalīl moved forward and occupied positions in front of them, while ʿAlī followed. As the Zanj outnumbered the government forces, the latter cut the pontoon bridge (from its moorings) and abstained from fighting. In the dark of night, ʿAlī b. Abān and his troops withdrew to al-Ahwāz, and al-Khalīl with his men remained in Masruqān. News now reached al-Khalīl that Aghartmish, Abbā and Maṭar b. Jāmiʿ were approaching and had landed on the eastern side of the Arbuk Bridge (*qanṭarah*),[6]

---

2. See Le Strange, *Lands*, 95.

3. He had been governor of Ṭabaristān and deputy of Muḥammad b. Ṭāhir in the reign of al-Mustaʿīn. In 255 (868-869) he was appointed chief of police of Baghdad and the surrounding areas. See Ṭabarī, III/3, 1524, 1706.

4. That is the two holy cities Mecca and al-Madīnah. See *EI*², s.v. al-Ḥaramayn.

5. ʿAskar Mukram was on the route from Baghdad to Tustar. See Le Strange, *Lands*, 246, 247, and index, 494.

6. This was a vaulted structure built of either brick or stone. See Yāqūt, *Muʿjam*, IV, 187.

intending to cross over and reach him. Al-Khalīl reported this [1938] to his brother ʿAlī b. Abān, whereupon ʿAlī set out for them and encountered them at the bridge. He then sent an order for al-Khalīl to come and join him. This he did. Those of ʿAlī's troops who were left in al-Ahwāz became terror-stricken and dismantled his camp, retreating to Nahr al-Sidrah.[7] The battle between ʿAlī and the government commanders took place with the government forces carrying the day. The latter abstained from further fighting, and ʿAlī returned to al-Ahwāz where, however, he found none of his men. Having discovered that they had reached Nahr al-Sidrah in good order he sent someone to retrieve them, but, since this was difficult, ʿAlī himself followed them and remained in Nahr al-Sidrah. The government forces then stationed themselves at ʿAskar Mukram.

ʿAlī b. Abān made preparations to resume fighting and summoned Bahbūdh b. ʿAbd al-Wahhāb who arrived with his troops. When Aghartmish and his men heard about the forces ʿAlī was bringing to bear against him, he and his army took the field against ʿAlī. The latter put his brother, al-Khalīl b. Abān, in command of his vanguard and assigned to him Bahbūdh and Aḥmad b. al-Zaranjī. The two parties came upon each other at Dawlāb,[8] whereupon, ʿAlī instructed al-Khalīl b. Abān to position Bahbūdh in ambush. Al-Khalīl marched until he engaged the enemy, and the battle flared between them. During the early part of the day the government forces were successful, but while manoeuvering on the battlefield they were attacked by the ambushers. The Zanj humbled the government forces, causing them to flee and Maṭar b. Jāmiʿ was taken prisoner; having fallen from his horse, he was seized by Bahbūdh and brought to ʿAlī. Sīmā, known as Ṣaghrāj, was killed with a group of officers. When brought before ʿAlī by Bahbūdh, Maṭar begged him to spare his life, but ʿAlī refused saying, "Had you spared the life of Jaʿfarawayh, I would indeed spare yours." Then he ordered that Maṭar be brought near him, and he beheaded him with his own hand. ʿAlī b. Abān now entered al- [1939]

7. See Le Strange, *Lands*, 237.

8. Presumably the waterwheel (*dawlab*) of al-Ahwāz. See Yāqūt, *Muʿjam*, II, 622.

Ahwāz, and Aghartmish and Abbā retreated with those men who had escaped with them until they reached Tustar. ʿAlī sent the heads (of the enemy) to the abominable one (that is, the leader of the Zanj) who ordered them displayed on the walls of his city.

Muḥammad b. al-Hasan reported: ʿAlī b Abān used to attack Aghartmish and his forces with mixed success. Then the abominable one sent most of his contingents to the assistance of ʿAlī b. Abān. As a result, the Zanj outnumbered the troops of Aghartmish, who was now forced to reconcile his differences with the enemy. Since ʿAlī b. Abān also wished for the same, they concluded a truce. ʿAlī b. Abān now started to attack the surrounding areas. One of his attacks brought him to the village known as Bayrūdh,[9] which he subdued, taking much booty. He wrote to al-Khabīth accounting for his actions, sent him the booty which he had acquired, and established himself in Bayrūdh.

In this year, Isḥāq b. Kundājīq deserted the camp of Aḥmad b. Mūsā b. Bughā because the latter, arriving in the Jazīrah, had appointed Mūsā b. Utāmish governor of Diyār Rabīʿah. This displeased Isḥāq b. Kundājīq, who left his camp and went to Balad,[10] where he attacked the Jacobite Kurds.[11] He routed them and seized their property and, as a result, greatly increased his strength. Thereupon he encountered the son of Musāwir al-Shārī and killed him.

In Shawwāl (May 15–June 12, 880), the people of Homs killed their governor ʿIsā al-Karkhī.[12]

In this year, Lu'lu', the page (*ghulām*) of Aḥmad b. Ṭūlūn, took Mūsā b. Utāmish prisoner. The former was staying in the hill country of the Banū Tamīm, while Mūsā b. Utāmish was at Ra's al-ʿAyn.[13] One night, while intoxicated, Mūsā set out to

9. Bayrūdh was situated between al-Ahwāz and al-Ṭīb. See Yāqūt, *Muʿjam*, I, 786.

10. Balad was a large settlement situated where the old Persian town Shahrābādh had been located. See Le Strange, *Lands*, 99, 125.

11. See Ṭabarī III/3, 1859.

12. So named because he had been governor of Karkh Sāmarrā during the reign of al-Muhtadī. See Ṭabarī, III/3, 1797.

13. A walled town famous for its gardens and parks on the banks of the Khabūr, a tributary of the Euphrates. See Le Strange, *Lands*, 95 ff.

attack Lu'lu''s forces by surprise, but they were lying in ambush. They captured him and delivered him to al-Raqqah. [1940]

In Shawwāl, Lu'lu' encountered Aḥmad b. Mūsā with his commander and their tribal levies. Lu'lu' was routed, and a great many of his troops were killed. Ibn Ṣafwān al-ʿUqaylī[14] and the tribesmen made for Aḥmad b. Mūsā's camp to loot the baggage, but Lu'lu''s troops returned to humble them in battle. Those who escaped the rout reached Qarqīsiyyā, and subsequently, in Dhū al-Qaʿdah (June 3-July 2, 880), they reached Baghdad and Sāmarrā. Ibn Ṣafwān fled into the desert.

In Shawwāl a battle took place between Aḥmad b. ʿAbd al-ʿAzīz b. Abī Dulaf and Buktimur. Aḥmad b. ʿAbd al-ʿAzīz routed Buktimur and the latter went to Baghdad.

Al-Khujustānī attacked al-Ḥasan b. Zayd in Jurjān, taking him by surprise. Al-Ḥasan fled, reaching Āmul, while al-Khujustānī seized Jurjān and some of the districts of Ṭabaristān. This took place in Jumādā II and Rajab 266 (January 18–March 16, 880).

Al-Ḥasan b. Muḥammad b. Jaʿfar b. ʿAbdallāh b. Ḥasan al-Aṣghar al-ʿUqayqī[15] summoned the people of Ṭabaristān to pledge allegiance to him because al-Ḥasan b. Zayd, before departing to Jurjān, had left him as his deputy in Sāriyyah.[16] After al-Khujustānī's attack on al-Ḥasan in Jurjān, and the flight of al-Ḥasan from there, al-ʿUqayqī announced in Sāriyyah that al-Ḥasan had been captured, and he called upon his followers to give their allegiance to him. Some people subsequently took the oath of allegiance to him; however, al-Ḥasan b. Zayd returned and fought against him. Then al-Ḥasan employed a ruse which allowed him to overpower al-ʿUqayqī, whom he then killed. Al-Khujustānī looted the property of the merchants of [1941] Jurjān and set fire to the city.

A battle between al-Khujustānī and ʿAmr b. al-Layth took place. The former gained the upper hand and routed ʿAmr. En-

---

14. Al-ʿUqaylī was Abū Aḥmad's governor of Qarqīsiyyā. His father, who had been governor of Diyār Muḍar, died in prison at Sāmarrā in 253 (867-868). See Ṭabarī above, 2029, 2149; Masʿūdī, *Muruj*, VII, 395 ff.

15. Ibn Kathīr, *Bidāyah*, XI, 39: al-ʿUqaylī.

16. See Le Strange, *Lands*, 370, 375.

tering Naysābūr, he ousted ʿAmr's governor and killed a number of those who had sympathized with ʿAmr.

In al-Madīnah and the surrounding areas hostilities broke out between Jaʿfarids and ʿAlīds.

The Cause of These Hostilities

According to reports, in this year Isḥāq b. Muḥammad b. Yūsuf al-Jaʿfarī was the guardian of al-Madīnah, and of the Wādī al-Qurā and surrounding areas.[17] He sent an agent (*ʿāmil*) to the Wādī al-Qurā, but the populace rebelled against the Jaʿfarid's agent, killing him along with two of Isḥāq's brothers. Isḥāq then went to the Wādī al-Qurā, but fell sick there and died. His brother Mūsā b. Muḥammad took over his office in al-Madīnah. Al-Ḥasan b. Mūsā b. Jaʿfar rebelled against him, but the latter was bought off with eight hundred dīnārs. Following this, Abū al-Qāsim Aḥmad b. Muḥammad b. Ismāʿīl b. al-Ḥasan b. Zayd, the son of the maternal uncle of al-Ḥasan b. Zayd, the governor of Ṭabaristān, staged a revolt. He killed Mūsā, gained control of al-Madīnah, and occupied the city.

At this time prices in the city rose steeply. Aḥmad b. Muḥammad went to the customs and lifted the duties on goods guaranteeing the merchants their money. Prices subsequently declined and the city became calm. The central authorties appointed the Ḥasanid governor of al-Madīnah until Ibn Abī al-Sāj arrived.

In this year, the tribesmen seized the carpet covering the Kaʿbah[18] and carried it off. Some of them went to the leader of the Zanj. This calamity shocked the pilgrims in the city.

[1942] In this year, the Byzantines invaded Diyār Rabīʿah. The population was summoned to take to the field, but they set out at a time when the cold weather made it impossible for them to enter the mountain passes.

In this year, Sīmā, Aḥmad b. Ṭūlūn's deputy, and three hundred men from Ṭarsūs raided the Syrian border region. In the

17. On his family connection with the government see Ṭabarī, III/3, 1358 ff.
18. See *EI*², s.v. al-Kiswah.

area of Hirqlah[19] they were met by the enemy—about four thousand men—and they fought a fierce battle. The Muslims inflicted heavy losses upon the enemy, but they themselves also sustained numerous casualties.

In this year, a battle took place between Isḥaq b. Kundājīq and Isḥāq b. Ayyūb.[20] Ibn Kundājīq defeated Isḥāq b. Ayyūb, forcing him to set up his defenses at Naṣībīn. The victor seized everything in Ibn Ayyūb's camp and killed a great many of his men. Pursuing Ibn Ayyūb, Isḥāq b. Kundājīq reached Naṣībīn and entered the city. The former fled and appealed for help to ʿIsā b. al-Shaykh, who was in Āmid,[21] and Abū al-Maghrā' b. Mūsā b. Zurārah, who was in Arzan.[22] They joined forces against Ibn Kundājīq, but then the central authorities sent Yūsuf b. Yaʿqūb to Ibn Kundājīq with the governor's insignias for Mosul, Diyār Rabīʿah and Armenia. Yūsuf bestowed the robes of honor on Ibn Kundājīq, whereupon the rebels sued for peace, paying him a sum of two hundred thousand dīnārs so that he might recognize their local authority.

In this year, Muḥammad b. Abī al-Sāj arrived in Mecca. Ibn al-Makhzūmī offered resistance, but Ibn Abī al-Sāj routed him and seized all his possessions on Tarwiyyah Day.[23]

In this year, Kayghalagh departed for al-Jabal, and Buktimur returned to Dīnawar.

In this year, the troops of the Zanj commander entered Rām-hurmuz.[24]

---

19. This city had been strongly fortified by Hārūn al-Rashīd, presumably because of his interest in a full-scale offensive against the Byzantines. It was turned into a station on the line uniting the border fortresses of the region. See Le Strange, *Lands*, 133, 136, 149.

20. For Ibn Ayyūb see Ṭabarī, III/4 2193.

21. See Le Strange, *Lands*, 108 ff.

22. For Abū al-Maghrā''s association with Ibn al-Shaykh, see Ṭabarī, III/3, 1685. Arzan was a fortified town near Āmid. See Le Strange, *Lands*, 112.

23. That is the eighth day of the pilgrimage. The day is so named because the pilgrims water their camels (*tarwiyyah*) this day, or because Abraham, who was to build the shrine, reflected (*rawwa*) on his dream of sacrificing Ishmael.

24. Three days journey east of al-Ahwāz. See Le Strange, *Lands*, 243, 247.

[1943] ## *Why the Zanj Journied to Rāmhurmuz*

We previously mentioned how Muḥammad b. ʿUbaydallāh al-Kurdī and ʿAlī b. Abān, the companion of the abominable one, agreed to the reconciliation. It has also been reported that, because of what happened, ʿAlī bore rancor in his heart against Muḥammad and was looking for a chance to wrong him. Muḥammad b. ʿUbaydallāh knew of this, and sought ways of evading him. He corresponded with the abominable one's son —the son known as Ankalāy—asking him to plead with his father to assign his, that is, Muḥammad b. ʿUbaydallāh's, district directly to him (Muḥammad) in order to remove ʿAlī's control over him. This request was granted, but it only increased ʿAlī's rage, and so he wrote to the abominable one, informing him that he was certain Muḥammad was plotting treachery. He requested permission to attack Muḥammad, and in order to create a pretext, he asked that the latter be ordered to deliver the tax revenues (*kharāj*) from his district to him (ʿAlī). This was granted and ʿAlī wrote to Muḥammad b. ʿUbaydallāh to transfer the money to him. The latter put off payment, delaying the execution of this order. ʿAlī therefore made preparations to engage him. He set out for him and attacked Rāmhurmuz where Muḥammad b. ʿUbaydallāh was stationed. As Muḥammad lacked the means of stopping ʿAlī, he fled. The latter thus entered Rāmhurmuz and ransacked the city, while Muḥammad b. ʿUbaydallāh clung to the most distant strongholds of Arbaq and al-Bīlam.[25] Extremely frightened by ʿAli's action, Muḥammad wrote to him asking for a reconciliation. ʿAlī in turn transmitted this request to the abominable one, and the latter instructed ʿAlī to accept the offer and to make sure that Mu-
[1944] ḥammad promptly delivered the money. Muḥammad b. ʿUbaydallāh delivered two hundred thousand dirhams to ʿAlī. The latter in turn, transferred the money to the abominable one and kept his distance from Muḥammad b. ʿUbaydallāh and from districts under the latter's jurisdiction.

In this year, a battle took place between the Kurds of al-

25. Arbaq was situated in the area of Rāmhurmūz. See Yāqūt, *Muʿjam*, I, 178. I have not succeeded in identifying Bīlam.

Dāribān and the Zanj of the abominable one. The Kurds were routed in this engagement.

The Battle Between the Zanj and the Kurds

After Muḥammad b. ʿUbaydallāh b. Azarmard surrendered the funds—the sum was previously reported—and after he had been left alone in the districts under his jurisdiction, he wrote to ʿAlī b. Abān asking for his assistance against a group of Kurds from a place called al-Dāribān. He suggested that the booty should go to ʿAlī and his troops.

ʿAlī wrote to the abominable one, asking permission to set out to do that. The latter replied, "Send al-Khalīl b. Abān and Bahbūdh b. ʿAbd al-Wahhāb, but you stay put. Don't dispatch your troops until you receive hostages from Muḥammad b. ʿUbaydallāh. The hostages will remain in your power and give you security against his treachery. You have irritated him, and he is not beyond seeking revenge."

In accordance with his instructions from the abdominable one, ʿAlī wrote to Muḥammad b. ʿUbaydallāh asking for hostages. Muḥammad b. ʿUbaydallāh gave him assurances and oaths, but evaded sending hostages. However, greed for the spoils which Muḥammad b. ʿUbaydallāh excited in him, induced ʿAlī to dispatch his troops alongside the former's forces. When the combined forces arrived at their destination, the lo- [1945] cal populace set out to fight and a battle ensued. At first the Zanj had the upper hand; but later the Kurds gallantly counterattacked, and the men of Muḥammad b. ʿUbaydallāh treacherously deserted the field and fled. The Zanj troops retreated in utter disorder.

Before that, Muḥammad b. ʿUbaydallāh had prepared a group who were specially instructed to intercept people in flight. This group interecepted and attacked those who had fled. They took spoils from them; they forced a contingent to dismount and took their horses. The men returned to ʿAlī in terrible condition.

Al-Muhallabī wrote to the abominable one about what had happened to his men, and the latter replied reproachfully, "I had instructed you not to rely on Muḥammad b. ʿUbaydallāh, but to have him send you hostages as a guarantee of cooperation. Now that you have disregarded my instructions and followed your own whim, you have brought ruin to yourself and your troops."

The abominable one also wrote to Muḥammad b. ʿUbaydallāh, "Your plot against the troops of ʿAlī b. Abān is no secret to me and the punishment you deserve will not fail to come." This message frightened Muḥammad b. ʿUbaydallāh, and he wrote the abominable one a letter filled with humility and submission. He also sent the horses which his men had taken from ʿAlī's troops during the flight, and (a message which) said, "With all my troops I went against those who attacked al-Khalīl and Bahbūdh. I threatened and intimidated them until I made them return these horses which I am sending to you."

The abominable one showed his anger, threatening Muḥammad in writing that he would throw a huge army against him. Again Muḥammad sent a letter of humility and self-effacement to him. He also sent a message to Bahbūdh guaranteeing him money; likewise he wrote to Muḥammad b. Yaḥyā al-Kirmānī, who at the time exerted the greatest influence
[1946] upon ʿAlī, and whose judgment was always accepted by him.

Bahbūdh, with the support of Muḥammad b. Yaḥyā al-Kirmānī, went to ʿAlī b. Abān to change his opinion in favor of Muḥammad b. ʿUbaydallāh. They softened the rage and rancor which he held in his heart. Then they went to the abominable one, reaching him just when he received the letter from Muḥammad b. ʿUbaydallāh. After lengthy discussions, he seemed to accept their view and thus agreed to reply favorably to Muḥammad b. ʿUbaydallāh. He said, "After all, that has happened, I am not going to accept less than a vow of allegiance to me in the sermons emanating from all the pulpits of the districts under his jurisdiction."

With this, Bahbūdh and al-Kirmānī left the abominable one and transmitted the result of their audience to Muḥammad b. ʿUbaydallāh. The latter answered that he would comply with every demand, but he acted evasively on the issue of vowing allegiance to the abominable one from the pulpits.

After all this, ʿAlī remained put for a time; then he prepared

to go against Mattūth[26] and marched there. He eagerly desired to take the city, but he could not do so because of its fortifications and the numerous defenders. Frustrated, he returned, assembled ladders and implements for scaling walls and, gathering his troops, he made himself ready. Masrūr al-Balkhī, who was then stationed in the districts of al-Ahwāz, knew that ʿAlī was going to Mattūth. When ʿAlī marched there for the second time, Masrūr also moved out and overtook him just near the city before sunset. When ʿAlī's men saw the advance units of Masrūr's cavalry, they fled in a most shameful manner, leaving all the implements which they had brought. Humiliated, ʿAlī retreated, suffering heavy losses. Soon the news followed that Abū Aḥmad was advancing. After his retreat from Mattūth, ʿAlī engaged in no more battles until Sūq al-Khamīs and Ṭahītā fell to Abū Aḥmad. Then, receiving a letter from the abom- [1947]
inable one which urgently summoned him, ʿAlī went to the latter's camp.

Leading the pilgrimmage this year was Hārūn b. Muḥammad b. Isḥāq b. Mūsā b. ʿIsā al-Hāshimī al-Kūfī.

---

26. A fortified place (*qalʿah ḥaṣīnah*) between al-Ahwāz and Wāsiṭ. See Yāqūt, *Muʿjam*, IV, 412–13.

The
Events of the Year
267
(August 12, 880–July 31, 881)

In this year, the government jailed Muḥammad b. Ṭāhir b. ʿAbdallāh and some members of his household. This occurred soon after Aḥmad b. ʿAbdallāh al-Khujustānī routed ʿAmr b. al-Layth. The latter had brought accusations against Muḥammad b. Ṭāhir. He accused him of corresponding with al-Khujustānī and al-Ḥusayn b. Ṭāhir. He also accused al-Ḥusayn and al-Khujustānī of using the pulpits of Khurāsān to exhort the populace to give allegiance to Muḥammad b. Tāhir.

In this year, Abū al-ʿAbbās b. al-Muwaffaq seized all the towns of the Tigris districts, among them ʿAbdasī[27] and others, which Sulaymān b. Jāmiʿ, companion of the commander of the Zanj, had conquered.

---

27. A town in the Kaskar district north of Wāsiṭ. See Le Strange, *Lands*, 43.

The Victory of Abū Al-ʿAbbās and His Activity Against the Zanj in This Area[28]

According to Muḥammad b. Al-Ḥasan—Muḥammad b. Ḥammād[29]: When news of how the Zanj entered Wāsiṭ and carried on (as reported above) reached Abū Aḥmad b. al-Mutawakkil, he urged his son Abū al-ʿAbbās, to proceed to the area and fight against them. Abū al-ʿAbbās did so promptly. At the [1948] time of Abū al-ʿAbbās's departure, Abū Aḥmad rode to Bustān Mūsā al-Hādī[30] to inspect the troops and their equipment. This was during Rabiʿ II 266 (November 20–December 18, 879). There were altogether ten thousand cavalry and infantry, all decked out in the most beautiful and elegant uniforms, and outfitted with the best equipment. They were provided with barges (*shadhdh*), galleys (*sumayriyyah*) and ferrys (*maʿābir*) for the infantry.[31] Everything was of the best construction.

Abū al-ʿAbbās left Bustān al-Hādī accompanied by Abū Aḥmad and travelled until he reached al-Firk.[32] Abū Aḥmad then departed and Abū al-ʿAbbās stayed on for several days to finish his preparations and to rally his troops. Following this, he departed for al-Madā'in, where he stayed for a time, and from there he went to Dayr al-ʿAqūl.[33]

Muḥammad b. Ḥammād reported: My brother Isḥāq b. Ḥammād and Ibrāhīm b. Muḥammad b. Ismāʿīl al-Hāshimī, who is known as Burayh, and Muḥammad b. Shuʿayb al-Ishtiyām and a large group of people who had accompanied Abū al-ʿAbbās in

28. For an analysis of this campaign see Popovic, *Révolte*, 123 ff.

29. A close companion of Abū Aḥmad and hence an eye witness to events. After the suppression of the Zanj revolt he was appointed over the judiciary of several districts. See Ṭabarī below, 2097.

30. Presumably the Bustān Mūsā at Baghdad. See Lassner, *Topography*, 295–96.

31. The designated translation for the various river vessels mentioned in the text is somewhat arbitrary. Any attempt to fix precise equivalents for the Arabic terms is hazardous. See Kindermann, *Schiff*, 42–43, 48, 54–55, 102.

32. A village near the Kalwādhā district of Baghdad. It may have been in the area subsequently known as al-Shammāsiyyah which served as a staging ground for troops. See Yāqūt, *Muʿjam*, III, 882; Lassner, *Topography*, index, 322.

33. See Yāqūt, *Muʿjam*, II, 676.

his march, told me what amounts to the following: Upon his arrival in Dayr al-ʿAqūl, Abū al-ʿAbbās received a letter from Nuṣayr Abū Ḥamzah, the commander of the barges and galleys—he had been sent ahead with the vanguard. The letter informed him that Sulaymān b. Jāmiʿ had already reached the island, in the vicinity of Bardūdā. He had with him calvalry, infantry, barges and galleys. Al-Jubbāʾī was in the vanguard. Moreover Sulaymān b. Mūsa al-Shaʿrānī had reached Nahr Abān with infantry, cavalry, and galleys. Abū al-ʿAbbās therefore departed for Jarjarāyā. From there he proceeded to Fam al-Ṣilḥ,[34] whence he travelled until he reached the canal. From there he sent out advance parties to gather information. They
[1949] brought him word that the enemy's armies were approaching, and that their advance units were in the Ṣilḥ, while their rearguard was in Bustān Mūsā b. Bughā, below Wāsiṭ.

When he digested this report, Abū al-ʿAbbās turned from the main routes and changed course. His troops came upon the enemy's advance units, feigned retreat and provoked the latter into a headlong pursuit. The enemy soldiers started shouting, "Look for a general to lead you in battle. Yours is busy with hunting." As soon as they came close to Abū al-ʿAbbās at the Ṣilḥ, he attacked them with horsemen and infantry. At his command, the call went out to Nuṣayr, "How long will you run from these dogs? Get them!" Then Nuṣayr turned to face them. Abū al-ʿAbbās, along with Muḥammad b. Shuʿayb al-Ishtiyām, boarded a galley, while the troops encircled the enemy from all directions and then inflicted a crushing defeat upon them. God put the enemy to flight before Abū al-ʿAbbās and his troops, and they killed and chased the Zanj until they reached the village ʿAbdallāh, which was some six *farsakhs*[35] (thirty-six km) from the place where the clash had started. They seized five barges and a number of galleys. Many of the enemy surrendered, others were taken prisoners, and the aforementioned ships were sunk. This was the first victory for Abū al-ʿAbbās, the son of Abū Aḥmad.

34. A town at the mouth of the Nahr al-Ṣilḥ above Wāsiṭ. See Le Strange, *Lands*, 38.

35. One *farsakh* = three Arabic *mīl*, or six kms.

After the battle was over that day, his officers and close associates, fearful of the proximity of the enemy, advised Abū al-ʿAbbās to set up his camp at the place which he had reached along the Ṣilḥ Canal, but he insisted on stopping in Wāsiṭ. After Sulaymān b. Jāmiʿ and his troops were routed—a rout in which God had struck them severely—Sulaymān b. Mūsā al-Sharʿrānī retreated from Nahr Abān to Sūq al-Khamīs, while Sulaymān b. Jāmiʿ went to Nahr al-Amīr.[36] Before they encountered Abū al-ʿAbbās, the enemy held, "This is an immature youngster without much experience and training in warfare. The right thing for us to do is to fall upon him with all our strength and try to eliminate him in the very first encounter. Then, perhaps, he will be so terrified that he will withdraw altogether." [1950]

This they did, they rallied all their troops and concentrated their efforts, but God smote them with His power and vengeance. The day after the battle, Abū al-ʿAbbās entered Wāsiṭ in splendid attire. This being Friday, he remained there to say Friday prayers, and a great many people put themselves under his protection. Then he marched on to al-ʿUmr,[37] one *farsakh* (six km) away, and established his camp there, saying, "I will establish my camp below Wāsiṭ so that those who are above the camp will be safe from the Zanj." It was Nuṣayr Abū Ḥamzah, and al-Shāh b. Mīkāl, who advised him to establish his position above Wāsiṭ, but he declined, saying, "I am only camping at al-ʿUmr. Both of you, go down to the mouth of the Bardūdā." Thus Abū al-ʿAbbās, shunning the counsel of his companions, and refusing to listen to any of their views, stopped at al-ʿUmr and started constructing barges.

Thereafter he began raiding the enemy incessantly. He assigned his special pages to galleys, placing two on each vessel. Sulaymān, as well, made ready and rallied his troops. He divided them into three columns: one coming from Nahr Abān,

---

36. The original name of this canal was Nahr Amīr al-Muʾminīn; that is, the Canal of the Commander of the Faithful. The reference is to the Caliph Abū Jaʿfar al-Manṣūr who had the canal dug in the area of al-Baṣrah. See Yāqūt, *Muʿjam*, IV, 835.

37. This place is identical with ʿUmr Kaskar, although it is also referred to as ʿUmr Wāsiṭ. See Yāqūt, *Muʿjam*, III, 724, 726.

another from Barrtumartā,[38] and still another from Bardūdā. Abū al-ʿAbbās encountered them, and shortly thereafter they were put to flight. One contingent of the enemy remained behind at Sūq al-Khamīs, and another at Māzarwān.

Some of Abū al-ʿAbbās's troops started (to chase the Zanj) [1951] from Barrtumartā, while others took hold of al-Madiyān. Abū Aḥmad did not stop until he reached Nahr Bar Musāwir. Thereupon, with the help of guides, he began inspecting the villages and roads until he returned to his camp and remained there to rest himself and his troops.

While there, an informant came with a report that the Zanj had assembled their forces, preparing to take his army by surprise, and that they were approaching from three directions. He further reported that they said that Abū al-ʿAbbās was a heedless youngster who would rush headlong into peril, and therefore they had decided to set up an ambush and to proceed towards him from three directions as mentioned above. Abū Aḥmad showed caution and prepared for this contingency.

Indeed, the Zanj had marched out towards him, after having placed some ten thousand men at Barrtumartā and about the same number at Quss Ḥathā.[39] They sent out twenty galleys against the (government) camp to lure the defenders past the positions of the ambushers. But Abū al-ʿAbbās prevented his men from chasing after them. When the foe perceived that their ruse failed, al-Jubbāʾī and Sulaymān came into the open with their barges and galleys. Abū al-ʿAbbās, however, had his troops realigned superbly; he instructed Nuṣayr Abū Ḥamzah to set forth with his barges against the enemy. Abū al-ʿAbbās himself dismounted and summoned one of his barges, which he named "the Gazelle [al-Ghazāl]." He instructed the captain Muḥammad b. Shuʿayb to select oarsmen for this vessel, which he boarded. He also selected from among his special troops and pages a detachment which he armed with spears. Then he ordered the cavalry to march before him along the bank of the river, warning them, "As far as possible do not slow your

---

38. Read: Bar Tumartā (?)

39. Perhaps confused with Qusyathā, mentioned by Yāqūt, *Muʿjam*, IV, 99, as a place in Iraq.

march until waterways obstruct your passage." He also ordered the transfer of some of the horses which were in Bardūdā. [1952]

The battle between the opposing factions flared up. The field of conflict ran from the limits of the village al-Raml to al-Ruṣāfah.[40] The Zanj were defeated and Abū al-ʿAbbās's troops seized fourteen barges. Sulaymān and al-Jubbā'ī fled that day, escaping death on foot. Their horses with all their ornaments and harnesses were seized. The entire government army, without losing a single soldier, reached Ṭahīthā and delivered their equipment. Abū al-ʿAbbās returned to his camp in al-ʿUmr and remained there. He ordered that all the seized barges and galleys be repaired and manned. For twenty days after that, none of the Zanj appeared. Every three days al-Jubbā'ī would go out with his scouts and return. Above the Sindād Canal he dug pits and at the base of the pits he planted iron rods and covered them with rush mats, thus concealing their position. These pits, intentionally scattered along the route usually taken by horsemen, were to trap bypassers. Then he would approach the flanks of Abū al-ʿAbbās's camp, showing himself to the troops there so that their horsemen would go out to pursue him.

One day, he came and the horsemen started to pursue him as usual, when the horse of an officer from Farghānah tumbled into one of those pits. Abū al-ʿAbbās's troops therefore became aware of the ruse that al-Jubbā'ī had conceived, and they took precautions to avoid passing along that road. The Zanj harassed the camp in the early morning every day to provoke an engagement; they even camped at Nahr al-Amīr in force, but all this was to no avail. They abstained from fighting for about a month. [1953]

Now Sulaymān wrote to the leader of the Zanj, requesting the latter to reinforce him with galleys of forty oarsmen each. And, indeed, within some twenty days forty galleys arrived, each carrying two army men. All the sailors were provided with swords, spears and shields. Al-Jubbā'ī established his position opposite the army of Abū al-ʿAbbās, and the opposing

---

40. That is, Ruṣāfat Wāsiṭ. A village in the adminsitrative district of Wāsiṭ some ten *farsakh*s (sixty kms) from the city. See Yāqūt, *Muʿjam*, II, 788.

forces resumed contact daily. But whenever the troops of Abū al-ʿAbbās set out against al-Jubbāʾī's forces, the latter, instead of holding fast to their positions, would retreat, while their skirmishers destroyed bridges, shot at horsemen appearing within the range of their arrows, or set fire to vessels of Nuṣayr which they found out on patrol. This went on for about two months, after which Abū al-ʿAbbās saw to it that an ambush was set up for the enemy at the village of Raml and several galleys were advanced ahead of the troops to serve as bait. Abū al-ʿAbbās also ordered two galleys, one for himself and one for Zīrak, and selectd for these vessels a number of his pages whom he knew to be gallant fighters. He assigned Badr and Mūʾnis to one galley, Rashīq al-Ḥajjājī and Yumn to another, Khafīf and Yusr to a third, and Nadhīr and Wasīf to a fourth. He prepared fifteen galleys, with two army men in each, and sent them ahead of the armed force.

Muḥammad b. Shuʿayb al-Ishtiyām reported: On that day, I was among those who were sent ahead. The Zanj seized a number of the advancing galleys and took prisoners. I hastily called out in a loud voice, "The enemy has seized our galleys." Upon hearing this, Abū al-ʿAbbās, who was taking his breakfast,
[1954] rushed toward the galleys which had been prepared for him. The army moved forward, but Abū al-ʿAbbās did not wait for his men to join him; only those who were prepared to move swiftly followed him. We reached the Zanj and when they saw us, God filled their hearts with terror, and they plunged into the water and fled. We rescued our troops and captured thirty-one of the Zanj galleys, however, al-Jubbāʾī escaped with three of them. That day Abū al-ʿAbbās fired so many shots from his bow that his thumbs started bleeding, and he withdrew. I think that if we had persisted making a maximum effort in pursuing al-Jubbāʾī on that day, we could have seized him; but we refrained from doing so because of extreme fatigue.

Abū al-ʿAbbās and most of his troops returned to their places at the mouth of the Bardūdā, without having lost a single man. Upon arriving at his camp, Abū al-ʿAbbās bestowed on all those who had gone with him necklaces, robes of honor, and rings, and ordered that the galleys seized from the Zanj be repaired.

He instructed Abū Ḥamzah to take up positions with his men and barges on the Tigris in front of Khusrūsābūr.[41]

Abū al-ʿAbbās then decided to penetrate (enemy territory) along the Māzarwān Canal to the town called al-Ḥajjājiyyah, and then on to Nahr al-Amīr. Positioning himself at these places, he would find out about the routes followed by the Zanj galleys. Nuṣayr was ordered to move out with his barges and galleys. He went on this mission, leaving the road to Māzarwān for the area of Nahr al-Amīr. Abū al-ʿAbbās now summoned his galley and sailed with Muḥammad b. Shuʿayb; then he entered Māzarwān. Believing that Nuṣayr was in front of him, he said to Muḥammad, "Go ahead up the river so that I might have news of Nuṣayr." Then he ordered the barge and galleys to follow Muḥammad.

Muḥammad b. Shuʿayb reported: We proceeded until, close [1955] to al-Ḥajjājiyyah, we came upon a transport (*ṣalghah*) with ten Zanj. We rushed toward it and the Zanj threw themselves into the water. Taking possession of the boat, we discovered that it was full of barley. When we discovered there was a Zanj in it, we seized him and questioned him about Nuṣayr and his barges. But he told us "No barge or galley has entered this waterway." We were perplexed. Meanwhile, the Zanj who had slipped through our hands went and informed their comrades of our whereabouts. Our sailors noticed some sheep and went ashore to carry them off.

Muḥammad b. Shuʿayb reported: I alone remained with Abū al-ʿAbbās. Before long a Zanj commander named Muntāb appeared with a group of men on one side of the canal, and ten of the Zanj appeared on the other. Seeing this, we rushed out, Abū al-ʿAbbās with his bow and arrows and I with my spear. I covered him while he shot arrows at the Zanj, wounding two of them. But they pressed the attack and their numbers increased. We espied Zīrak with the barges and the pages accompanying him. By that time, some 2,000 Zanj were around us on both

41. Yāqūt, *Muʿjam*, II, 442, indicates that the general populace referred to it as Khussābūr. It was a village situated some five *farsakh*s (thirty kms) from Wāsiṭ.

sides of Māzarwān. But God meted out their due and drove the Zanj back, utterly humiliated. Abū al-ʿAbbās returned to his camp. His troops had seized great numbers of sheep, cows and water buffaloes. He ordered that three of the sailors who had been with him, and had then left to seize the cattle, be beheaded; those who had stayed on duty were to be given a month's pay. Abū al-ʿAbbās also issued a warning that none of
[1956] the sailors were to leave their galleys in time of battle, and that the death penalty would be imposed upon those who violated this order. The Zanj fled together to Ṭahīthā. Abū al-ʿAbbās stayed in his camp at al-ʿUmr while patrols fanned out over all the surrounding areas. This situation lasted for some time.

Meanwhile, Sulaymān b. Jāmiʿ gathered his troops and officers and entrenched himself at Ṭahīthā, while al-Shaʿrānī did the same at Sūq al-Khamīs. At al-Ṣīniyyah[42] they also had a huge army comanded by one Naṣr al-Sindī. They began to ransack everything within reach, carrying off whatever they could of the crops, and fortifying the places where they were stationed.

Abū al-ʿAbbās sent out some of his commanders on horseback to the environs of al-Ṣīniyyah. Among them were al-Shāh, Kumushjūr, al-Faḍl b. Mūsā b. Bughā and his brother Muḥammad. Abū al-ʿAbbās, along with Nuṣayr and Zīrak, sailed on the barges and transports. He ordered that the cavalry be transferred from Bar Musāwir to the road to al-Ẓuhr. The army advanced until it reached al-Hurth, whereupon Abū al-ʿAbbās ordered that the beasts of burden be transferred there. The animals were transported across the water, thereby reaching the western side of the Tigris. Abū al-ʿAbbās then instructed the army to march along the road to Dayr al-ʿUmmāl.[43]

When the Zanj noticed the cavalry, they were seized with terror and escaped to the water and their vessels. Before long they were overtaken by (Abū al-ʿAbbās's) barges and galleys. Seeing that there was no escape, the Zanj sought to surrender.

---

42. Al-Ṣīniyyah was reportedly a small town (*bulaydah*) below Wāsiṭ. See Yāqūt, *Muʿjam*, III, 458.

43. A town below Nahr Abān in the vicinity of Wāsiṭ. See Le Strange, *Lands*, 41.

A group of them were killed, others were captured, and some jumped into the water. The troops of Abū al-ʿAbbās seized their vessels which were filled with rice that now fell into the hands of the government forces. They also seized the galley of the [1957] Zanj commander known as Naṣr al-Sindī. The rest of the Zanj fled, one contingent to Ṭahīthā, and the other to Sūq al-Khamīs. Abū al-ʿAbbās thus returned to his camp filled with booty. He had conquered al-Ṣīniyyah and expelled the Zanj from there.

Muḥammad b. Shuʿayb reported: While we were fighting the Zanj at al-Ṣīniyyah, Abū al-ʿAbbās noticed a Numidian crane in flight. He aimed at it and pierced it with his arrow. The crane fell to the ground in front of the Zanj, who picked it up and, examining the hole of the wound, perceived that it was caused by the arrow of Abū al-ʿAbbās. This heightened their fear and was the reason for their flight.

Some reliable sources report that Abū al-ʿAbbās shot the arrow at the crane on another occasion.

Word reached Abū al-ʿAbbās that a huge force led by two Zanj, Thābit b. Abī Dulaf and Lu'lu', was stationed at ʿAbdasī.[44] With a detachment of horsemen selected from his most valiant pages and courageous officers he marched to ʿAbdasī to engage the enemy. At dawn he reached the spot where they were located, and dealt them a crushing blow, killing a great many of their best men. The Zanj force was routed. Abū al-ʿAbbās captured its leader, Thābit b. Abī Dulaf and, sparing his life, he entrusted him to one of his officers. The one named Lu'lu' was struck by an arrow which killed him. A great many women who were in the hands of the Zanj were rescued on that day. Abū al-ʿAbbās ordered that they be set free and returned to [1958] their families. He seized everything that the Zanj had collected.

Abū al-ʿAbbās then returned to his camp and ordered his troops to rest in preparation for marching against Sūq al-Khamīs. He summoned Nuṣayr and instructed him to get his men ready to march. Nuṣayr said to him, "The canal to Sūq al-Khamīs is narrow. Stay here and allow me to go there to check

44. A city in the Kaskar district. See Le Strange *Lands*, 42, 43.

it out." But Abū al-ʿAbbās refused to permit this because he was expecting the arrival of his father, Abū Aḥmad, from whom he had received a letter saying that he had decided to come.

Muḥammad b. Shuʿayb reported: Abū al-ʿAbbās called me and said, "I must take Sūq al-Khamīs." To this I retorted, "If, as you say, it is absolutely necessary for you to do this, do not take a great number of people in the barge. At any rate, take no more than thirteen pages, ten archers and three spear bearers, since I would hate to have the barge overcrowded in this narrow canal."

Abū al-ʿAbbās made himself ready and marched out with Nuṣayr in the lead. When they reached the mouth of (the canal to) Bar Musāwir, Nuṣayr said: "Send me ahead." Abū al-ʿAbbās concurred, and Nuṣayr proceeded with fifteen barges. One of the officers from among the mawlās (clients), Mūsā Daljawayh, who had asked permission to go forward, was allowed to do so, and he went along.

Abū al-ʿAbbās advanced until his journey took him to Basāmī; from there he went to the mouth of the Barātiq, then to the Riqq Canal, and finally to the waterway crossing Rawāṭā and ʿAbdasī.[45] These three waterways led to three divergent
[1959] roads. Nuṣayr set out on the road along the Barātiq Canal, that is, the road leading to Madīnat Sulaymān b. Mūsā al-Shaʿrānī, which he named The Fortress of Sūq al-Khamīs (al-Manīʿah bi-Sūq al-Khamīs). Abū al-ʿAbbās stayed at the mouth of this canal and Nuṣayr (advanced until he) disappeared from sight, and nothing further was heard of him. Now a great many of the Zanj came out against us at this place, and hindered us from entering the canal. They positioned themselves between us and the approaches to the walls—the distance between the place which we had reached and the walls surrounding Madīnat al-Shaʿrānī was about two *farsakh*s (twelve km) They stood their ground there and engaged us in combat. The battle between us—they fighting on land, and we aboard ships at the edge of the canal—raged from the beginning of the day to noon, by which time we still had no word from Nuṣayr. Then the

45. Other than ʿAbdasī, I have not succeeded in identifying these locations.

Zanj began shouting, "We caught Nuṣayr. What are you going to do? We shall follow you wherever you go!"

Abū al-ʿAbbās became very worried when he heard this, and Muḥammad b. Shuʿayb asked permission to go and find out what had happened to Nuṣayr. This being granted, he went off in a galley with twenty oarsmen and reached Nuṣayr Abū Ḥamzah who had approached the dam which the profligates had set up. They discovered that he had just set fire to the dam and to their city (*madīnah*), and that he had engaged in a violent but victorious struggle with them. The Zanj had initially seized some of Abū Ḥamzah's barges, but he succeeded in recovering them.

Muḥammad b. Shuʿayb returned to Abū al-ʿAbbās and reported the good news that Nuṣayr and his men were safe, and told him of their exploits. Abū Aṃmad rejoiced at this. On that day Nuṣayr captured a great many Zanj and then returned to the place where Abū al-ʿAbbās was positioned. [1960]

Upon Nuṣayr's return, Abū al-ʿAbbās said, "I am not leaving this place until I fight them again tonight." And this he did. He instructed his men to expose one of his barges in full view of the Zanj, while concealing the rest. At the sight of the vessel, the Zanj, anxious to capture it, started off in pursuit. Now the crew of that barge kept it to a slow course so that the Zanj overtook it and held fast to the rudder. Then the sailors started to race so as to reach the position of the barges which lay in ambush.

Abū al-ʿAbbās, wearing a felt vest above his coat of mail, was aboard a galley—he had placed his barge behind him. When he noticed the barge which the Zanj clung to, he rushed toward it. He perceived it just as the Zanj grasped its rudders, surrounding it from all sides, and showered it with arrows and stone.

Muḥammad (continued): On that day we extracted twenty-five arrows from the felt vest of Abū al-ʿAbbās. I extracted forty arrows from the felt cap I had on, and from the rest of the sailor's felt caps twenty-five to thirty arrows. God rendered into the hands of Abū al-ʿAbbās six Zanj galleys; the barge was rescued and the Zanj fled. Abū al-ʿAbbās and his men repaired to the bank and charged the Zanj warriors with their swords and shields. The enemy fled in panic without looking back. Safely, and with booty, Abū al-ʿAbbās returned. He clothed his sailors with robes of honor and bestowed gifts upon them. Then he returned to his camp at al-ʿUmr and remained there until the arrival of al-Muwaffaq.

On the eleventh of Ṣafar (September 22, 880) Abū Aḥmad b.
[1961] al-Mutawakkil camped at al-Firk. Then he departed from Baghdad (Madīnat al-Salām) heading towards the camp of the leader of the Zanj, intending to do combat with him. The reason for this, according to reports, was that word had reached Abū Aḥmad that the leader of the Zanj had written to his lieutenant, ʿAlī b. Abān al-Muhallabī, instructing him to march with all his troops to the location of Sulaymān b. Jāmiʿ, in order to join forces with the latter in fighting Abū al-ʿAbbās b. Abī Aḥmad.

Abū Aḥmad remained in al-Firk for several days to permit his troops, and any others who wanted to proceed with him, to join on. He had prepared the barges, galleys, ferries and boats. Then, on Tuesday, the second of Rabīʿ I (October 11, 880), he and his clients, pages, cavalry and infantry reportedly left al-Firk, bound for Rūmiyat al-Madāʾin.[46] From there they journeyed on stopping at al-Sīb,[47] Dayr al-ʿAqūl,[48], Jarjarāyā, Qunnā,[49] Jabbul,[50] al-Ṣilḥ and a place one *farsakh* (six km) from Wāsiṭ. He remained at the latter for one day and one night and was met by his son Abū al-ʿAbbās and a squadron of cavalry including his leading officers and men. Abū Aḥmad inquired about the state of his men, and getting from his son a picture of their gallantry and devotion in fighting, he ordered that robes of honor be bestowed upon them and Abū al-ʿAbbās. Thereupon, the son returned to his camp at al-ʿUmr where he remained throughout the day. In the early morning of the next day, Abū Aḥmad took

46. According to Muslim authors, al-Madāʾin, "the cities," received its name because it was an urban center formed from seven cities, one of which was Rūmiyyah. See Le Strange, *Lands*, 34.

47. Le Strange, *Lands*, 41.

48. Ibid., 35.

49. Ibid., 36.

50. Ibid., 38.

to the water where he was met by his son, Abū al-ʿAbbās, and all his troops in military formation, as fully equipped as they would be when confronting the traitor's forces. Abū Aḥmad sailed on until he reached his camp on the waterway called Shīrzād, where he stopped. On Thursday, the twenty-eighth of [1962] Rabīʿ I (November 6, 880), he departed from there and stopped at the canal called Nahr Sindād, opposite the village called ʿAbdallāh. He instructed his son Abū al-ʿAbbās to halt on the eastern side of the Tigris, opposite the mouth of the Bardūdā, and put him in charge of the vanguard. Then he allotted the soldiers' allowances and paid them. Following that, he instructed his son to advance in front of him with the equipment that he had in his possession, toward the mouth of the Bar Musāwir Canal.

Abū al-ʿAbbās set out with the best of his officers and troops, including Zīrak al-Turkī, the commander of his vanguard, and Nuṣayr Abū Ḥamzah, the commander of the barges and galleys. After this it was Abū Aḥmad who set out with his selected cavalry and infantry, leaving the bulk of his army and many of his horsemen and foot soldiers behind in his place of encampment.

His son Abū al-ʿAbbās met him with a show of captives, heads and bodies of slain enemies from among the troops of al-Shaʿrānī. For, on that same day, before the arrival of his father Abū Aḥmad, Abū al-ʿAbbās had been attacked by al-Shaʿrānī who came upon the former's camp. Abū al-ʿAbbās dealt him a severe blow, killing a great many of his men and taking captives. Abū Aḥmad ordered that the captives be beheaded, which was done. Then Abū Aḥmad descended to the mouth of the Bar Musāwir, where he stayed for two days. From there, on Tuesday, the eighth of Rabīʿ II (November 17, 880), he departed from Sūq al-Khamīs with all his men and equipment bound for the city which the leader of the Zanj had named al-Manīʿah bi-Sūq al-Khamīs. He proceeded with his ships along the Bar Musāwir while the cavalry marched before him along the eastern side of the waterway until they reached the waterway called Barātiq, which led to Madīnat al-Shaʿrānī. Abū Aḥmad [1963]
preferred to begin fighting against Mūsā al-Shaʿrānī before he

fought Sulaymān b. Jāmiʿ because he feared that al-Shaʿrānī, who was to his rear, might attack and thus divert him from the adversary in front of him. That is why he set out against al-Shaʿrānī. He ordered the cavalry to cross the canal and proceed along both banks of the Barātiq. Abū Aḥmad also instructed his son Abū al-ʿAbbās to advance with a flotilla of barges and galleys, and he himself followed with barges along with the bulk of his army.

When Sulaymān, his Zanj troops and others noticed the cavalry and infantry proceeding on both banks of the canal and the ships advancing along the waterway—this was after Abū al-ʿAbbās had met them and engaged them in a skirmish—they fled and scattered. The troops of Abū al-ʿAbbās climbed the walls killing those who opposed them. When the Zanj and their supporters scattered, Abū al-ʿAbbās and his forces entered the city, killed a great many of its people, took many prisoners and laid hold of whatever was there. Al-Shaʿrānī and the others who escaped with him fled; they were pursued by Abū Aḥmad's men up to the marshes where many drowned. The rest saved themselves by fleeing into the thickets.

Thereupon, Abū Aḥmad instructed his troops to return to their camp before sunset of that Tuesday, and he withdrew. About five thousand Muslim women and some Zanj women, who were taken in Sūq al-Khamīs, were saved. Abū Aḥmad gave instructions to take care of all the women, to transfer them to Wāsiṭ and return them to their families.

[1964] Abū Aḥmad spent that night opposite the Barātiq Canal and in the early morning of the next day, he entered the city and gave the people permission to take all the Zanj possessions there. Everything in the city was seized. Abū Aḥmad ordered the walls razed, the trenches filled, and the remaining ships burned. He left for his camp at Bar Musāwir with booty taken in the districts (*rustāq*) and villages previously possessed by al-Shaʿrānī and his men; this included crops of wheat, barley and rice. He ordered that the crops be sold and the money realized from the sale be spent to pay his mawlā's pages, the troops of his regular army, and other people of his camp.

Sulaymān al-Shaʿrānī escaped with his two brothers and others, but he lost his children and possessions. Upon reaching al-Madhār he reported to the traitor (that is, the leader of the Zanj) what had befallen him and that he had taken refuge in al-Madhār.[51]

According to Muḥammad b. al-Ḥasan—Muḥammad b. Hishām, known as Abū Wāthilah al-Kirmānī: I was in the presence of the traitor—he was having a discussion—when the letter from Sulaymān al-Shaʿrānī arrived with the news of the battle and his flight to al-Madhār. As soon as he had the letter unsealed and his eye fell on the passage describing the defeat, his bowel muscles loosened and he got up to relieve himself, then he returned. As his Assembly came to order, he took the letter and began reading it again, and when he reached the passage which had disturbed him the first time, he left once more. This repeated itself several times. There remained no doubt that the calamity was great, and I refrained from asking him questions. After some time had elapsed, I ventured to say, "Isn't this the letter from Sulaymān b. Mūsā?" He replied, "Yes, and a piece of heartbreaking news, too. Indeed, those who fell upon him dealt him a crushing blow 'that will not spare nor leave unburned.'[52] He has written this letter from al- [1965] Madhār, and he has barely saved his own skin."

I deemed this news momentous and only God knows what a joy filled my heart, but I concealed it and refrained from rejoicing at the prospect of the approaching relief. However, the traitor regained self-control in face of vicissitude, and showed firmness. He wrote to Sulaymān b. Jāmiʿ, cautioning him against al-Shaʿrānī's fate and instructing him to be vigilant and watchful concerning what might lie before him.

According to Muḥammad b. al-Ḥasan—Muḥammad b. al-Ḥammād: Al-Muwaffaq stayed in his camp at Bar Musāwir for two days to gather information about al-Shaʿrānī and Sulaymān b. Jāmiʿ and to discover the latter's base. When some of those

51. Ibid., 42, 43.
52. That is, a crushing blow. See Qur'ān LXXIV: 28; Lane, *Lexicon*, I, 298.

sent out for this purpose brought him information that Sulaymān b. Jāmiʿ was encamped in the village called al-Ḥawānīt,[53] he immediately ordered the cavalry to cross to the Kaskar area on the western bank of the Tigris. He himself journeyed by boat and ordered the barges and infantry transports to proceed down to al-Kathīthah. Al-Muwaffaq left the bulk of his army, including a large troop of infantry and horses, at the mouth of Bar Musāwir and instructed Bughrāj to remain positioned there. Upon his arrival in al-Ṣīniyyah, Abū Aḥmad instructed Abū al-ʿAbbās to advance promptly with barges and galleys to al-Ḥawānīt in order to verify the information about Sulaymān b. Jāmiʿ's whereabouts. If the enemy were to display slackness, Abū al-ʿAbbās was to attack him. That same evening Abū al-ʿAbbās arrived in al-Ḥawānīt and, instead of Sulaymān, he found the black officers, Shibl and Abū al-Nidā'—two of the earliest companions of the rebel. Both were famous for their
[1966] courage and bravery, and were associated with him from the very beginning of his revolt. The officers had been left there by Sulaymān b. Jāmiʿ to guard vast crops in the area. Abū al-ʿAbbās engaged them, moving his barges into a narrow spot in the waterway. He killed some of their infantry, and injured many others with arrows. These were the most valiant of Sulaymān b. Jāmiʿ's men, the chosen ones on whom he relied. The battle between the opposing factions lasted until night intervened.

According to Muḥammad b. Ḥammād: This was the battle in which Abū al-ʿAbbās shot the crane, and to which Muḥammad b. Shuʿayb referred as the Battle of al-Ṣīniyyah—the bird passed on his right side.

On that day a man surrendered to Abū al-ʿAbbās. When Abū al-ʿAbbās asked him about Sulaymān b. Jāmiʿ's location, he reported that the latter was stationed in Ṭahīthā. At this, Abū al-ʿAbbās returned to his father with the news that Sulaymān's true location was the city which he named al-Manṣūrah, and which was in the place known as Ṭahīthā.[54] In addition, he told

53. Le Strange, *Lands*, 41.

54. The term for "city" is *madīnah*, which very often means administrative center.

his father that all of Sulaymān's officers were with him there except for Shibl and Abū al-Nidā', who were at al-Ḥawānīt which they had been ordered to guard. As soon as he learned this, Abū Aḥmad gave the order to set out for Bardūdā, since from there the road led to Ṭahīthā. Abū al-ʿAbbās went ahead with barges and galleys and instructed all those left behind at Barr Musāwir to march to Bardūdā. On the day after he had given instructions to Abū al-ʿAbbās, Abū Aḥmad left for Bardūdā and, after two days' march, on Friday the seventeenth of Rabīʿ II, 267 (November 26, 880), he arrived there. He remained to make whatever repairs were needed for his army, to effect the payment of the soldiers, and to repair the ferries that were [1967] to be taken along. He also picked up numerous workers and the equipment needed to block canals and repair roads for the horses. He left Bughrāj al-Turkī behind in Bardūdā.

When Abū Aḥmad decided to go to Bardūdā, he ordered a page of his called Juʿlān—he had been left with Bughrāj in his camp—to take down his tents and forward them and the weapons to Bardūdā with the animals which had been left at his camp. At the time of the late evening prayer, when the people did not expect it, Juʿlān disclosed the order he had received. This made them suspect that the order was given because of a defeat, and thus they ran headlong from the camp abandoning their tents and provisions. Fearful that the enemy was very close, they scattered so that no two remained together and, in the dark of the night, they all fled towards their camp in Bardūdā. Subsequently, they learned the true state of affairs and, calming down, they regained composure.

In the month of Ṣafar (September 11–October 8, 880), the troops of Kayghalagh al-Turkī and those of Aḥmad b. ʿAbd al-ʿAzīz b. Abī Dulaf engaged in a battle in the vicinity of Qarmāsīn. Kayghalagh emerged victorious and proceeded to Hamadhān. But in the same month, Aḥmad b. ʿAbd al-ʿAzīz, with the troops which he had rallied to his side, came upon Kayghalagh and attacked him; the latter was routed and set off for al-Ṣaymarah.

On the twenty-sixth of Rabīʿ II (December 4, 880), Abū Aḥmad and his troops entered Ṭahīthā and ousted Sulaymān b. Jāmiʿ. In this battle Aḥmad b. Mahdī al-Jubbā'ī was killed.

[1968]
How Abū Aḥmad and His Troops Occupied Ṭahīthā and How al-Jubbā'ī Was Killed[55]

According to Muḥammad b. al-Ḥasan—Muḥammad b. Ḥammād: In Bardūdā, Abū Aḥmad paid his troops and repaired the equipment of those going to fight against the leader of the rebellion. Having done so, he set out in the direction of Ṭahīthā. This was on Sunday, the eighteenth of Rabīʿ II, 267 (November 26, 880). He proceeded on horseback with his cavalry. The vessels were sent on with whatever they carried as regards infantry, weapons, and equipment. Also sent on were ferries, barges and galleys. They proceeded until he met them at the waterway called Nahr Mahrūdh[56] in the vicinity of the village called Qaryat al-Jawziyyah. Here Abū Aḥmad camped and ordered that a pontoon bridge be moored at the above-mentioned waterway. He remained there for a day and night. On the next day, he sent the horses and equipment over the bridge in his presence; then he crossed too and gave the order to his officers and troops to march to Ṭahīthā. They advanced to a place which Abū Aḥmad chose as quarters for himself, within two miles of the city of Sulaymān b. Jāmiʿ. Here, facing the troops of the perifidious one (that is, the leader of the Zanj), they stayed during Monday and Tuesday, the twenty-first of Rabīʿ II (November 29–30, 880). Then a heavy downpour began, and an intense cold afflicted his troops during the days of his stay there. Rain and cold prevented him from fighting, and they did not engage in battle until the end of the week. It was only on Friday evening that Abū Aḥmad with a small group of his officers and clients set out in search of a place to deploy his cav-
[1969] alry. He advanced close to the walls of (the city of) Sulaymān b. Jāmiʿ, where numerous troops of the enemy confronted them. Ambushers attacked them from different positions, and an engagement which gave rise to heavy fighting broke out. A detachment of horsemen dismounted and fought back until they

55. See Popovic, *Révolte*, 130 ff.

56. Yāqūt mentions a canal of this name in the Baghdad region. See *Muʿjam*, IV, 700, It is difficult to see how this waterway can be identified with the canal of this text.

escaped from the straits into which they had gotten themselves. One of Abū Aḥmad's pages and officers, Wasīf ʿAlamdār by name, and a number of Zīrak's officers were taken prisoner. Abū al-ʿAbbās fired an arrow which hit Aḥmad b. Mahdī al-Jubbā'ī in one of his nostrils and penetrated all the way to his brain. Hit, al-Jubbā'ī fell from his horse and was carried back on his final journey to the camp of the perfidious one. The latter was very distressed by this calamity because al-Jubbā'ī had been his most steadfast and indispensable lieutenant, and had the most foresight of all his followers. Al-Jubbā'ī lingered for a few days while being treated, and then he died. Griefstricken, the perifidious one took charge of the final ablutions, of putting the body in a shroud and of the funeral service. Then he stood by al-Jubbā'ī's grave until he was buried. Following this, he addressed his troops with a sermon in which he spoke of the death of al-Jubbā'ī. This death occurred on a night of thunder and lightning, and the perfidious one was reported to have said; "I knew the time of his soul's ascent before word of his death came to to me, because I heard the chant of the angels praying for him and pleading for mercy for him."

Muḥammad b. al-Ḥasan reported: Abū Wāthilah,[57] who was among those present at the sermon, came to me and began to amaze me with stories he had heard; then, Muḥammad b. Simʿān came to me and told me stories similar to those of Muḥammad b. Hishām. The perfidious one left the interment of al-Jubbā'ī grieved and broken-hearted.

According to Muḥammad b. al-Ḥasan—Muḥammad b. Ḥammād: when Abū Aḥmad returned from the engagement [1970] which took place Friday night, the twenty-fifth of Rabīʿ II (December 2, 880), news of it had already reached his camp. All of his army went out to meet him and they encountered him on his way back. As it was already sunset, Abū Aḥmad had them return to camp. When all the people of his camp were together, he instructed them to be on the alert that night in alternate shifts and to get ready for battle. When they arose on the morning of Saturday, the twenty-sixth of Rabīʿ II (December 3, 880), Abū Aḥmad arrange his troops in military formations, alter-

57. That is, Muḥammad b. Hishām al-Kirmānī.

nating squadrons of cavalry with infantry. He ordered that the barges and galleys proceed with him along the waterway called Nahr al-Mundhir, which bisects the city of Ṭahīthā.

Thus he advanced toward the Zanj until he reached the walls of the city; there he assigned officers from among his pages to the places from which he feared the Zanj might attack him. He positioned the infantry in front of the horsemen and assigned them to positions from which he feared ambushers might strike. Then he stopped and performed four *rakʿahs*, imploring God to extend his help to him and to the Muslims. Following that, he called for his arms. He put them on, and ordered his son Abū al-ʿAbbās to advance to the walls and rouse the pages to combat; this was done.

Sulaymān b. Jāmiʿ had a moat prepared before the walls of his city, that is, the city which he named al-Manṣūrah. When they reached this moat, the pages were startled and hesitated to cross, but the officers urged them on. Along with them, the officers dismounted from their horses, and with daring they rushed into the moat and crossed it. They came upon the Zanj, looking down the walls of their city and put them to the sword.
[1971] A party of horsemen also waded through the moat. When the Zanj saw these people who (had already) encountered them, coming again, they turned about and fled. Abū Aḥmad's men chased after them and entered the city from all sides. The Zanj had fortified it with five moats, each with a (protective) wall to make them impassable. The enemy made his stand behind each wall and moat reached by the government troops, but Abū Aḥmad's men drove them from every defensive position. The barges and galleys penetrated the city by the waterway traversing it, after the Zanj had been put to flight. Now the government ships started to sink every barge and galley which they passed. They chased the enemy on both sides of the canal, killing and capturing until they ousted him from the city and from about a *farsakh* (six km) of the adjacent territory. Abū Aḥmad then took control of the entire area.

Sulaymān b. Jāmiʿ escaped with only a small group of his men, losing the rest to death and captivity in this violent fight. Abū Aḥmad rescued about ten thousand women and children (taken captive) from the people of Wāsiṭ and the adjacent vil-

lages as well as from surroundings at al-Kūfah. He ordered them placed under protection and care. They were then transferred to Wāsiṭ and delivered to their families. Abū Aḥmad and his men took hold of all stores, money, food and cattle in the city, which came to an enormous amount; the crops and other things obtained he ordered sold, and the proceeds of the sale were transferred to his treasury to be disbursed as pay to the mawlās and troops of his camp. They carried away everything transportable, and captured a number of Sulaymān's wives and children. On that day, Waṣīf ʿAlamdār and others who were captured with him on that Friday eve were rescued and taken [1972]
from the prison, thus preventing their death at the hands of the Zanj.

A great many of the Zanj who escaped fled into the thickets around the city. On Abū Aḥmad's order, a pontoon bridge was laid across the waterway known as Nahr al-Mundhir and the people passed over it to the western side. Abū Aḥmad remained in Ṭahīthā for seventeen days, and ordered that the walls be razed and the moats filled. This being done, he ordered a search for the fugitives in the thickets, establishing a prize for everyone bringing in a prisoner. The people thus vied with one another in searching for them. Now, if one was brought in, Abū Aḥmad would pardon him, bestow upon him robes of honor, and assign him to the officers in charge of the pages. By doing this, he won them over, causing them to defect from their master.

Abū Aḥmad directed Nuṣayr to take his barges and galleys and pursue Sulaymān b. Jāmiʿ and the fugitives, that is, Zanj and others who were with him. He ordered Nuṣayr to pursue them vigorously through the marshes until entering that part of the Tigris which was called the Blind Tigris (Dijlat al-ʿAwrā').[58] Then he proceeded to open up the dams which the profligate had built, in order to cut off the barges on the Tigris from access to the area between his position and the waterway known as Abū al-Khaṣīb. He sent word to Zīrak to stay in Ṭahīthā so that its inhabitants, who had been driven away by the profligate (that is, the leader of the Zanj), might gradually re-

58. See Le Strange, *Lands*, 26, 43.

turn, and instructed him, as well, to search for the rest of the Zanj who still remained in the thickets and to capture them.

In the month of Rabīʿ II (November 9–December 7, 880), Umm Jabīb, the daughter of al-Rashīd passed away.

Having accomplished what he wanted, Abū Aḥmad returned to his camp in Bardūdā; he had set his mind on going to al-Ahwāz to put the affairs of that province in order. For a long [1973] time he had been concerned with the actions of al-Muhallabī, who by his attacks harassed the government troops stationed there and established his domination over most of the districts of al-Ahwāz. Abū al-ʿAbbās had already gone on before him on this journey of his.

When Abū Aḥmad arrived in Bardūdā, he remained for several days, and issued instructions to prepare everything he needed for a cavalry march to the districts of al-Ahwāz. He sent people ahead to repair the roads and residences, and to store up provisions for the troops accompanying him. Just before his departure from Wāsiṭ, Zīrak arrived on his way back from Ṭahīthā, where the population of the districts once occupied by the Zanj were back (in their places) and living securely. Abū Aḥmad instructed him to get ready and to bring his best and most valiant men, as well as the barges and galleys down to the Blind Tigris. They were to join forces with Abū Ḥamzah in order to reconnoiter the Tigris, pursue the Zanj fugitives, and attack such troops of the profligate as they might come upon along the route to the latter's city on the Abū al-Khaṣīb Canal. If they thought it a proper place for battle, they were to fight the profligate in his city and to report to Abū Aḥmad, so that he might further instruct them how to proceed. Abū Aḥmad appointed his son Hārūn as his deputy over the people he left behind at his camp in Wāsiṭ and decided to depart with a mobile group of his officers and troops. He did this after having forwarded an order to his son Hārūn. The latter was to have the troops and boats which Abū Aḥmad had left behind set course for a base on the Tigris. This was to occur as soon as word to this effect was received from Abū Aḥmad.

[1974] On the first of Jumādā II, 267 (January 7, 881), Abū Aḥmad left Wāsiṭ bound for Al-Ahwāz and its districts. (En route) he camped at Bādhibān,[59] Jūkā,[60] al-Ṭīb,[61] Qurqūb,[62] and Darustān. Next he stopped at Wādī al-Sūs where a pontoon bridge had been placed across the water for him.[63] He stayed from morning to late afternoon until all his men had crossed the waterway. Then he continued his march until he arrived at al-Sūs and camped there. Before that, he had sent an order to Masrūr, his governor in al-Ahwāz, to come to him. Masrūr met him with his troops and officers the day after Abū Aḥmad stopped at al-Sūs. Abū Aḥmad gave him and his men robes of honor, and stayed for three days.

Among the profligate's companions at Ṭahīthā was Aḥmad b. Mūsā b. Sa'īd al-Baṣrī, who was known as al-Qalūṣ. The latter was one of his adjutants and one of his earliest followers. He was captured after being severely injured, and he died of his wounds. Abū Aḥmad ordered his head cut off and displayed on the Wāsiṭ Bridge.

Among the prisoners taken that day was 'Abdallāh b. Muḥammad b. Hishām al-Kirmānī. The abominable one, having forced al-Kirmānī to come to him, sent him to Ṭahīthā, putting him in charge of the judiciary and worship there. In addition, many choice black troops were captured, men of courage and valor. When the abominable one learned about their fate, his control began to come apart and he lost his ability (to act wisely). In a fit of anxiety, he sent a letter with a companion of his to al-Muhallabī, who, at the time, was positioned in al-Ahwāz with some thirty thousand men. The letter contained an order to abandon all the provisions and equipment that 'Alī had and to proceed to him (that is, to the abominable one).

Al-Muhallabī received the letter having already learned [1975]
about the march of Abū Aḥmad to al-Ahwāz and its districts. As a result, he lost his senses and left everything he had at his disposal to Muḥammad b. Yaḥyā b. Sa'īd al-Karnabā'ī, whom

59. Ibid., 82.
60. Ibid., 42.
61. Ibid., 64, 82, 241, 247.
62. Ibid., 241, 246.
63. Ibid., 233.

he appointed as his deputy. Muḥammad became seized with fear, abandoned everything that had been entrusted to him and followed al-Muhallabī. At the time, large quantities of various kinds of grain, dates and livestock were stored in Jubbā, in al-Ahwāz, and the areas surrounding it. All this they gave up.

The profligate wrote also to Bahbūdh b. ʿAbd al-Wahhāb, who was at the time his governor of al-Fandam, and al-Bāsiyān, and the surrounding villages between al-Ahwāz and Fārs.[64] Bahbūdh was stationed in al-Fandam. The profligate ordered him to come (to his camp), whereupon Bahbūdh abandoned huge quantities of wheat and dates which he had at his disposal. Abū Aḥmad seized all of this, strengthening himself thereby and weakening the profligate.

When al-Muhallabī departed from al-Ahwāz, his men scattered about the villages between the city and the abominable one's camp, plundering them and banishing their inhabitants, even though the latter were at peace with the rebels. Many cavalry and infantry of al-Muhallabī failed to join him and remained behind in the districts of al-Ahwāz. Having heard about the pardon granted to those of the abominable one's men who had fallen into captivity in the region of Ṭahīthā, they wrote to Abū Aḥmad requesting him to take them under his protection. Meanwhile, al-Muhallabī and those of his troops who followed him reached the Abū al-Khaṣīb Canal.[65]

That which had induced the profligate to order al-Muhallabī and Bahbūdh to march to him hastily was his apprehension lest Abū Aḥmad and his troops reach him in his present state. That is, he would reach him at a time when his own men were
[1976] stricken with terror and weariness, while al-Muhallabī and Bahbūdh and their troops were cut off from him. But things did not turn out as he had reckoned.

Abū Aḥmad stayed as long as it was necessary to take over everything left by al-Muhallabī and Bahbūdh, to open the dams which the abominable one had erected on the Tigris, and to repair the highways and roads. Then he left al-Sūs and went to

64. Ibid., 242, 243, 247.
65. Ibid., 48.

Jundaysābūr,[66] where he stayed for three days. Since the army was short of fodder, he sent out men to look for it and bring it in. Thereupon he departed from Jundaysābūr and went to Tustar where he ordered that the taxes from the districts of al-Ahwāz be collected, sending to every district an officer to speed the delivery of the money. He sent off Aḥmad b. Abī al-Aṣbagh to Muḥammad b. ʿUbaydallāh al-Kurdī—al-Kurdī was afraid that the troops of the abominable one might reach him before Abū Aḥmad reached the territory of al-Ahwāz. Abū Aḥmad instructed the former to treat Muḥammad al-Kurdī kindly, and to let him known that Abū Aḥmad was determined to forgive him and to exonerate him from his errors. Al-Kurdī was to come forward with the money quickly and to proceed to Sūq al-Ahwāz. Abū Aḥmad commanded Maṣrur al-Balkhī, his governor of al-Ahwāz, to send all his mawlās, pages, and regular troops so that he might inspect them, pay them their allotments and urge them on to fight against the abominable one. This, Masrūr did, and his troops were inspected one by one and given their pay.

Abū Aḥmad then left for ʿAskar Mukram, where he set up his temporary quarters. From there he went to al-Ahwāz, seeing that the provisions which his troops were transporting would reach al-Ahwāz before his arrival. But he miscalculated this time, and his men became greatly agitated. He spent three days expecting the food to arrive, and still it did not come. Conditions grew bad and dissension broke out among the troops. Then, Abū Aḥmad made an inquiry into the reasons for the delay, and found that the troops had ruined an ancient Per- [1977]
sian bridge, called Qanṭarat Arbuk,[67] which was between Sūq al-Ahwāz and Rāmhurmuz. This had blocked the way for the merchants and those who were transporting the food, preventing them from going further. Abū Aḥmad set out for that bridge, which was two *farsakhs* (twelve km) from Sūq al-Ahwāz. Gathering the black soldiers who remained in his camp, he ordered them to carry rocks and stones to repair it. He

66. Ibid., 237, 238, 247.
67. See Ṭabarī, III/2, 1835.

paid them generously and did not leave the spot until the bridge was repaired and restored completely that same day. Then the people took the bridge route, and the caravans with the food arrived. The army was resuscitated and conditions improved.

Abū Aḥmad now ordered that boats be assembled and put together to span the Dujayl.[68] The boats were gathered from the districts of al-Ahwāz and the bridge building began. Abū Aḥmad remained in al-Ahwāz several days until his troops put their affairs in order and repaired the necessary equipment. He also waited for their animals to round into good shape, thus making up for the suffering caused by the delay in the supply of fodder. Meanwhile, messages reached al-Muwaffaq from al-Muhallabī's men who had deserted. They remained in the area of Sūq al-Ahwāz and were now requesting guarantees of safe conduct from al-Muwaffaq. This being granted, about one thousand men came to him. Abū Aḥmad treated them kindly, assigned them to officers of his pages and allotted them military pay.

Now, when the Dujayl bridge was tied,[69] Abū Aḥmad sent his troops across, then he himself followed, and established his camp on the western bank of the river in the place called Qaṣr al-Ma'mūn.[70] He remained for three days. One night there was a terrible earthquake, May God preserve us from its evil and save us from its adversity! Before crossing the bridge over the Dujayl, Abū Aḥmad sent his son Abū al-ʿAbbās to the place where
[1978] he planned to camp in the area of the Blind Tigris. This was the place known as the Nahr al-Mubārak of Furāt al-Baṣrah.[71] He wrote to his son Hārūn to go there, as well, with all the troops

68. That is, the Dujayl which was known as the Dujayl of al-Ahwāz. It was better known as the Kārūn. See Le Strange, *Lands*, index, 524.

69. It was a pontoon bridge (*jisr*), and hence portable.

70. Not to be confused with any of the palaces of that name in Baghdad. See Lassner, *Topography*, index, 321.

71. Presumably the canal leading to al-Mubārak, a town which lay on the western side of the Tigris in the general vicinity of the fighting. See Le Strange, *Lands*, 38. Note that Yāqūt also mentions a canal of this name located in the Baṣrah region. See Yāqūt, *Muʿjam*, IV, 408–409. Furāt al-Baṣrah was, however, an administrative region (*kūrah*) in Sassanian times, op. cit, III, 863.

that had been left behind with him, so that the armies would gather there.

Abū Aḥmad departed from Qaṣr al-Ma'mūn and, when he stopped at Qūraj al-ʿAbbās, he was met by Aḥmad b. Abī al-Aṣbagh, who brought him word about the settlement with Muḥammad b. ʿUbaydallāh, as well as presents from the latter, such as animals and beasts trained for the hunt, and other things. At this, he departed from al-Qūraj and next stopped at Jaʿfariyyah.[72] There was no water in this village exccept for the wells which Abū Aḥmad had dug earlier in his camp. He had sent Saʿd al-Aswad, the mawlā of ʿUbaydallāh b. Muḥammad b. ʿAmmār from Qūraj al-ʿAbbās to do the job, and the wells were dug. Abū Aḥmad stayed at this place for a full day. He came upon stored-up provisions which the troops found more than sufficient for their needs and they partook of them. From there they went to the place called al-Bushīr, where they found a pool of rainwater. Abū Aḥmad stayed there for a day and a night, then late in the night they departed bound for Nahr al-Mubārak. After a rather long and strenous march, they arrived there after the midday prayer. On the way, Abū Aḥmad was met and welcomed by his two sons, Abū al-ʿAbbās and Hārūn,and they accompanied him on his journey until reaching Nahr al-Mubārak. This was on a Saturday, in the middle of Rajab, 267 (February 5–March 6, 881).

Meanwhile, between Abū Aḥmad's departure from Wāsiṭ and his arrival at Nahr al-Mubārak, Zīrak, Nuṣayr and their men carried out an impressive action, fulfilling their task of pursuing the Zanj fugitives from Ṭahīthā. (According to) Muḥammad b. al-Ḥasan—Muḥammad b. Ḥammād: When Zīrak and Nuṣayr met on the Blind Tigris they marched together until they reached al-Ubullah, where one of the abominable one's [1979] men asked for a guarantee of safe-conduct. He informed the two of them that the abominable one had sent out a great number of galleys, skiffs (*zawraq*) and boats (*ṣalghah*) loaded with Zanj under the command of one of his lieutenants, Muḥammad b. Ibrāhīm. The latter's patronymic was Abū ʿĪsā. This

72. Not to be confused with the various places of this name mentioned in Yāqūt, *Muʿjam*, V, 88.

Muḥammad b. Ibrāhīm, who hailed from al-Baṣrah, had been brought to the abominable one at the time al-Baṣrah was destroyed by a Zanj officer named Yasār. Yasār had been in charge of the profligate's security force. This Baṣran served Yasār as his scribe until the latter died. Meanwhile Aḥmad b. Mahdī al-Jubbā'ī prospered under the abominable one, who appointed him governor over most of his districts. This Muḥammad b. Ibrāhīm was assigned to him and served as his scribe until al-Jubbā'ī perished.

Muḥammad b. Ibrāhīm coveted the latter's rank and desired that the abominable one arrange for him to replace al-Jubbā'ī. He thus forsook the ink and the pen and took to arms, applying himself exclusively to military affairs. At this juncture the abominable one sent him out with these troops, ordering him to take up positions across the Tigris in order to repel any (enemy) force which might arrive. At times Muḥammad stayed on the Tigris, and at times he went out with his men to the waterway known as Nahr Yazīd.[73] Among these troops of his were Shibl b. Sālim and ʿAmr, who was known as Ghulām Būdhā, the most valiant of his black troops and others. One man from this force surrendered to Zīrak and Nuṣayr and informed them of Muḥammad's designs. He told them that Muḥammad b. Ibrāhīm had targeted the area of Nuṣayr's camp—Nuṣayr was, at the time, stationed at Nahr al-Mar'ah.[74] He told them that Muḥammad and his troops were intending to pass along the
[1980] waterways which cross Nahr Maʿqil[75] and Bathq Shīrīn in order to reach the place known as al-Shurṭah[76] so as to emerge from behind and flank Nuṣayr's army. No sooner did this news reach Nuṣayr, than he hurriedly left al-Ubullah for his camp. At the same time, Zīrak took off for Bathq Shīrīn and appeared from behind him at a place called al-Mīshān, thinking that Muḥammad b. Ibrāhīm and his men would go to Nuṣayr's camp along this course. It was as he had surmised, and he encoun-

73. It is possible that this is the Nahr Yazīd in the area of al-Baṣrah mentioned by Yāqūt, *Muʿjam*, IV, 846.

74. An ancient canal in the Baṣrah area. See Yārūt, *Muʿjam*, IV, 844.

75. Ibid., 845.

76. A large village between al-Baṣrah and Wāsiṭ. See Yāqūt, *Muʿjam*, III, 275.

tered them on the way. After he had gone through violent battle, God granted him the upper hand, and the enemy (forces) were routed. They escaped to a canal where an ambush of theirs had been prepared—this was the Nahr Yazīd. However, Zīrak was guided there, and his galleys and barges deeply penetrated their positions. Some of the enemy (troops) were killed; some were captured. Among the captured were Muḥammad b. Ibrāhīm, whose patronymic was Abū ʿĪsā, and ʿAmr, who was called Ghulām Būdhā. They were seized along with some thirty galleys. Shibl and the others who escaped fled to the abominable one's camp. Victorious, Zīrak left Bathq Shīrīn, taking along the captives, the severed hands of the dead, and the galleys, skiffs and other boats that he had seized. Zīrak thus made his way from the Blind Tigris to Wāsiṭ, and wrote to Abū Aḥmad about the battle, the victory, and the (ultimate) conquest.

As a result of Zīrak's action, all the partisans of the profligate that were in the districts along the Tigris were filled with fear. It is said that about two thousand men requested guarantees of safe-conduct from Abū Ḥamzah, while he was stationed at Nahr al-Mar'ah. Abū Ḥamzah wrote of this to Abū Muḥam- [1981]
mad, and the latter instructed Zīrak to receive them and confirm their safe conduct. Moreover, he was to grant them a military allotment, integrate them with his own troops and use them against the enemy.

Zīrak remained in Wāsiṭ up to the time a dispatch arrived from Abū Aḥmad, ordering his son Hārūn to march to Nahr al-Mubārak with the troops that had remained with him; Zīrak then went with Hārūn. Abū Aḥmad now wrote to Nuṣayr, who was stationed at Nahr al-Mar'ah, ordering the latter to come to him at Nahr al-Mubārak. Abū Aḥmad then met him there.

In going to Nahr al-Mubārak, Abū al-ʿAbbās advanced with his barges and galleys to the camp of the profligate. He then attacked him in his city on the Abū al-Khaṣīb Canal. The battle between the two forces raged from early morning to late afternoon. One of the abominable one's officers called Muntāb, who had been attached to Sulaymān b. Jāmiʿ, asked Abū al-ʿAbbās for a guarantee of safe-conduct. With him were a contingent of his men. This defection was the kind of thing that shattered the abominable one and his army. Abū al-ʿAbbās withdrew with booty. He clothed Muntāb with robes of honor, treated him generously, and gave him a mount to ride. When Abū al-ʿAbbās reached his father, he told him about Muntāb, and how he had come to him, asking for guarantees of safe-conduct. At this, Abū Aḥmad also ordered robes of honor for Muntāb, as well as presents and a mount to ride. Muntāb was the first of the Zanj officers to seek a guarantee of safe-conduct.

According to Muḥammad b. al-Ḥasan b. Sahl—Muḥammad b. Ḥammād b. Isḥāq b. Ḥammād b. Zayd: When Abū Aḥmad reached Nahr al-Mubārak on a Saturday, in the middle of Rajab, 267 (February 5–March 6, 881), the first thing he reportedly did concerning the abominable one was to write him a letter calling upon him to repent and return to God Almighty and to desist from bloodshed and crimes. He was to stop
[1982] devastating regions and centers of population, and desist from rape and the violation of property. Moreover, he was to stop boasting that he was a prophet or apostle—an honor which God had not bestowed upon him. In addition, he informed him that he would extend him forgiveness and guarantees of safe-conduct if he would desist from those actions which God abhors. If he would but join the community of the Muslims, all his grave crimes of the past would be forgotten and he would earn for himself a life of plenty.

He forwarded this letter to the abominable one by way of his (that is, Abū Aḥmad's) messenger. The latter tried to deliver it, but was prevented from doing so by the abominable one's men. So, the messenger threw the letter to them, and they presented it to the abominable one who read it. The warning contained in the message did nothing but augment his hatred and obstinacy. He gave no reply at all, and persisted in his errors. The messenger returned to Abū Aḥmad, reported his action and the abominable one's refusal to reply to the letter.

Now, from Saturday through Wednesday, Abū Aḥmad was busy inspecting the barges and galleys, assigning to them his officers, clients and pages, and selecting archers for the vessels. On Thursday, Abū Aḥmad and his men, accompanied by his son Abū al-ʿAbbās, set out by the Abū al-Khaṣīb Canal for the city of the abominable one, which the latter had named al-

Mukhtārah.[77] Abū Aḥmad observed the city, and studied its defenses and fortifications, including the walls and surrounding moats. He studied the barricaded roads leading to it, the array of ballistas, catapults, and Nawukiyyah bows and other equipment on the city walls. The likes of these he had never seen in any previous revolt against the central authorities. Seeing the arrayed multitudes of enemy warriors, he realized how diffi- [1983] cult his task was. When the abominable one's troops saw Abū Aḥmad, they raised their voices so that the earth trembled.

Abū Aḥmad instructed his son, Abū al-ʿAbbās to proceed to the walls of the city and shower the defenders with arrows; this he did. He moved so close to the city that his barges struck the quay of the profligate's fortress. The profligate's (troops) rushed to the spot where the barges approached. The enemy banded together and hurled a succession of arrows and stones from their ballistas, catapults and slings, while the rank and file threw stones with their hands until there was no spot at which an observer from the barges could glance without seeing an arrow or a stone. Abū al-ʿAbbās endured all this, and the profligate and his companions saw the government force displaying perseverance and zeal such as no one fighting against them had ever done. Then Abū Aḥmad ordered Abū al-ʿAbbās and his men to return to their positions in order to rest and attend to their wounds; this they did.

At this point, two of the troops from the galleys asked Abū Aḥmad for guarantees of safe-conduct and they brought him their boat with its equipment and sailors. Abū Aḥmad ordered that brocade robes of honor and jewel-bedecked belts and other gifts be bestowed upon them. At his command, their sailors were given robes of red silk and white garments; all were showered with generous gifts. In this way Abū Aḥmad won their sympathy; then he posted them in a place from which they could be seen by their former comrades. This was the most humilitating stratagem ever employed against the profligate. For, when the remaining Zanj saw how their companions had been pardoned and granted kindness, they too wished eagerly for safe-conduct. They then rushed towards Abū Aḥmad, desir-

77. On the seige of al-Mukhtārah, see Popovic *Révolte*, 134 ff.

[1984] ing to obtain what he had made available for the others. On that day, a number of troops from the galleys went over to Abū Aḥmad, and upon his order they all received the same treatment as their predecessors. When the abominable one saw that the troops from his galleys were inclined to surrender and were seizing every opportunity to do so, he ordered all of them to return from the Tigris to Nahr Abī al-Khaṣīb; at the mouth of this canal he placed men to prevent their leaving. At this, he had the barges brought forward, for which purpose he summoned Bahbūdh b. ʿAbd al-Wahhāb, one of his most loyal champions; the latter had under his command the largest and the best equipped vessels. Bahbūdh and his men responded to this call. It happened to be full tide, and the barges of Abū Aḥmad were dispersed. Abū Ḥamzah with his ships clung to the eastern bank of the Tigris. Establishing his position there, he felt that the fight was over and he was no longer needed. But when Bahbūdh and his barges appeared, Abū Aḥmad ordered Abū Ḥamzah to advance with his barges; he also ordered Abū al-ʿAbbās to attack Bahbūdh with his vessels, while sending word to the officers and pages to attack with him. Twelve barges, manned by the officers and pages who were with Abū al-ʿAbbās and Zīrak, bore the brunt of the battle. As the battle flared, the abominable one's men chose to attack Abū al-ʿAbbās and his force, for they had only a few barges. However, when the Zanj were confronted with a counter-attack and put to flight, Abū al-ʿAbbās and his men turned to chase Bahbūdh, whom they drove to an enclosure near the abominable one's fortress. Bahbūdh suffered two lance thrusts and received many arrow wounds; his limbs were badly injured by stones. But his men saved him, for they protected him until he reached
[1985] Abū al-Khaṣīb; thus he narrowly escaped death. Among the officers who were with him and were slain that day was one called ʿAmīrah, a man brave and valiant, who was always in the forefront of the battle. The men of Abū al-ʿAbbās seized one of Bahbūdh's barges whose men had been killed or drowned. The ship was taken and, in accordance with Abū Aḥmad's instructions, Abū al-ʿAbbās and his men set their ships toward the eastern bank of the Tigris as the force withdrew.

When the profligate perceived that Abū Aḥmad's force was withdrawing, he ordered those who had fled in their barges to Nahr Abū al-Khaṣīb, to come forward so as to allay his men's fear by creating an impression of an orderly retreat and not a flight in defeat. At this, Abū Aḥmad quickly instructed some of his pages to turn the fore of their barges toward them in pursuit. No sooner did the Zanj see this than they fled in great panic. One of their barges remained behind and the troops in it asked Abū Aḥmad for guarantees of safe-conduct. Displaying a white flag that they had, the Zanj came to him in their barge and were granted safe-conduct. They were given various presents and garments. This induced the profligate to order the Zanj barges brought back into the canal and to bar their exit from it. Since it was near the end of the day, Abū Aḥmad ordered his men to return to their camp at the Nahr al-Mubārak. On that day, during his withdrawal, a great many of the Zanj and others sought guarantees of safety from Abū Aḥmad. He welcomed them and had them transported on his barges and galleys. Then he ordered robes of honor for them, as well as various presents, and their names were inscribed in the registers of Abū al-ʿAbbās's troops.

Abū Aḥmad went to his camp, which he reached after the late evening prayer. He stayed there during Friday, Saturday [1986]
and Sunday, and then decided to transfer his camp to a place which would be nearer for him to carry on the campaign against the abominable one. On Monday, the twenty-fourth of Rajab, 267 (February 28, 881), Abū Aḥmad together with Abū al-ʿAbbās, his clients, pages and officers—among them Zīrak and Nuṣayr—boarded barges and sailed until they reached the waterway called Nahr Jaṭṭa,[78] east of the Tigris. It was opposite the canal called Nahr al-Yahūdī.[79] He stopped there, made whatever arrangements he felt were necessary, and then pushed on, leaving behind Abū al-ʿAbbās, Nuṣayr and Zīrak. Abū Aḥmad

78. One of the canals of the Baṣrah area. Its banks were heavily settled. See Yāqūt, *Muʿjam*, IV, 837.

79. This does not seem to be the Yahūdī Canal which was in the vicinity of Sāmarrā. See Le Strange, *Lands*, 58. I have found no reference to this particular waterway.

returned to his camp, and upon his command, it was announced among the men that they were going to journey to the place he had chosen on the Jaṭṭā Canal. After the roads were put in good order for the tranport animals and the bridges on the canals were secured, he moved out, with the animals in the lead. Early on the morning of Tuesday, the twenty-fifth of Rajab (March 1, 881), he and all his troops travelled to Nahr Jaṭṭā and set up camp there.

They remained there until Saturday, the fourteenth of Shaʿbān, 267 (March 21, 881), having engaged in no combat. It was only on that day that Abū Aḥmad set out with his infantry and cavalry—he took along all his horsemen. He put the infantry men and the volunteers—every one of them in uniform and breastplate—aboard vessels and barges, and journeyed to the Euphrates, reaching a place opposite the profligate's camp. At the time, Abū Aḥmad had fifty thousand or more troops and auxiliaries, while the profligate had some three hundred thousand, all of whom were active warriors or defenders, such as
[1987] swordsmen, lancers, archers, sling-shooters and artillerymen for the catapults and ballistas. The weakest were charged with flinging stones by hand, and, as assembled onlookers, they added to the tumult by screaming and shouting, a task shared by the women.

Abū Aḥmad remained opposite the profligate's camp until late in the morning, when, at his command, heralds cried out that guarantees of safe-conduct were being offered to everyone without discrimination, except for the abominable one. He then called for arrows upon which were fastened sheets containing the text of the guarantees which had been announced. In it he promised to treat kindly those people (who surrendered). The sheets were then shot into the abominable one's camp. Now, the hearts of the heretics were swerving towards Abū Aḥmad out of awe and eagerness for the good-will and pardon which he had promised them. A great many of them came to him on that day, carried by barges; whereupon, he presented them with various gifts. Abū Aḥmad then returned to his encampment on the Jaṭṭā Canal, and no fighting took place that day. Two of his mawlā officers, one of them Buktimur and the other Jaʿfar b. Yaghlaʿuz, arrived with all their troops, strengthening the forces with Abū Aḥmad. Abū Aḥmad departed from the Jaṭṭa Canal to an encampment which he had prepared in advance. He constructed bridges along its waterways and had the river spanned so that the camp could expand to Furāt al-Baṣrah, opposite the city of the profligate. It was on a Sunday, in the middle of Shaʿbān, 267 (March 7–April 4, 881), that Abū Aḥmad settled at this encampment; he made it his base and positioned himself there, assigning his officers and commanders to their various positions. He placed Nuṣayr, the commander of the barges and galleys, together with his troops, in the first range of the camp, whose outer limit was a place di- [1988] rectly opposite the waterway known as Nahr Juwayy Kūr. Zīrak al-Turkī, the commander of the vanguard of Abū al-ʿAbbās, was assigned with his troops to a position opposite the area between the Abū al-Khaṣīb Canal, which is also known as Nahr al-Atrāk, and the waterway known as Nahr al-Mughīrah. Zīrak was followed by Abū Aḥmad's chamberlain (*ḥājib*), Yaʿlā b. Juhistār, and his troops. The tents of Abū Aḥmad and his two sons were in front of Dayr Jābīl.[80] Abū Aḥmad sent his client Rāshid at the head of his (Abū Aḥmad's) clients and his pages down to the waterway called Nahr al-Maṭmah—his pages consisted of Turks, Khazars, men from al-Rūm, Daylam, Ṭabaristān, the Maghrib and Zanzibar. He placed his wazīr Sāʿid b. Makhlad with a force of clients and page above Rāshid's force, and sent Masrūr al-Balkhī with his troops down to the waterway called Nahr Sindādān. Similarly, he sent al-Faḍl and Muḥammad, the sons of Mūsā b. Bughā, with their armies down to the waterway known as Nahr Hālah. These two were followed by Mūsā Dāljawayh with his soldiers and officers. Bughrāj al-Turkī was assigned to the rearguard camped at the Jaṭṭa Canal. In this way they established their base camp and remained there.

Now, observing the position of the abominable one, his fortifications and the vastness of the army, Abū Aḥmad realized that he must wear him out in a long siege and bring about a split among his troops by offering good-will to those who would turn away from their master, and by treating harshly

80. In the Baṣrah region. See Yāqūt, *Muʿjam*, II, 650.

those who stuck to their errors. He further realized that he needed more barges and other equipment for river fighting. He
[1989] therefore sent agents to collect provisions and let them come by land and water to his camp in the city which he named al-Muwaffaqiyyah. He wrote to the governors of the surrounding districts to bring the money to his treasury in this city. He also sent a messenger to Sīrāf[81] and Jannābā[82] about building the numerous barges which he needed in order to post them where they could cut off the flow of provisions to the traitor and his cohort. He also wrote to his governors in the surrounding districts to dispatch to him anyone fit and willing so that they might be inscribed on his roll. Then he spent a month or so waiting. Provisions kept on arriving regularly, transport after transport, and the merchants provided various kinds of wares and produce for the city of al-Muwaffaqiyyah. Markets sprang up in that city, and the number of merchants and contractors from every land grew in number. After more than ten years of brigandage on the waterways by the profligate and his men, boats began to arrive again.

Abū Aḥmad built a Friday Mosque and ordered the people to worship there; then he established mints that issued gold and silver coins. Various resources and amenities were concentrated in Abū Aḥmad's city, and its inhabitants missed nothing that was available in the older cities. Money flowed into it and pay was distributed on time. As the situation improved, people lived in comfort, and everyone was eager to travel to the city of al-Muwaffaqiyyah and stay there.

[1990] Two days after Abū Aḥmad's arrival in al-Muwaffaqiyyah, the abominable one ordered Bahbūdh b. ʿAbd al-Wahhāb (to attack). He crossed (the water) to the edge of Abū Ḥamzah's camp, catching the troops in the galleys unaware. Bahbūdh charged Abū Ḥamzah and killed many of his men, capturing many others. He set fire to the reed huts they had put up before buildings were erected there. At this, Abū Aḥmad instructed Nuṣayr to rally all his men and to grant no one leave from the

81. The great seaport of the Persian Gulf. See Le Strange, *Lands*, index, 530.

82. Ibid., index, 509.

camp. He also ordered him to use his barges, galleys, skiffs, and infantry to guard the perimeter of his camp up to the outer reaches of Māyān Rūdhān,[83] al-Qindal[84] and Abrusān, and to engage whatever troops the profligate had there.

At Māyān Rūdhān was one of the profligate's officers, an Ibrāhīm b. Jaʿfar al-Hamdānī along with four thousand Zanj; and in al-Qindal, Muḥammad b. Abān, who was known as Abū al-Ḥasān, the brother of ʿAlī b. Abān, was stationed with three thousand men. Similarly, the one known as al-Dūr was stationed in Abrusān with a force of fifteen hundred, made up of Zanj and men of al-Jubbāʾī's contingent.

Abū al-ʿAbbās opened operations with an attack on al-Hamdānī. In a series of engagements, al-Hamdānī lost many men who were killed or captured.He himself escaped in a galley he had held ready and reached the brother of al-Muhallabī, the one whose patronymic was Abū al-Ḥāsan. The troops of Abū al-ʿAbbās took hold of everything the Zanj had in their possession and transported it to their camp. Abū Aḥmad had sent word to his son to grant safe-conduct to everyone appealing for it and to treat kindly all who came out to him. A band of Zanj deserted Alī b. Abān, seeking guarantees of safe-conduct and Abū al-ʿAbbās granted them their request. Then he sent them to his father, who ordered robes of honor an gifts for everyone of them according to their personal merits. He also ordered that [1991]
they be placed opposite the Abū al-Khaṣīb Canal so that their (former) compatriots could see them. Thus, Abū Aḥmad continued to trap the traitor, granting safe-conduct to all Zanj and others deserting him, and besieging and blockading the rest by cutting off their supplies and necessities.

The provisions from al-Ahwāz and the various kinds of merchandise from it, its districts, and the surrounding areas that fell under the jurisdiction of its officials, used to come along the waterway known as Nahr Bayān. Bahbūdh once got wind of a caravan with a variety of merchandise and food, so with a select team he set out one night to a palm grove and lay there in wait. As the caravan, unaware of the ambush, was passing,

83. See Yāqūt *Muʿjam*, IV, 708–709.

84. A place situated in the Baṣrah region. See Yāqūt, *Muʿjam*, IV, 183.

Bahbūdh fell upon it, killing some and capturing others while seizing goods to his heart's content. Abū Aḥmad had dispatched with the caravan an officer with a convoy of troops to guard it, but they were unable to do so, because of the size of Bahbūdh's force and the terrain which was unfavorable for the use of cavalry that was indispensible.

When word of this reached Abū Aḥmad, he was shocked by the losses in money, men and goods, and he gave instructions to compensate the men in full. He now posted barges at the mouth of the Bayān and other canals, places which could not be reached by horsemen. He also ordered that additional barges be built and sent to him, and a goodly number of them arrived. He manned them and put them under the command of his son, Abū al-ʿAbbās, instructing him to take care of every spot through which provisions could flow to the profligate (forces). For this purpose Abū al-ʿAbbās, sailed with his barges to the mouth of the sea, placing officers on all the roads. Having done so, he fully acquitted himself of this task.

In Ramaḍān (April 5–May 4, 881) a battle took place be-
[1992] tween Isḥāq b. Kundāj, and Isḥāq b. Ayyūb, ʿĪsā b. al-Shaykh, Abū al-Maghrāʾ, Ḥamdān al-Shārī and the tribes of Rabīʿah, Taghlib, Bakr and Yaman that were connected with them. Ibn Kundāj routed them and chased them to Naṣībīn and beyond there to the vicinity of Āmid. He seized their possessions and they camped at Āmid. Further engagements ensued.

In this month Ṣandal al-Zinjī was killed. The reason for his being killed (is as follows). On the second of Ramaḍān, 267 (April 6, 881) troops of the abominable one reportedly made their way toward the camps of Nuṣayr and Zīrak with the intention of attacking them; but warned by people, Nuṣayr and Zīrak gave battle and, driving the Zanj back, they took Ṣandal prisoner. They say, this Ṣandal used to unveil the faces and heads of free-born Muslim women and treat them as if they were handmaids. And if one would resist, he would strike her in the face and pass her to some savage Zanj for a very low price. When he was delivered to Abū Aḥmad, the latter ordered him tied, and in his presence the man was ordered pierced with arrows and killed.

In Ramaḍān, (April 5–May 4, 881) a great many of the Zanj requested safe-conduct from Abū Aḥmad.

The Reason for These Requests

It is reported that Muhadhdhab, one of the abominable one's most prominent followers, and a leading and courageous figure among them, sought a guarantee of safe-conduct from Abū Aḥmad. A barge brought him to Abū Aḥmad while the latter was breaking his fast. Muhadhdhab reported that he came [1993] bearing good advice and seeking safety, and indicated that at that very moment the Zanj were on their way to Abū Aḥmad's camp in order to attack him by night. For this purpose the profligate had summoned his most valiant men. At this, Abū Aḥmad gave an order to send barges arrayed with a force to combat the Zanj and prevent their passage. When the Zanj perceived that their plan was disclosed, they withdrew in panic and scores of Zanj and others surrendered and continued to do so. By the end of Ramaḍān, 267, (April 5–May 4, 881) the number of people, white and black, who arrived at the camp of Abū Aḥmad reached five thousand.

In Shawwāl (May 5–June 2, 881), news arrived that al-Khujustānī had entered Naysābūr and that ʿAmr b. al-Layth and his men had fled. The former had treated the people there harshly; he demolished the houses of the Muʿādh b. Muslim's clan, and killed those of its members who fell into his hands. Their estates were given to others as fiefs. He eliminated the name of Muḥammad b. Ṭāhir from the sermons in the pulpits of the cities which he seized in Khurāsān, and had the people pledge allegiance only to himself and to al-Muʿtamid, leaving out all others.

In Shawwāl, (May 5–June 2, 881) Abū al-ʿAbbās engaged in a fight with the Zanj, and inflicted heavy losses upon them.

The Reason For This Fight

According to information which reached me, the profligate selected from all his troops, men of courage and valor, and in-

[1994] structed al-Muhallabī to cross (the waterway) with them for a night raid on the camp of Abū Aḥmad. This he did.

The number of the Zanj and others who crossed the water was about five thousand, mostly blacks, among them some two hundred officers. They crossed to the eastern side of the Tigris, and decided that some of their forces should go behind the palm grove near the lagoon, so as to be in the rear of Abū Aḥmad's army. A large detachment was to pass with barges, galleys and ferries in front of Abū Aḥmad's camp. Should fighting break out between the two forces, the abominable one's commanders who reached the lagoon were to attack the camp of Abū Aḥmad al-Muwaffaq with great vigor, surprising him and his men in the midst of battle.

The rebels counted on the success of this scheme. Their troops stayed all night on the Euphrates[85] in order to attack the army at the break of day. But a young sailor from their ranks sought safety from Abū Aḥmad and disclosed to him the plan which the rebels had conceived against him. Abū Aḥmad instructed Abū al-ʿAbbās and the officers and pages to set out for the area of the abominable one's troops. He dispatched a group of officers from among his pages with cavalry to the lagoon behind the palm grove on the Euphrates, in order to cut off the enemy's retreat to the lagoon. The men of the barges and galleys were instructed to block the Tigris, while the infantry were ordered to move toward the enemy from the palm grove.

When, contrary to their expectations, the rebels became aware of these measures taken against them, they fled along the same way they had come, and sought safety in the direc-
[1995] tion of Jawwīth Bārūbah.[86] Informed of their retreat, al-Muwaffaq instructed Abū al-ʿAbbās and Zīrak to go with their barges and reach the river before the Zanj so as to prevent them from crossing. He instructed one of his pages—he was called

85. Presumably where the river turns into The Great Swamp.

86. The text reads: Barawayh; it should read: Bārūbah, as in Yāqūt, *Muʿjam*, II, 163. The latter indicates it to be a town in the Baṣrah region opposite al-Uballah.

Thābit—who had under his command an extensive force of black pages, to transport his men with bridging equipment and skiffs to the place where the enemies of God were positioned in order to attack them in place. Thābit overtook the Zanj at Jawwīth Bārūbah and attacked them. He engaged them in sustained combat, but the Zanj stood fast, and then pressed the attack against his combined force. His troops consisted of only some five hundred men because his contingent was not fully mobilized. The enemy sought them out, but then Thābit counterattacked them gallantly, forcing them back. God granted him the sight of them running away, bearing heavy losses in dead, wounded, and drowned; those who plunged into the water, relying upon their ability to swim, were picked up by the barges and galleys in the Tigris and the canal. Of this army, only a few escaped. Abū al-ʿAbbās and Thābit returned victorious. The heads of the killed were hung from the barges; similarly, the captives were crucified. They passed near the enemy city in order to terrify the compatriots of the dead and captured. Upon seeing this, the Zanj fell into despair and were seized by foreboding. After he had come with the prisoners and the heads into the city of al-Muwaffaqiyyah, Abū al-ʿAbbās heard that the leader of the Zanj was deluding his men with false stories that the heads displayed were only effigies to frighten them, and that the crucified captives were deserters who had surrendered to the government army. At this, al-Muwaffaq instructed Abū al-ʿAbbās to gather the heads and go with them in front of the profligate's fortress. He was then to hurl them into the latter's camp by means of a catapult at- [1996]
tached to a vessel. This was done. Now, when the heads dropped into the Zanj city, the friends of the dead recognized the heads of their compatriots and broke out in tears. The lies and duplicity of the sinner thus became evident to all.

In Shawwāl, (May 5–June 2, 881) the troops of Ibn Abī al-Sāj fought with al-Hayṣam al-ʿIjlī, destroying his vanguard; then they seized his camp and pillaged it.

In Dhū al-Qaʿdah, (June 3–July 2, 881), Zīrak fought with troops of the leader of the Zanj at Nahr b. ʿUmar and inflicted heavy losses upon them.

The Reason for This Engagement

It is reported that the leader of the Zanj ordered the procurement of barges. These were constructed for him and added to those used in military operations. He divided his barges into three groups led by Bahbūdh, Naṣr al-Rūmī and Aḥmad b. al-Zaranjī respectively. Each commander was made responsible for his group. There were some fifty barges to a squadron. He manned them with archers and lancers, and an effort was made to bring their equipment and arms into perfect condition. Then they were ordered to set out upon the Tigris, cross to the eastern side and challenge the troops of al-Muwaffaq in combat.

Al-Muwaffaq, at this time, had only a small number of barges, since not all that he had ordered prepared for him had arrived, and those which he had at his disposal were scattered about the mouth of the sea and mouths of the canals along which provisions flowed to the Zanj. The henchmen of the sinner went about their task brutally, and as a result, it was possible to seize one after another of al-Muwaffaq's barges. Nu-
[1997] ṣayr, who was known as Abū Ḥamzah, at the time commanded the major part of al-Muwaffaq's barges; he refrained from engaging the enemy in combat or from advancing towards them, as he would otherwise have done, because the number of his barges was not sufficient. Therefore, people in al-Muwaffaq's camp were terrified, fearing that the Zanj with their superiority in barges might set out against them.

But at this juncture, barges which al-Muwaffaq had built in Jannābā arrived. Fearing the Zanj might intercept them on the Tigris, Abū Aḥmad instructed Abū al-ʿAbbās to set out with his barges to meet them and safely convey them to the camp. Abū al-ʿAbbās then brought these barges to Nuṣayr's camp.

When the Zanj noticed the barges, they were anxious to seize them. The abominable one ordered his barges and men out to challenge the enemy. The barges of Nuṣayr and Abū al-ʿAbbās went into action in an effort to cut them off.

One of Abū al-ʿAbbās's pages, a brave man called Waṣīf, who was known as al-Ḥijrā'ī, rushed forward with his barges and attacked the Zanj vigorously. They fled and he pursued them until he encountered them in the Abū al-Khaṣīb Canal, and was

cut off from his force. The barges of the Zanj turned about to attack him, and he found himself in a grave situation. Some of the Zanj barges clung with their oars to the oars of Waṣīf's barge and pulled it toward the bank, while others surrounded him and his men from all sides. More Zanj rushed down from the walls, and although Waṣīf and his men fought vigorously, they were killed. Then the Zanj withdrew with their barges into the Abū al-Khaṣīb Canal. Abū al-ʿAbbās met the Jannābā barges that had arrived safely with their armament and men. Abū Aḥmad ordered Abū al-ʿAbbās to take complete command of all the military operations involving the barges, and cut off [1998]
the flow of supplies to the enemy from any quarter; this he did.

The barges were outfitted and manned with the best archers and lancers. When everything was fully prepared, Abū al-ʿAbbās posted the vessels in places where the barges of the abominable one sought loot, following their usual pattern. Abū al-ʿAbbās set out against them with his barges and the other commanders were ordered to join him in the attack. This they did, penetrating the enemy formations, showering them with arrows and stones, and reaching them with lances. God smote the enemy who fled in panic, while Abū al-ʿAbbās and his men chased them, forcing them to seek refuge in the Abū al-Khaṣīb Canal. Three of their ships were sunk, and two others were captured with all their fighting men and sailors. At the order of Abū al-ʿAbbās, they were all beheaded. When the abominable one saw the fate of his men, he held his barges back in the enclosure of his fortress and forbade his men to sail them into the Tigris except when the river was free from al-Muwaffaq's vessels.

After Abū al-ʿAbbās had attacked them in this fashion, the panic among the Zanj increased and prominent companions of the abominable one sought to surrender. They were granted safe conduct. It is reported that among the prominent Zanj seeking safety was Muḥammad b. Ḥārith al-ʿAmmī, who was charged with defending the camp at Munkā and the walls close to the camp of al-Muwaffaq. He deserted at night with a number of his companions, and al-Muwaffaq received him with generous gifts, clothed him with robes of honor, and gave him a number of horses with harnesses and equipment. He also put [1999] him on the payroll. Muḥammad b. al-Ḥārith also attempted to take along his wife, who was his cousin, but the woman failed in her attempt to join him. Caught by the Zanj, she was returned to the abominable one, who kept her in jail for a time, then he had her auctioned off in the market and sold.

Among those seeking a guarantee of safe-conduct was Aḥmad, who was known as al-Bardhaʿī. It is said that he was one of the most valiant companions of the abominable one and a close friend of al-Muhallabī. Among the Zanj commanders who sought safety were Madbad, Ibn Ankalawayh and Manīnah. They were all bestowed with robes of honor, and given numerous gifts and horses. All the soldiers who came with them were also accorded excellent treatment.

As the flow of provisions to the abominable one was cut off, and all the roads leading to him and his men were blocked, he instructed Shibl and Abū Nidā', two of his earliest followers—commanders upon whom he could rely and whose advice he trusted—to set out with ten thousand Zanj and others to the Dayr, Mar'ah and Abū al-Asad canals.[87] From there they were to go to the Great Swamp (*al-Baṭīḥah*)[88] to raid the Muslims, seize any provisions they might find, and cut off the provisions and other supplies flowing to the camp of al-Muwaffaq from Baghdad (Madīnat al-Salām) and Wāsiṭ and the surrounding areas. When news of their journey reached al-Muwaffaq, he summoned his client Zīrak, the commander of Abū al-ʿAbbās's vanguard, and instructed him to proceed against them with his troops. He also attached a select group of men to Zīrak's command.

Zīrak moved out quickly with his barges and galleys, and transported his infantry in skiffs and light vessels, reaching
[2000] Nahr al-Dayr.[89] Having found no trace of the Zanj, he moved on to Bathq Shīrīn, and then worked his way along the ʿAdī Canal.[90] When he came out to the Ibn ʿUmar Canal,[91] he met up

87. See Le Strange, *Lands*, 26, 41, 42; Yāqūt, *Muʿjam*, IV, 839.
88. See Le Strange, *Lands*, 41.
89. See above, n. 87
90. See above, n. 88.
91. See Yāqūt, *Muʿjam*, IV, 830.

with the Zanj force, the size of which terrified him. Zīrak implored God to help him against the Zanj, then charged upon them with the most seasoned and stalwart of his men. God cast terror into the hearts of the Zanj, and they collapsed under the blows of Zīrak's arms. An enormous number of them were killed, as many drowned and a great number of them were captured. Zīrak took hold of as many vessels as he could, and sank as many as he could. The number of vessels he seized reached about four hundred. He took the captives and the heads of the slain and proceeded to the camp of al-Muwaffaq.

On the twenty-third of Dhū al-Ḥijjah (July 26, 881), al-Muwaffaq himself crossed with his troops to the city of the profligate to fight him.

The Reason Why He Crossed Over to the Profligate

The reason for this was as follows: It is reported that when the commanders of the profligate's troops perceived the misfortune which had befallen them—death for those who emerged from the city (to fight), a harsh siege for those who had remained within its limits—none of them ventured out. And as they saw the excellent treatment accorded to those who sought safety from Abū Aḥmad and the pardon granted them, they too tended to surrender. They started to flee by every means possible. This filled the abominable one with terror and a certain feeling of his own doom.

In every sector where he suspected there was an escape route [2001]
from his camp, he appointed guards and security men. He gave them the task of policing these areas and assigned men to the mouths of the canals to prevent boats from leaving. He was anxious to block any road, pass and opening so as to eliminate any temptation to leave his city.

A group of the deviate's commanders, that is, the leader of the Zanj, sent a message to al-Muwaffaq, requesting a guarantee of safe-conduct, and asking him to send out an army to fight the abominable one, so that they would have an opportunity to change allegiance. Then al-Muwaffaq instructed Abū al-ʿAbbās to go with a body of his troops to the place known as

Nahr al-Gharbī, which was patrolled at the time by ʿAlī b. Abān.

Abū al-ʿAbbās set out for Nahr al- Gharbī with a select force, taking with him barges, galleys and ferries. ʿAlī b. al- Muhallabī and his men volunteered to go out against him and the two forces thus engaged in combat. Abū al-ʿAbbās's force gained the upper hand and subdued the enemy. The profligate sent Sulaymān b. Jāmiʿ to reinforce al-Muhallabī with a large contingent of Zanj. The battle continued that day from early in the morning into the late afternoon; the victory went to Abū al-ʿAbbās and his men. That group of the abominable one's commanders who had sought safe-conduct from Abū al-ʿAbbās came over to him now, joined by a great many Zanj horsemen and others. Abū al-ʿAbbās then ordered his troops to return to the barges and boats, and he left. On the way back he passed the city of the abominable one and reached the place known as Nahr al-Atrāk. His troops, noticing that there were few Zanj in that section of the canal, were tempted to attack and set off in the direction of the enemy—this was after the major part of the government troops had already withdrawn to al-Muwaffaqiyyah. They approached the bank, climbed up and quickly ad-
[2002] vanced along the paths there. A group of them climbed the walls and came upon a small band of Zanj and their supporters. They killed those who came within their reach there. The profligate became aware of them, however, and bands of Zanj rallied to fight them, answering the call. When Abū al-ʿAbbās saw the growing concentration of the enemy against his small band of troops, he himself rushed back with his men from the barges to join them, while dispatching a message to al-Muwaffaq to send reinforcements. The latter immediately sent a force of pages to assist him; they came on barges and galleys. The pages gained the upper hand and put the Zanj to flight.

When Sulaymān b. Jāmiʿ noticed how Abū al-ʿAbbās's men were victorious over the Zanj, he rushed to the canal with a large body of troops, and travelled upstream until he reached the canal called Nahr ʿAbdallāh. There he tracked the troops of Abū al-ʿAbbās, who were fighting the Zanj in front of them. As they were pursuing the fleeing Zanj, Sulaymān emerged behind them and beat his drums. At this, the troops of Abū al-ʿAbbās turned to flee, and the Zanj who were running away turned about. A detachment of al-Muwaffaq's pages and other units of his army were attacked, and the Zanj thus acquired a number of flags and spears. Abū al-ʿAbbās protected the rest of his men; most of them were unharmed and he withdrew with them. This skirmish encouraged the Zanj and their followers, and strengthened their spirits.

Again al-Muwaffaq resolved upon crossing with all his troops to fight against the abominable one. He instructed Abū al-ʿAbbās and the rest of the officers and pages to prepare for the crossing. He also gave orders to assemble the boats and crossing equipment and to distribute them among different units. He then set the date on which he wanted to cross. This, however, was upset by stormy weather which lasted for many days. Delaying until these winds subsided, al-Muwaffaq re- [2003] sumed the preparations for crossing and fighting against the deviate. When they were completed, on Wednesday, the twenty-fourth of Dhū al-Ḥijjah, 267 (Tuesday, July 28, 881), he crossed with a huge and fully-equipped army, and gave the order for many horses to be ferried over by boat. He commanded Abū al-ʿAbbās to march with the cavalry and to take with him all his officers from among the horsemen and infantry so as to attack the enemy in the rear on the lower part of the canal known as Nahr Munkā. He instructed his mawlā Masrūr al-Balkhī to go to the canal known as Nahr al-Gharbī, thereby forcing the abominable one to split his force. He ordered Nuṣayr Abū Ḥamzah and Rashīq, Abū al-ʿAbbās's page—he was one of his companions—who had almost as many ships as Nuṣayr, to sail to the mouth of the Abū al-Khaṣīb Canal and to fight whatever vessels of the abominable one they might come across. In the meanwhile, the latter increased the number of his vessels and manned them with the best of his fighting men. Abū Aḥmad advanced with his entire force to one of the fortresses of the abominable one's city—the latter had it reinforced by his own son, the one known as Ankalayh. He flanked Ankalayh with ʿAlī b. Abān, Sulaymān b. Jāmiʿ and Ibrāhīm b. Jaʿfar al-Hamdānī, and provided the fortress with ballistas, catapults, and Nawukiyyah bows. He placed the archers in position and concentrated the major part of his army there. When

the two parties came upon each other, al-Muwaffaq commanded the archers and lancers among the pages and blacks to draw nearer to the fortress in which the profligates were assembled. Between them was the canal known as Nahr al-
[2004] Atrāk, which was wide and deep. When they arrived there, al-Muwaffaq's men began to waver, but after being encouraged by shouting, they moved ahead, swimming while the profligates were shooting at them from ballistas, catapults, and slings, and hurling stones by hand, shooting arrows from the Nawukiyyah bows, foot-bows and various other launching devices. Al-Muwaffaq's men bore up against all this, crossed the canal, and reached the walls; but the men who were outfitted for demolition operations failed to join them. Then the pages of Abū al-ʿAbbās were put in charge of breaking walls with the weapons at hand. God granted them success and facilitated their ascent. By specially adapted ladders, which were delivered to the spot, they mounted the fortress and planted one of al-Muwaffaq's flags there. After the heaviest of fighting, in which both parties bore great losses, the profligates surrendered their wall and left the battle-ground. In this operation, Thābit, a page of al-Muwaffaq who had been one of the most illustrious commanders among the pages, was struck by an arrow in the stomach and died. Al-Muwaffaq's troops succeeded in seizing the walls of the rebels; they burned down all the ballistas, catapults, and Nāwukiyyah bows, and then, evacuating that sector, they withdrew.

Abū al-ʿAbbās with his men and cavalry had moved toward the canal known as Nahr Munkā, when they came upon ʿAlī b. Abān al-Muhallabī and his troops. The enemy had come out to oppose them and push them back from their objective. Abū al-ʿAbbās charged ʿAlī and routed him, killing a great many of his troops; but al-Muhallabī escaped. Abū al-ʿAbbās reached the spot from which he thought he might penetrate the city of the abominable one on the lower part of the Munkā Canal. He believed that the entrance into the city from this approach would
[2005] be easy, but when he entered the trench he found it wide and impeding. However, he urged his men on and they crossed —the horsemen on their horses and the infantry by swimming—until they reached the wall, where he made a breach

wide enough to enable them to get through. The first group to penetrate came upon Sulaymān b. Jāmiʿ who had come to defend this sector as soon as he learned that al-Muhallabī had fled. The government troops fought him. Ten pages of al-Muwaffaq who were in front of the men, repelled Sulaymān and his force, though there were many of them. They turned the enemy aside many times, defending their comrades until they withdrew to their positions.

Muḥammad b. Ḥammād reported: When al-Muwaffaq's troops seized the position that the profligate had entrusted to his son and his aforementioned men and officers, they scattered from the wall, as best they could, those who rushed them. Then the special demolition detachment arrived with tools and implements, and made a number of breaches in the wall. Al-Muwaffaq had prepared a special pontoon bridge to span the trench of the profligates. The bridge was set in place and all the people passed over it. Seeing this, the abominable ones became terrified and fled from a second wall to which they had been holding fast. Al-Muwaffaq's troops entered the city of the perfidious one. The deviate and his supporters fled, with al-Muwaffaq's troops in pursuit. They killed whoever came within their reach, and continued their chase until they came to the canal known as Nahr Ibn Simʿān. The residence of Ibn Simʿān fell to al-Muwaffaq's men, who burned everything in it and demolished it. The deviates held their position for a long time at Nahr Ibn Simʿān, putting up stubborn resistance. [2006]
One of al-Muwaffaq's pages pressed hard towards ʿAlī b. Abān al-Muhallabī and seized him by his cloak, but the latter disentangled himself, slipped out of the cloak which he flung at the page and narrowly escaped death. Al-Muwaffaq's troops charged the Zanj gallantly and forced them from Nahr Ibn Simʿān, reaching the fringe of the profligate's review ground. When the abominable one heard that his troops had been routed and that al-Muwaffaq's force had penetrated into the outskirts of his city, he took to his mount together with his men; but here, on the fringe of the review ground, the troops of al-Muwaffaq came upon them and recognized them. They charged him, and dispersed his troops and others who were with him, separating him and leaving him isolated. One of the

infantry got so close to the rebel that he struck the head of his horse with his shield. It was already sunset, and al-Muwaffaq ordered his men to return to their ships. They returned safely, carrying along a great many heads of slain rebels after having killed and wounded at random, and after having put (the enemy's) houses and markets to the torch. At the beginning of that day, a group of officers and horsemen of the deviate surrendered to Abū al-ʿAbbās, and he now had to transport them by boat. When night fell, a strong northern wind stirred, and the ebb tide became more pronounced causing most of the ships to be stuck in the mud. The abominable one urged his supporters on, encouraging them to act, and a group of them set out to attack some of the various vessels that remained behind. They seized them, killing some of the troops in them. Bahbūdh, who had been facing Masrūr al-Balkhī and his troops at Nahr al-Gharbī that day, attacked him, killing a number of his men,
[2007] seizing captives as well as some of their animals. This broke the fighting spirit of al-Muwaffaq's men.

The same day, the abominable one brought all his barges out into the Tigris to fight against Rashīq, but Rashīq seized some of his ships; others, he sank and burned. The rest fled to the Abū al-Khaṣīb Canal.

It is reported that on that day the profligate and his men were forced to disperse and flee at random to the al-Amīr, and to al-Qindal, Abrusān, ʿAbbādān and the other villages. On that day two brothers of Sulaymān b. Mūsā al-Shaʿrānī, Muḥammad and ʿĪsā, fled to the desert and remained there until word reached them that al-Muwaffaq's troops had withdrawn; only then did they return. A group of tribesmen who were at the profligate's camp also fled, and upon reaching al-Baṣrah, they sent a delegation to Abū Aḥmad seeking a guarantee of safe-conduct from him. Abū Aḥmad accepted this and sent out vessels to transport them to al-Muwaffaqiyyah. He ordered them clothed with robes of honor, gave them presents and provided them with allotments and a place to stay. Among those who surrendered was also one of the most illustrious commanders of the deviate, Rayḥān b. Sāliḥ al-Maghribī, a man of leadership and authority, who held the chamberlain's office for the son of the abominable one, that is, the son called Ankalayh.

Rayḥān applied in writing for his own safety and for the safety of a group of his men. This he was granted, and a large number of barges, galleys and ferries were sent out to him with Zīrak, the officer who commanded the vanguard of Abū al-ʿAbbās. Zīrak sailed along the canal known as Nahr al-Yahūdī, and reached the place known as al-Muṭṭawiʿah where he encountered Rayḥān and his men. [2008] This was the place where Zīrak had formerly arranged for them to meet. Zīrak escorted them to al-Muwaffaq's quarters, and robes of honor were ordered for Rayḥān. He was also presented with a number of horses and full equipment, and was assigned a generous yearly pension. His men also were clothed with robes of honor and allotted pensions according to their ranks; then they were assigned to Abū al-ʿAbbās and he ordered them transported to a position facing the palace of the abominable one. They were posted in a ship there and the abominable one's men thus learned about Rayḥān's desertion and that of his men, and about the kind reception they had been accorded.

Immediately, other troops of Rayḥān who had remained behind in the camp of the abominable one, as well as many others, surrendered. They were treated with the same generosity and kindness as their comrades. Rayḥān's desertion took place after the skirmish which occurred on Sunday, the twenty-eighth of Dhū al-Ḥijjah, 267(July 30, 881).

In this year Aḥmad b. ʿAbdallāh al-Khujustānī, so he asserted, set out for Iraq. He reached Simnān[92] and learned that the people of al-Rayy had entrenched themselves against him and fortified their city. Then he withdrew from Simnān and returned to Khurāsān.

At the beginning of the year, a great many people turned back while en route to Mecca due to the oppressive heat. A large number who continued their journey died because of the heat and thirst. Also in this year, the Fazārah fell upon the merchants and, reportedly, seized seven hundred loads of cloth.

In this year, at the pilgrims' station in Mecca, an agent (*ʿāmil*) of Aḥmad b. Ṭulūn with his horsemen, and an agent of [2009] ʿAmr b. al-Layth with his horsemen, arrived simultaneously.

92. A town in the Qūmis region. See Le Strange, *Lands*, 360.

Each of them claimed his master's right to plant his flag to the right side of the pulpit in the Mosque of Ibrāhīm Khalīl al-Raḥmān,[93] since each claimed that the rights of guardianship belonged to his patron. They brandished their swords and most of the people fled the mosque. The Zanj clients of Hārūn b. Muḥammad backed the agent of ʿAmr b. al-Layth, and he was able to do as he wished. Hārūn, who was governor of Mecca, cut his sermon short and the people were saved from harm. The one called Abū al-Mughīrah al-Makhzūmī was then in charge of maintaining security in the congregation.

Also in this year al-Ṭibāʿ was expelled from Sāmarrā.

Also in this year, al-Khujustānī minted dīnārs and dirhams, each dīnār being ten dāniqs in weight and each dirham, eight. The legend ran, "Rule and Power are with God. He is the Lord of strength and might. There is no God but God, and Muḥammad is the messenger of God." Next to it was written, "The one who relies upon God dwells in happiness and prosperity;" the other side read, "The Faithful, Aḥmad b. ʿAbdallāh."

Leading the pilgrimage this year was Hārūn b. Muḥammad b. Isḥāq b. Mūsā b. ʿĪsā al-Hāshimī.

---

93. That is Abraham, the patriarch.

The Events of the Year 268

(August 1, 881–July 20, 882)

On Tuesday,the first day of al-Muḥarram (August 12, 881), Jaʿfar b. al-Ibrāhīm, who was known as al-Sajjān, sought safe-conduct from Abū Aḥmad al-Muwaffaq. It is mentioned that [2010]
the reason for this was Abū Aḥmad's battle at the end of Dhū al-Ḥijjah 267 (July 3-31, 881), to which we have referred above, as well as the flight of Rayḥān b. Ṣāliḥ al-Maghribī and his men from the camp of the deviate, and their linking up with Abū Aḥmad. The abominable one became completely discouraged at this; al-Sajjān was, reportedly, one of his trustworthy associates.

Abū Aḥmad conferred on this al-Sajjān robes of honor, various gifts, as well as a military allotment, and a place of lodging. Al-Sajjān was assigned to Abū al-ʿAbbās, who was ordered to transport him in a barge to a position in front of the abominable one's fortress so his (former) compatriots could see him. Al-Sajjān addressed them and told them that they were misled by the abominable one; he informed them what he had experienced because of the latter's lies and immoral behavior. The same day that al-Sajjān was placed in front of the abominable one's camp, a great many Zanj officers and others sought guarantees of safety; all of them were treated kindly. One after another the enemy sought safety and abandoned the abominable one.

After that battle which I have mentioned as having taken place on the last day of Dhū al-Ḥijjah of the year (2)67 (July 31, 881), Abū Aḥmad did not cross over to fight the abominable one, thus giving his troops a respite until the month of Rabīʿ II (November 9–December 7, 881).

In this year, ʿAmr b. al-Layth went to Fārs to fight Muḥammad b. al-Layth, his own governor in this province. ʿAmr routed Muḥammad b. al-Layth and auctioned off the spoils of his camp; the latter escaped with a small group of his men. ʿAmr entered Iṣṭakhr, which was looted by his troops, and then sent a force to chase after Muḥammad b. al-Layth. They seized him, and then delivered him to ʿAmr, a prisoner. Thereupon, ʿAmr went to Shīrāz where he remained.

On the eighth of Rabīʿ I, 268 (Monday, October 10, 881) an
[2011] earthquake shook Baghdad. This was followed by a heavy rain which lasted for three days. Four thunderstorms hit the city.

In this year, al-ʿAbbās b. Aḥmad b. Ṭūlūn marched to fight his father, who went out to meet him at Alexandria. Aḥmad seized him and they returned together to Miṣr.

On the fifteenth of Rabīʿ II (Nov. 23, 881), Abū Aḥmad al-Muwaffaq crossed over to the city of the rebel. This took place after Abū Aḥmad had weakened the rebel by carrying out severe actions against him. He blockaded his city, and cut off his food supplies, so that a great many of the rebel's troops sought guarantees of safe-conduct. He was able to accomplish this because he was positioned at his city, al-Muwaffaqiyyah.

When he decided to cross over to the enemy's city, Abū Aḥmad, reportedly, instructed his son Abū al-ʿAbbās to go to that section of the city's fortification, where the abominable one had entrusted the defenses to his son and his most stalwart troops and officers. Abū Aḥmad himself made for the section of the wall between the canals known as Nahr Munkā and Nahr Ibn Simʿān. He ordered Saʿīd, his wazīr, to go to the mouth of the canal known as Nahr Juwway Kūr with Zīrak at his flank, then he ordered Masrūr al-Balkhī to go to the Nahr al-Gharbī.

He assigned each of them a team of sappers to demolish the walls facing them, but at the same time, he instructed them not to carry out excessive demolition work, and not to enter the abominable one's city. To every area where he sent his commanders, Abū Aḥmad also assigned barges with archers. He instructed them to use their arrows to protect the sappers and the infantry from the Zanj. Many breaches were made in the walls and Abū Aḥmad's troops poured through all of them into the rebel's city. The men of the abominable one came to do [2012] combat, but Abū Aḥmad's troops routed them. The government force followed on their heels, pursuing them into the city, where the diverging roads, streets and ravines forced them to split up and separate. Setting fires and killing, Abū Aḥmad's men penetrated further than previously.

But the abominable one's men counterattacked and pressed Abū Aḥmad's troops. Their ambushers emerged from prepared positions which the others had not known, and thus Abū Aḥmad's men who were inside the city were caught unaware. Defending themselves, they retreated toward the Tigris; most of them reached the river. Some of them boarded vessels, others threw themselves into the water and were picked up by the men of the barges, and some of them were killed. The abominable one's troops captured arms and (other) booty.

A detachment of Abū Aḥmad's pages made a stand near the residence of Ibn Simʿān. Among them were Rashīd, Mūsā, the son of Mufliḥ's sister, and a group of officers. They were the last of the troops to stand fast. The Zanj surrounded them, and with a superior force, they stood between them and the barges. However, the government troops defended themselves and their men and fought their way back to the barges, upon which they embarked. Some thirty pages from Daylam stood facing the Zanj and their allies, covering the retreating forces and assuring their safety. These thirty Daylamites were killed to the last man, after taking as many of the rebels as they could. The government troops were very grieved by the losses they had suffered in this battle, as Abū Aḥmad returned with his men to his city al-Muwaffaqiyyah. He assembled all his men and censured them for disobeying his instruction without consulting him about his plan and how to execute it. He threatened them [2013] with the most severe punishment if they disregarded his orders again. Then he ordered a count of the missing of his troops, and when this was done and their names presented to him, Abū Aḥmad made arrangement so that what was due the missing would be transferred to their children and families. When the men saw his care for the heirs of those who had perished in his service, they were favorably impressed. They respected him all the more, and their good faith increased.

In this year Abū al-ʿAbbās fought and exterminated a band of tribesmen who were smuggling provisions to the profligate.

The Battle against the Tribesmen

It is said that when the abominable one had devastated al-Baṣrah, he appointed Aḥmad b. Mūsā b. Saʿīd, the one called al-Qalūṣ, one of his earliest companions, as governor of the city. While al-Qalūṣ conducted the affairs of al-Baṣrah, it became the profligate's port. The tribesmen and merchants travelled to the city and carried off provisions and merchandise, which they then transferred to the camp of the abominable one. This lasted until Abū Aḥmad conquered Ṭahīthā and al-Qalūṣ was captured. Then, the abominable one appointed Mālik b. Bishrān, the son of al-Qalūṣ's sister, to govern al-Baṣrah and its surroundings. When now, Abū Aḥmad descended upon Furāt al- Baṣrah, the rebel feared that Abū Aḥmad would attack this Mālik—he was at the time stationed at Sayḥān[94] on the canal known as Nahr Ibn ʿUtbah. He thus wrote to Mālik instructing him to transfer his camp to the canal known as Nahr al-Dīnārī, and to dispatch a detachment of his men to catch fish and to deliver the catch to his, that is, the abominable one's camp. He ordered him to send another group to the road which the tribesmen took from the desert, and to learn whether any of them
[2014] were carrying provisions. In case a party of tribesmen with provisions was encountered, the instructions were to go to them and to deliver their provisions to the abominable one.

94. Not to be confused with the town of that name located in Bilād al-Rūm. See Le Strange, *Lands*, 131. I have not found any reference to a Sayḥān in the vicinity of the battles.

Complying with these instructions, Mālik, the nephew of al-Qalūṣ, sent two inhabitants to the Great Swamp from the village Basmā.[95] One of them was al-Rayyān, the other al-Khalīl; both were staying in the camp of the abominable one. Al-Khalīl and al-Rayyān set out and gathered a band of people from theṬaff[96] and went to Basmā. They remained there, transporting catches of fish, one catch at a time. The fish were shipped from the Great Swamp,[97] to the abominable one's camp. They used small skiffs which could pass through the narrow canals and small waterways (*al-arkhanjān*),[98] which no barge or galley could traverse. As long as the two men stayed in the aforementioned place, a constant supply of fish moved from the Great Swamp to the abominable one's camp. Also reaching him were the provisions and other supplies brought by the tribesmen by way of the desert. This was sufficient for his army. In this way the situation of the people of his camp was eased. This continued on until ʿAlī b. ʿUmar, who was known as al-Nazzāb— he was one of the rebel's men who had been posted with al-Qalūṣ—sought safe-conduct with al-Muwaffaq and reported to him about Mālik b. Bishrān. He told him of Mālik's position on the Dīnārī Canal, how the latter supplied the abominable one's camp with fish from the Great Swamp, and of the deliveries by the tribesmen.

Al-Muwaffaq directed his mawlā Zīrak to take barges and galleys to the location where al-Qalūṣ's nephew was situated, whereupon Zīrak pounced upon him and his men. Zīrak killed some of them and captured others. The rest scattered, leaving Mālik, who fled and returned to the abominable one. The latter sent him back with a force to the lower part of the canal [2015]
known as Nahr al-Yahūdī. Mālik then camped there, at a spot close to the canal known as Nahr al-Fayyāḍ, and as a result provisions from the area adjacent to the marshes of the Fayyāḍ again were arriving at the abominable one's camp.

When word reached al-Muwaffaq that Mālik was stationed

95. See above, n. 1.

96. For the Ṭaff region of the Euphrates, see Yāqūt, *Muʿjam*, III, 539.

97. The Great Swamp was famous for its fish which were easily caught. See Le Strange, *Lands*, 43.

98. For *al-arkhanjān*, see Ṭabarī, *Introductio et al*, CXI.

at the lower part of the Yahūdī Canal and that provisions from that sector were reaching the rebel's camp, he instructed his son Abū al-ʿAbbās to go to the Nahr al-Amīr and the canal called Nahr al-Fayyāḍ to verify the report which had reached him. The troops marched out and came upon a band of tribesmen under the command of an officer who was conveying camels, sheep, and other food-stuff from the desert. Abū al-ʿAbbās attacked, killing some of them and taking the rest prisoner. Only their leader escaped, for he was riding a fast mare. All the camels, sheep, and food which these tribesmen were conveying were seized. Abū al-ʿAbbās cut off a hand of one of the captives and let him go, whereupon the man arrived at the abominable one's camp and brought to him the news of what had befallen him. Abū al-ʿAbbās's attack on these tribesmen so terrified Mālik, the nephew of al-Qalūṣ, that he sought a guarantee of safe-conduct from Abū Aḥmad. He was granted protection, and gifts were bestowed upon him. Mālik was also given robes of honor and assigned to Abū al-ʿAbbās. In addition he received a military allotment and lodging.

In place of Mālik, the abominable one appointed one of al-Qalūṣ's companions, Aḥmad b. al-Junayd, and he instructed him to camp at the place known as Dahrshīr, and at the lower part of Nahr Abū al-Khaṣīb. Aḥmad was to proceed with his
[2016] men to a place from where he could procure the fish from the Great Swamp and then transport it to the camp of the abominable one.

A report about Aḥmad b. al-Junayd reached Abū Aḥmad who sent one of his mawlā commanders, called al-Tarmudān, with a body of troops. This force encamped on the island known as al-Rūḥiyyah, whereupon the supply of fish from the Great Swamp to the camp of the abominable one was cut off. Al-Muwaffaq also directed Shibāb b. al-ʿAlā' and Muḥammad b. al-Ḥasan, both ʿAnbarīs, to take cavalry and prevent the tribesmen from transporting food to the camp of the abominable one. He gave further instructions that the market of al-Baṣrah be opened to the tribesmen so that they could transport the dates they wanted to sell to that market, since the desire for profit was what had induced them to journey to the abominable one's camp.

Now, Shihāb and Muḥammad proceeded as instructed, and stationed themselves at Qaṣr ʿĪsā.[99] The tribesmen brought them the dates they had taken from the desert and began selling them on behalf of the two officers. Abū Aḥmad then dismissed al-Tarmudān from al-Baṣrah, replacing him with one of his Farghānī officers, a man called Qayṣar b. Urkhūz Ikhshādh Farghānah. He also sent out Nuṣayr,the one called Abū Ḥamzah, with barges and galleys, ordering him to position himself at Fayḍ al-Baṣrah[100] and Nahr Dubays. In addition, he was to penetrate to the Ubullah, Maʿqil and Gharbī canals. He carried out these orders.

According to Muḥammad b. al-Ḥasan———Muḥammad b. Ḥammād: When Nuṣayr and Qayṣar were positioned at al-Baṣrah, they used barges to cut the flow of provisions to the abominable one and his supporters. That is, they cut off those provisions which had been brought from the Great Swamp and the sea. The rebels therefore devised a scheme by which they travelled the Nahr al-Amīr to al-Qindal, then the Masīḥī Canal to [2017] the roads leading to the hinterland and the sea. In this way, their provisions came by sea and land, as did their supplies of sea fish.

When word of this reached al-Muwaffaq, he instructed Rashīq, Abū al-ʿAbbās's page, to establish a camp at Jawwīth Bārūbah, east of the Tigris, in front of Nahr al-Amīr. He also ordered him to dig and fortify a trench. In addition, he instructed Abū al-ʿAbbās to assign to Rashīq five thousand of his best men and thirty barges. Al-Muwaffaq then ordered Rashīq to position these barges at the mouth of the Amīr Canal and to establish a patrol of fifteen barges with which to penetrate the waterway up to the intersection by which the Zanj were passing to Dubbā, al-Qindal and the canal known as Nahr al-Masīḥī. The patrols were to remain there, and if any of the abominable ones (men) were to appear, the government troops were to attack them. After the patrol was completed, they

99. Not to be confused with the famous Qaṣr ʿĪsā in Baghdad. See Lassner, *Topography*, index, 321. I have not succeeded in identifying a Qaṣr ʿĪsā in the region of the battles.

100. The fayḍ (Estuary of) al-Baṣrah is identical with the Blind Tigris. See Le Strange, *Lands*, 43.

withdrew immediately, to be replaced by the other patrol waiting at the mouth of the canal. They acted according to these instructions. Rashīq camped at the place to which he was ordered and the routes the rebels used to pass to Dubbā, al-Qindal and the Masīḥī Canal were seized. Thus, the enemy no longer had access to the hinterland or the sea; the rebels' sphere of operation narrowed and the blockade became more severe.

In this year, the brother of Sharkab attacked al-Khujustānī and seized his mother, and Ibn Shabath b. al-Ḥasan rebelled and captured ʿUmar b. Sīmā, governor of Ḥulwān.

[2018] In this year, Aḥmad b. Abī al-Aṣbagh left ʿAmr b. al-Layth. The latter had sent him to Aḥmad b. ʿAbd al-ʿAzīz b. Abī Dulaf carrying funds. ʿAmr sent on what was demanded of him: more than three hundred thousand dīnārs and gifts, among them fifty manns[101] of musk, fifty manns of saffron, two hundred manns of aloes, three hundred embroidered and other garments, gold and silver vessels, and two hundred thousand dīnārs worth of animals and slaves. The total value of what he sent in gifts amounted to five hundred thousand dīnārs.

In this year, Kayghalagh appointed al-Khalīl Rīmāl governor of Ḥulwān. The new governor treated the rebels harshly on account of ʿUmar b. Sīmā and the crime commited by Ibn Shabath. They guaranteed Ibn Sīmā's release and set right the business concerning Ibn Shabath.

In this year, Rashīq, the page of Abū al-ʿAbbās b. al-Muwaffaq, attacked a band of the Banū Tamīm who had cooperated with the Zanj when the latter had occupied and burned al-Baṣrah. The reason for this was as follows. Word reached Abū al-ʿAbbās that some of these tribesmen were bringing provisions, such as wheat, camels and sheep from the hinterland to the abominable one's city. It was also indicated that they were in the lower part of the Amīr Canal, expecting ships which were to come to them from the lower part of the rebel's camp in order to transport them and their goods. Rashīq set out with

101. One *mann* = 2 *raṭl*, according to the established legal weight. In reality, the *mann* varied in different places and in different periods. See Hinz, *Islamische Masse und Gewichte*, 16 ff.; also, see below, nn. 109, 127.

his barges and came upon them at the place where they had stopped, that is, the canal known as Nahr al-Isḥāqī.[102] He attacked them, taking them unawares. He killed most of them, and took a group prisoner—there were merchants who had left the camp of the abominable one in order to bring the provi- [2019]
sions. Rashīq seized all kinds of provisions from them, as well as the water buffalos, camels and asses which they used to transport them. He then sent the prisoners and heads (of the slain) in his barges and vessels to al-Muwaffaqiyyah. On al-Muwaffaq's order, the heads were fastened on the barges and the prisoners hung for display so that everyone could see the success of Rashīq and his men. As a result they were paraded throughout the camp. Following this the order was given, and the heads and captives were taken past the camp of the abominable one so that those in the camp might know about Rashīq and his attack on those who bring provisions to them. Among those seized by Rashīq was one of the tribesmen who used to travel between the leader of the Zanj and the tribesmen, negotiating the supply of provisions. Al-Muwaffaq had one of the man's hands and feet cut off; then he was thrown into the abominable one's camp. The command was given to behead the captives and it was carried out. All that Rashīq's troops had obtained was placed at their disposal. The order was given for Rashīq to receive robes of honor and presents, and return to his camp. The number of troops seeking safe-conduct from Rashīq increased, and on the instructions of Abū Aḥmad, all of them were assigned to the former's command. Their numbers grew to the point that his base had become as crowded as any of the largest camps. Supplies to the abominable one and his men were cut off from all directions, as all roads to them were blocked. The blockade hit them hard, and weakened them physically. The captives and deserters among them were asked when they had last seen bread. Surprised, they would say they had not seen bread for a year or two. [2020]

102. This does not seem to be the Isḥāqī Canal which flowed near Sāmarrā. See Le Strange, *Lands*, 52. I have not succeeded in identifying a canal of this name in the region of the battles.

With the troops of the perfidious one reaching this condition, al-Muwaffaq decided to resume attacking them in order to aggravate their injured state and fatigue. At this time, great throngs came to Abū Aḥmad, seeking guarantees of safe-conduct. Those who remained in the lines of the profligate had to resort to devious schemes by which to obtain their daily nourishment. They would scatter about villages and canals that were distant from their camp to look for food. When news of this reached Abū Aḥmad, he instructed a group of commanders and officers from the ranks (*ʿarīf*) drawn from among his black pages to go to the places frequented by the Zanj. They were to try and win their confidence, and ask for their loyalty. Any one among the Zanj who refused was to be killed, and his head delivered to Abū Aḥmad. He offered them a reward so that they became zealous in executing their duty by day and night. Not a day passed without a group coming over to them, or without the heads of slain being delivered, or prisoners taken.

According to Muḥammad b. al-Ḥasan——Muḥammad b. Ḥammād: When the number of the Zanj prisoners in al-Muwaffaq's camp became great, he ordered a review of them. Whosoever was strong, stalwart, and able to carry arms, he favored with kindness. He integrated them with black pages causing them to take cognizance of his generosity. Those who were feeble and infirm, or worn out, or aged and unable to bear arms, or disabled by wounds, were each given two garments, some dirhams and food. They were then transported back to the camp of the abominable one, where they were left after being instructed to describe al-Muwaffaq's kind treatment to all who came to him. They were also instructed to say that he intended to offer the same treatment to anyone seeking safety
[2021] with him or falling into his hands.

By these measures al-Muwaffaq succeeded in attaining his goal of causing the troops of the Zanj leader to become preoccupied with coming over to him, and making peace and offering their allegiance. Time and again, al-Muwaffaq and his son Abū al-ʿAbbās began to lead their troops in person while engaging the abominable one and his men in combat. They killed, captured, and inflicted many casualties. In one of these skirmishes, Abū al-ʿAbbās was hit and wounded by an arrow.[103] However, he recovered from this wound.

In Rajab of this year (January 25–February 23, 882), Bahbūdh, the companion of the abominable one, was killed.

How Bahbūdh Was Slain

It is reported that among the companions of the profligate, Bahbūdh b. ʿAbd al-Wahhāb was the one who held the record for the most raids, and was the most successful in cutting the highways and expropriating money. He had amassed a great fortune in this way. Frequently he would go out with his swift galleys, passing through the canals leading to the Tigris. If he would come upon a vessel belonging to the troops of al-Muwaffaq, he would seize it and bring it into the canal from which he had emerged. If someone pursued him for a long way, a specially prepared detachment of his men would emerge from the canal, cutting off the enemy and attacking him. Since this occurred quite often, and people were becoming more careful, he began riding in a barge which he made to resemble the barges of al-Muwaffaq, planting on it flags similar to those of the latter. He would go with this vessel to the Tigris, and if he took the government troops by surprise, he would attack, killing and taking prisoners. He would also penetrate the Ubullah, Maʿqil, Bathq Shīrīn, and Dayr canals; whereupon, he would cut the roads and waylay travellers, taking their money and lives.

When information about all these actions of Bahbūdh [2022] reached al-Muwaffaq, he decided to block all the canals which lent themselves to this movement and place barges at the mouths of the large canals to secure them from the actions of Bahbūdh and his accomplices. In addition, he would make the roads and highways safe for the people.

Thus, when the routes were placed under guard, and those canals which could be blocked had been blocked, and when Bahbūdh's freedom to maneuver was thus curtailed, he stayed

103. See Popovic, *Révolte*, 142 ff.

waiting for an opportunity to exploit the carelessness of the barge crews which were entrusted with (securing) the mouth of the Nahr al-Ubullah. He waited until such a chance presented itself, and then he slipped through from the lower part of the Abū al-Khaṣīb Canal with his barges and galleys resembling those of al-Muwaffaq's forces, as they hoisted similar flags. He manned his flotilla with his strongest, boldest and most courageous troops, and he led it from the lower part of the Abū al-Khaṣīb Canal into an intersecting waterway, leading to the Yahūdī and from there to the Nāfidh. When he finally reached the Ubullah, he came upon barges and galleys that had been arrayed to safeguard the canal. The crews of the barges were completely unaware and unprepared. Bahbūdh attacked, killing some and capturing others, while six barges were seized. Following this, he retreated along the Ubullah Canal.

When news about Bahbūdh reached al-Muwaffaq, he instructed Abū al-ʿAbbās to set out against him with barges from the canal known as Nahr al-Yahūdī. He hoped that his son would beat Bahbūdh to the intersecting canal, cutting the rebel's escape route. Abū al-ʿAbbās reached the place called al-Muṭṭawwiʿah but Bahbūdh had beaten him to it and entered the canal called Nahr al-Saʿīdī, which led to Nahr Abū al-Khaṣīb.

Abū al-ʿAbbās caught sight of Bahbūdh's barges and, eagerly desiring to reach them, he increased his speed, coming abreast with the enemy. They engaged in a fight in which Abū al-ʿAb-
[2023] bās killed a number of Bahbūdh's men while taking others prisoner. One contingent asked Abū al-ʿAbbās for safety but a great many of Bahbūdh's force stood by the Zanjid, steadfastly protecting him. Since all this took place when the water level tended to be low, the government barges ran into the mud in those sections of the canals and junctions where the water was receding. Bahbūdh and the rest of his men thus escaped by the skin of their teeth.

Al-Muwaffaq continued to besiege the abominable one and his men, blocking his supply lines; the number of those seeking safe-conduct from the government increased. Al-Muwaffaq saw to it that all of them were accorded robes of honor and presents, and paraded on excellent horses with saddles, bridles, and other equipment. In addition military allotments were issued to them.

Reports reached al-Muwaffaq afterwards that want and misery had impelled a party of the abominable one's men to scatter about the villages in search of food, such as fish and dates. So, he ordered his son Abū al-ʿAbbās to hurry to these villages and places with his barges, galleys, and his swift skiffs. He was to take his strongest, most courageous and steadfast men and intercept those people, thus preventing their return to the city of the leader of the Zanj. Abū al-ʿAbbās set forth to carry out these orders.

The abominable one learned about this expedition of Abū al-ʿAbbās against him, and he instructed Bahbūdh to set out with his men in secret along the intersections and deserted canals as far as al-Qindal, Abrusān and the surrounding areas. As instructed by the abominable one, Bahbūdh went out to his destination with a Zanj detachment, but blocking his way was one of Abū al-ʿAbbās's galleys filled with archers drawn from [2024]
his pages. Bahbūdh was eager to get the galley and went after it. Its defenders gave battle, and one of the black pages of the galley thrust at Bahbūdh with his lance and hit him in the stomach. Bahbūdh fell into the water, but his men ran and picked him up. They fled carrying him to the camp of the abominable one. God had taken his life, however, before they reached the camp.

The profligate and his leading men were overwhelmed by this loss, and their grief increased because of it. Bahbūdh's death was one of Abū Aḥmad's greatest victories, but he was unaware of his end until one of the sailors surrendering to him told him the news. Abū Aḥmad rejoiced with this report and ordered the page who had killed Bahbūdh brought to him. He was presented to Abū Aḥmad, who gave him presents, raiment and a neck ring, as well as an increase in his allotment. All the others in that galley were presented with special gifts, robes of honor, and other presents.

In this year, the month of Ramaḍān (March 25–April 23, 882) began on a Sunday. The second Sunday of Ramaḍān was

Palm Sunday, the third Sunday was Easter, the fourth was Nayrūz,[104] and the fifth was the last day of the month.

In this year, Abū Aḥmad captured al-Dhawā'ibī—he had been collaborating with the leader of the Zanj.

In this year, a battle took place between Yadkūtakīn b. Asātakīn and Aḥmad b. ʿAbd al-ʿAzīz.[105] Yadkūtakīn routed the latter and took Qumm from him.

In this year, ʿAmr b. al-Layth, on the order of Abū Aḥmad, sent an officer to capture Muḥammad b. ʿUbaydallāh b. Azārmard al-Kurdi.[106] The officer captured him and delivered him to ʿAmr.

[2025] In Dhū al-Qaʿdah of this year (May 23–June 21, 882), one of the descendants of ʿAbd al-Mālik b. Ṣāliḥ al-Hāshimī—he was called Bakkār—revolted in Syria (in the region) between Salamyah, Aleppo and Homs. He called upon the people to pledge allegiance to Abū Aḥmad, but Ibn ʿAbbās al Kilābī fought against him and was routed. Then, Lu'lu', Ibn Ṭūlūn's companion, sent a general called Būdan against him with a vast army, but on his return he scarcely had one soldier left.

In this year, Lu'lu' declared his revolt against Ibn Ṭūlūn.

In this year, the leader of the Zanj killed Ibn Mālik the Zanjid because word reached him that the latter intended to join Abū Aḥmad.

In this year, Aḥmad b. ʿAbdallāh al-Khujustānī was killed. He was killed by a page of his in Dhū al-Ḥijjah (June 22–July 20, 882).

In this year, the troops of Ibn Abī al-Sāj killed Muḥammad b. ʿAlī b. Ḥabīb al-Yashkarī,[107] in a village near Wāsiṭ. His head was displayed in Baghdad.

In this year, Muḥammad b. Kumushjūr fought against ʿAlī b. al-Ḥusayn Kuftimur and captured him, but he subsequently set him free. This was in Dhū al-Ḥijjah (June 22–July 20, 882).

In this year, the ʿAlid, known as al-Ḥarūn, was imprisoned. The reason for this was that he had intercepted and seized a

104. That is, the Persian New Year also known as Nawrūz.
105. That is, the son of Abū Dulaf.
106. See Ṭabarī, III/3, 1908 ff.
107. Ibid., 1920 ff.

dispatch case containing a report on the state of the pilgrimage. The deputy of Ibn Abī al-Sāj sent his men out to the Mecca [2026] Road and they seized al-Ḥarūn and delivered him to al-Muwaffaq.

In this year, Abū al-Mughīrah al-Makhzūmī marched on Mecca, where Hārūn b. Muḥammad b. Isḥāq al-Hāshimī was governor. Hārūn rallied an army of about two thousand men, and with their help he thwarted al-Makhzūmī. The latter now turned toward ʿAyn Mushāsh[108] and spoiled its well. From there, he went to Jidda, looted its food, and burned down its houses. The price of bread in Mecca rose to a dirham for two *ūqiyah.*[109]

In this year Ibn Ṣaqlabiyyah, the emperor of the Byzantines, took the field and besieged Malaṭyah, but the people of Marʿash and al-Ḥadath[110] assisted the people of Malaṭyah, and routed the emperor, chasing him up to al-Sarīʿ.

Khalaf al-Farghānī, the governor of Ibn Ṭūlūn, conducted the annual summer expedition along the Syrian frontier. He killed some ten thousand Greeks and took booty. The share for each participant in the raid reached forty dīnārs.

Leading the pilgrimage this year was Hārūn b. Muḥammad b. Isḥāq al-Hāshimī; Ibn Abī al-Sāj was in charge of security and safety on the road.

---

108. This well provided Mecca with a major part of its drinking water. See Yāqūt, *Muʿjam*, IV, 536.

109. One *ūqiyah* = 1/12 of a *raṭl*. At this time in history, it would have been about 125 gr. See Hinz, *Islamische Masse und Gewichte*, 34–35; also, see above, n. 101, and below, n. 127.

110. Marʿash was situated on the Syrian border; al-Ḥadath was a fortress nearby. See Le Strange, *Lands*, 122.

The Events of the Year 269

(July 21, 882–August 9, 883)

Among the events, the ʿAlid known as al-Ḥarūn was brought into the camp of Abū Aḥmad in al-Muḥarram (July 21–August 19, 882). He was carried on a camel, wearing a brocade cloak (*qabā'*), and a tall hat (*qalansuwah*). He was then transported in a barge to a position where the leader of the Zanj could see him and hear the speech of the messengers.

[2027] In al-Muḥarram of this year, the tribesmen waylaid and plundered a caravan of pilgrims between Tūz and Sumayrā'.[111] They seized some five thousand camels with their loads and abducted many people.

On the fourteenth night of al-Muḥarram (Wednesday, August 1, 882), a total eclipse of the moon took place. On the twenty-eighth of the same month (August 17, 882)—which was a Friday—at sunset, there was a total eclipse of the sun. Thus, in the month of al-Muḥarram, the eclipse of both sun and moon took place.

---

111. Two places situated along the pilgrimmage route. See Yāqūt, *Muʿjam*, I, 893.

In Ṣafar of this year (August 20–September 17, 882), the mob attacked Ibrāhīm al-Khalījī and plundered his house in Baghdad. The reason for this was that one of his servants had shot a woman with an arrow and killed her. Al-Khalījī implored the authorities for protection but when they recommended that he deliver the servant, he refused. His servants shot at the people, killing some and wounding others, among them two police officers. Ibrāhīm then fled, but his servants were seized and his house and stables were plundered. Muḥammad, the son of ʿUbaydallāh b. ʿAbdallāh b. Ṭāhir, who was stationed at the Main Bridge for his father,[112] gathered the animals and anything else he could of Ibrāhīm's plundered property. He did this because ʿUbaydallāh had instructed him to deliver all these things to Ibrāhīm. He confirmed the fact that all these things were returned.

In this year, having reached al-Ṭā'if in the course of his withdrawal from Mecca, Ibn Abī al-Sāj dispatched a force to Jidda which seized two boats of al-Makhzūmī loaded with both money and weapons.

In this year, Rūmī b. Khashanaj seized three Farghānī offi- [2028]
cers, one of them was named Ṣadīq, the other Ṭakhshā, and the third Tughān, and put them in chains. Ṣadīq was wounded but he escaped.

In Rabīʿ I of this year (September 18–October 17, 882), Khalaf, the companion of Aḥmad b. Ṭūlūn and his governor for the Syrian frontier, attacked Yāzamān al- Khādim, the mawlā of al-Fatḥ b. Khāqān, and imprisoned him. A group of inhabitants from the frontier fell upon Khalaf and rescued Yāzamān; whereupon, the former fled and the people withdrew their allegiance from Ibn Ṭūlūn and cursed him from the pulpits. When this reached Ibn Ṭūlūn he left Egypt for Damascus, and from there he went to the Syrian frontier, stopping in Adhanah. In the meanwhile, Yāzamān and the inhabitants of Ṭarsūs dammed all the flood-gates of the city except for the Bāb al-Jihād and the Bāb al-Baḥr.[113] The water then overflowed near

112. That is, at the headquarters of the *ṣaḥib al-shurṭah*, the prefect of police, who was in charge of security. See Lassner, *Topography*, 151.
113. These were two fortresses. See Le Strange, *Lands*, 131.

Adhanah and the surrounding area. They entrenched themselves in Ṭarsūs, while Ibn Ṭūlūn positioned himself in Adhanah for some time. Then he returned to Antioch, and from there he went to Homs and then on to Damascus where he remained.

In this year, Lu'lu', the page of Ibn Ṭūlūn, opposed his patron. At the outbreak of the dispute, Lu'lu' held Homs, Aleppo, Qinnasrīn and Diyar Muḍar. He went to Bālis[114] and looted the city, capturing Saʿīd and his brother, the sons of al-ʿAbbās al-Kilābī. Then, Lu'lu' corresponded with Abū Aḥmad about going over to the latter's side and breaking with Ibn Ṭūlūn. He stipulated certain conditions which Abū Aḥmad accepted.
[2029] Lu'lu', who was in al-Raqqah, left the city, taking with him a group of inhabitants from al-Rāfiqah[115] among others. They went to Qarqīsiyyā, where Ibn Ṣafwān al-ʿUqaylī was stationed. Lu'lu' attacked Ibn Ṣafwān and seized the city which he turned over to Aḥmad b. Mālik b. Ṭawq. Ibn Ṣafwān fled and Lu'lu' set course for Baghdad.

In this year, an arrow shot by a Greek page of the abominable one—the page was called Qarṭās—hit Abū Aḥmad soon after he entered the abominable one's city in order to demolish its walls. The reason for this, according to reports, (is as follows). After the abominable Bahbūdh perished, the leader of the Zanj coveted the treasures and wealth which Bahbūdh had amassed. He had verified that his possessions amounted to two hundred thousand dīnārs, and jewels, gold and silver of great value. He used every strategem in searching for this, coveting it so much that he imprisoned all of Bahbūdh's leading men, relatives and companions. He flogged them, and ransacked house after house and destroyed building after building belonging to Bahbūdh, hoping to find anything buried there, but he found nothing.

That which he had done to Bahbūdh's leading men while

114. A town west of al-Raqqah, which was an important way station on the caravan route. See Le Strange, *Lands*, 107.

115. Raqqah-Rāfiqah was a composite city. The former was the private sector occupied by the civilian populace; the latter was the government sector that housed the local authority and garrison behind imposing walls. That is, al-Rāfiqah was an administrative center, al-Raqqah an integrated city.

searching for the wealth was one of the factors that turned the rebel's companions against him. It invited their anger, and caused them to shun the leader of the Zanj. Al-Muwaffaq gave orders to announce that he was offering safe-conduct to protect Bahbūdh's companions. When this was announced, they rushed to him gladly. They were then given favors, various gifts, robes of honor, and a military allotment according to their rank.

Abū Aḥmad observed that crossing to the camp of the rebel was difficult at those times when the winds stirred the waters [2030] of the Tigris. He therefore decided to prepare a place to serve as an encampment for himself and his troops on the western side of the Tigris between Dayr Jābīl and Nahr al-Mughīrah. He gave the order to cut down the palm trees and (prepare) the ground for a defensive perimeter. It was to be surrounded by defensive trenches and fortified with walls to make it safe from night raids and unexpected assaults by the rebels. He set up shifts supervised by his officers. Everyone took his turn in going with the infantry and the laborers who were with them to work from early morning all through the day, preparing the camp which Abū Aḥmad had decided to establish there.

To counter this, the profligate also set up shifts with ʿAlī b. Abān al-Muhallabī, Sulaymān b. Jāmiʿ and Ibrāhīm b. Jaʿfar al-Hamadānī, each of them taking a shift for the day. The abominable one's son, the one known as Ankalāy, used to accompany Sulaymān every day of his shift, and he often did the same with Ibrāhīm. Later, the abominable one appointed Ankalāy instead of Ibrāhīm b. Jaʿfar, and Sulaymān b. Jāmiʿ accomanpanied the former. The abominable one then assigned Sulaymān b. Mūsā al-Shaʿrānī and his brothers to Ankalāy and they were constantly with him.

The abominable one knew that, given the terror of his men as the two armies came close, should al-Muwaffaq draw near to him during the fighting, the former would close the gap between himself and those seeking to flee to the government forces. With this, the rebel's position would collapse and all his [2031] preparations would be compromised. Therefore, he instructed his men to do combat with the government officers crossing every day, and to thwart their attempts to prepare the camp to which the enemy wanted to transfer. On one of those days stormy winds broke out at a time when one of al-Muwaffaq's officers had crossed to the western side of the Tigris. The rebel, saw the captain isolated, cut off from his troops, and prevented from re-crossing by the stormy Tigris; he seized this opportunity to move against him with all his army, a group much larger than the government officer's contingent. The barges which had been assigned to the officer could not reach their assigned places because the wind tossed them against the rocks, and the crews feared their vessels would be torn apart. The Zanj overpowered this officer and his men, dislodging them from their positions. They overtook one detachment, and the government force stood fast and was killed to the very last man. The Zanj chased after another group which had fled to the water. They took prisoners and killed some men, but most of the enemy escaped. Reaching their ships they jumped in and crossed to al-Muwaffaqiyyah.

This success of the profligates caused much grief and became a matter of grave concern to the people of al-Muwaffaq's camp. Abū Aḥmad now thought that the plan of encamping on the western bank of the Tigris was unpromising and unsafe from the stratagems of the profligate and his men, who would always be able to raid by night or find some easy way to escape and gain a respite due to the many thickets of the terrain and the difficulty of passing through there. He realized that the Zanj were more able than his troops to pass those desolate
[2032] places and found it easier to do so. So he abandoned his plan of setting up camp on the western bank of the Tigris. He now set his goal at razing the walls of the profligate's city, and extending the roads and passes leading there for his troops. With that, he gave instructions to start with the demolition of the wall in the section adjacent to the canal known as Nahr Munkā.

To meet this threat the abominable one sent his son, the one known as Ankalāy, and ʿAlī b. Abān and Sulaymān b. Jāmiʿ to prevent this. Each of them was to take his shift on the same day. Should the troops of al-Muwaffaq outnumber them, the three were to pool their forces jointly to repel the attackers. When al-Muwaffaq noticed the gathering of the abominable ones and their joint-effort to prevent the demolition of the walls, he decided to take part in the action personally, thus inspiring his troops' greater dedication and zeal, and increasing their will to endure. This he did, and the battle was joined and became thick and heavy. Great losses in dead and wounded were suffered by both factions. Abū Aḥmad carried on against the profligates for several days without respite, but still his troops were unable to penetrate far into the positions of the abominable ones because of two bridges spanning the Munkā Canal. When the fighting seemed to reach its peak, the Zanj would pass over the bridges and take the road which led them to the rear of Abū Aḥmad's troops. They took their toll of the government force and diverted them from their goal of demolishing the walls.

Then, al-Muwaffaq sought a stratagem by which he would [2033] destroy these two bridges in order to block the profligates from the road they had taken in order to divert his troops when the fighting became intense. He instructed some of his officers from among the pages to go to these two bridges and lay in wait for the Zanj, with the intention of taking them by surprise when they became careless in their watch. He also ordered them to prepare pickaxes, saws and other tools which might be needed to destroy the two bridges and be helpful in speeding up the work. Acting upon these instructions, the pages set off and reached the Munkā Canal at midday, the Zanj appeared, and came forward, hastening to meet them. Among the Zanj hurrying toward them was Abū al-Nidā', with a party of more than five hundred men. Al-Muwaffaq's men and the Zanj force engaged in a battle which lasted until the turn of the day, when the pages of Abū Aḥmad overpowered the profligates, pushing them away from the two bridges. An arrow struck the one called Abū al-Nidā', in his chest. It pierced his heart and felled him. His soldiers shielded his body and carried it away, as they fled. The officers from al-Muwaffaq's pages were thus able to dismantle the two bridges. They cut the moorings and floated the pontoons to the Tigris while transporting the wooden planks to Abū Aḥmad. They returned safe and unharmed. The pages informed al-Muwaffaq of Abū al-Nidā''s death and the dismantling of the bridges, whereupon al-Muwaffaq and the people of his camp became filled with joy. The archer who shot Abū al-Nidā', was granted a generous gift.

Now, Abū Aḥmad pressed the fight against the abominable one and his followers. They razed those sections of the wall where they could penetrate, while keeping the enemy preoccupied in their city in order to divert them from the defense of
[2034] their wall. Thus they hastened its demolition. From the wall, they went to the residences of Ibn Simʿān and Sulaymān b. Jāmiʿ. All these places fell to al-Muwaffaq's troops, the profligates being unable to defend them and stem the advance of al-Muwaffaq's men. These two residences were demolished and everything in them looted. Al-Muwaffaq's troops also reached one of the markets of the leader of the Zanj. The latter had established it on the bank of the Tigris and named it al-Maymūnah. Al-Muwaffaq ordered Zīrak, the commander of Abū al-ʿAbbās's vanguard, to set out for this market. The latter moved out with his troops, and went about the task before him. This market was subsequently levelled and laid waste.

Al-Muwaffaq now went to the residence which the leader of the Zanj had established for al-Jubbā'ī and demolished it. He plundered it as well as the adjacent stores of the profligate. Then, he instructed his men to set off for the spot where the abominable one had built a structure which he named the Friday Mosque. The profligates persevered in their defense of this place, as the abominable one had spurred them on imbuing them with the belief that it was incumbent upon them to defend the structure and glorify it. The Zanj believed these statements of his and obeyed his exhortations, so that it was very difficult for the men of al-Muwaffaq to reach their objective. The fight for this place lasted for days; at this point, only the staunchest, most heroic, and persistent of men remained with the profligate. They defended (themselves) with zeal; so much so, that they would hold their positions. If one (of them) were hit by an arrow or sustained the blow of a spear or were struck by a sword, and fell, his neighbor would draw him aside and take up his position; they feared that if the position of any man
[2035] remained empty, (then) ill would befall the rest of his companions.

When Abū Aḥmad saw the endurance and defensive posture of this group, and that their resistance would last for days, he instructed Abū al-ʿAbbās to move to the strongest side of the building which the abominable one called the mosque, and to recruit for that purpose his most valiant troops and pages. He attached sappers to them, men who had been assigned to demolition duty. If preparations were made to demolish something, they would rush to carry out their task. Al-Muwaffaq ordered ladders placed against the walls, which archers climbed and then launched showers of arrows upon the profligates behind the walls. He spread his infantry from the limits of al-Jubbāʾī's residence to the position where he had assigned Abū al-ʿAbbās. Then he distributed money, medallions, and bracelets among those who rushed to demolish the walls and markets of the profligate, and the houses of his companions. What had been difficult before now. became easy after a long and violent fight—the building which the abominable one had named the mosque was demolished. The government troops reached its pulpit and carried it away, delivering it to al-Muwaffaq, who returned with it to al-Muwaffaqiyyah, in good spirits and happy. Then, al-Muwaffaq returned to the task of demolishing the walls, destroying the section (that ran) from Ankalāy's residence to that of al-Jubbāʾī. Al-Muwaffaq's men came upon some of the administrative offices and storehouses belonging to the abominable one; they were subsequently plundered and set to the torch. These events happened on a day of thick fog which obscured vision, so that the men could hardly see one another. This day was the beginning of victory for al-Muwaffaq. In the midst of the fighting a profligate arrow launched by Qarṭās, a Greek page who was with the rebel, struck al-Muwaffaq in the chest. That happened on Monday, [2036]
the twenty-fifth of Jumādā II, 269 (January 9, 883). Al-Muwaffaq kept his mishap secret and returned to al-Muwaffaqiyyah. He had his wound dressed that very night, and remained to spend the night at his city. Although his wound bothered him, he returned to the fight in order to rally the spirits of his leading men so that no apprehension or weakness would seize them. Because of this excessive activity, his illness intensified and complications set in; the matter took such a se-

rious turn that it caused concern for his life, and he was in need of the best possible care.

The entire camp, troops and subjects alike became disturbed. Their apprehension about the strength of the abominable one was so great, that one detachment of troops stationed in al-Muwaffaqiyyah left the city because of the fear that seized them. The gravity of his illness became a subject of discussion in government circles. Advisors from among his confidantes urged him to abandon his camp for Baghdad (Madīnat al-Salām) and leave behind someone in his place. He declined to do this, fearing that the abominable one's scattered forces could be reassembled. Therefore, despite the seriousness of his illness, and the discussion taking place in government circles, he remained. God in his mercy granted him good health, so that after lengthy seclusion he showed himself to his officers and his inner circle, causing them to feel strengthened. He remained in his retreat and continued to recover from his illness until Shaʿbān of this year (February 13–March 13, 883). When he recovered and felt able to resume the fight against the profligate, he became aroused, and returned to battle the rebel with his old perseverance.

[2037] When the abominable one ascertained what had happened to Abū Aḥmad, he started to give his men false promises and to stir false hopes. But after word reached him that Abū Aḥmad had reappeared, sailing in his barge, the rebel started to swear from his pulpit that this was an empty and baseless rumor, and what they had really seen in the barge was an effigy which in their confused minds seemed to be Abū Aḥmad.

In this year, on Saturday in the middle of Jumādā I (November 16–December 15, 882), al-Muʿtamid, who set out for Egypt, stopped at al-Kuḥayl[116] to hunt. On Jumādā II (December 16, 882–January 13, 883), Ṣāʿid b. Makhlad left Abū Aḥmad, and went to Sāmarrā with a group of officers. Two of Ibn Ṭūlūn's officers, one of them called Aḥmad b. Jayghawayh and the other Muḥammad b. ʿAbbās al-Kilābī, proceeded to al-Raqqah.

116. Yāqūt, *Muʿjam*, IV, 240, mentions this place in connection with al-Muʿtaḍid's journey to campaign against Khumarawayh in 271 (884/885). It was a large city on the west bank of the Tigris above Takrīt.

When al-Muʿtamid arrived in the province of Isḥāq b. Kundāj—he was governor of Mosul and of the Jazīrah—the latter fell upon al-Muʿtamid's retainers. These were the men who had left Sāmarrā with al-Muʿtamid for Egypt, namely Tīnak, Aḥmad b. Khāqān and Khaṭārmish. Isḥāq had them bound, and seized their money, animals and slaves. He had previously received a letter to arrest them and al-Muʿtamid. Their estates and those of Fārs b. Bughā were conferred upon Isḥāq b. Kundāj.

The reason for his detaining al-Muʿtamid and his retainers is as follows. When al-Muʿtamid arrived in Isḥāq's province, letters from Ṣāʿid ordering their detention had already reached Ibn Kundāj. He acted as though he sympathized with them and shared their feelings of loyalty to al-Muʿtamid, sihce the latter was the caliph, and it would be unlawful to oppose him. Now, some of al-Muʿtamid's officers cautioned him to bypass Ibn [2038] Kundāj, warning him that the latter would pounce upon them. But he insisted on stopping, as recorded above, saying, "Isḥāq is my mawlā and page. I want to hunt, and on the way to him there is bountiful game." When they reached his province, he met and accompanied them, reportedly to offer al-Muʿtamid hospitality before he passed into the province of Ibn Ṭūlūn. The next day, early in the morning, the retainers, pages, and the others who were with al-Muʿtamid and those who left Sāmarrā with him started to saddle their animals. Ibn Kundāj remained with al-Muʿtamid's officers, and said to them, "Now, you have neared the domain of Ibn Ṭūlūn and his commander who is stationed in al-Raqqah. As soon as you reach him, the power will be his and you'll be in his hands, as if you were one of his soldiers. Would you be content with this, knowing that he is one of you?"[117] They argued over this until daybreak. Al-Muʿtamid was not yet ready to depart, for his captains were involved in this argument in his presence without coming to any agreement. Then Ibn Kundāj suggested: "Let's go and discuss the matter at some other place, and let's respect the honor of the Commander of the Faithful and not raise our voices here." Clutching their hands, he took them out of al-Muʿtamid's tent

117. That is, they were equal in rank to Ibn Ṭulūn when he was stationed at the court in Sāmarrā.

and led them into his own. No other tent remained; all the tents but his had been removed. According to instructions he had forwarded to his attendants, pages, retainers and men, they were not to leave the place before he did. As soon as they entered Ibn Kundāj's tent, the bravest of his pages and troops entered into his presence and that of his officers. Chains were
[2039] also brought in, and Ibn Kundāj's pages seized and put chains on every one of al-Muʿtamid's officers who had accompanied him from Sāmarrā. After they were all fettered, and he had disposed of this task, Isḥāq b. Kundāj went to al-Muʿtamid and reproached him for leaving his capital[118] and that of his ancestors and for forsaking his brother at a time when he was conducting war against those who were attempting to kill him and all his family, and to abolish their empire. Thereupon, he delivered him and his chained attendants to Sāmarrā.

In this year, Rāfiʿ b. Harthamah established himself in districts and villages of Khurāsān which al-Khujustānī had seized. Rāfiʿ b. Harthamah had taken ten years worth of taxes on advance from a number of districts of Khurāsān, by which he brought destitution upon the people and devastation upon the districts.

In this year, a skirmish took place between the Ḥusaynīs, Ḥasanīs and Jaʿfarīs. The Jaʿfarīs had eight people killed in the battle, but they gained the victory and released al-Faḍl b. al-ʿAbbās al-ʿAbbāsī, the governor of al-Madīnah.

In Jumādā II (December 16, 882–January 13, 883), Hārūn b. al-Muwaffaq appointed Ibn Abī al-Sāj governor of al-Anbār, the Euphrates Road, and Raḥbat Ṭawq. Aḥmad b. Muḥammad al-Ṭāʾī, was appointed governor of al-Kūfah and its environs. He acted as paymaster and collector of taxes there, distributing
[2040] the pay in the name of ʿAlī b. al-Ḥusayn, the one known as Kuftimur. Aḥmad b. Muḥammad encountered al-Hayṣam al-

118. The reference here is to forsaking Baghdad. There was a very likely polemical exchange between the partisans of the old capital, and the supporters of the new capital at Sāmarrā. This was also reflected in poetry. See, for examples, the verses of ʿUmārah b. ʿAqīl b. Bilāl b. Jarīr al-Khaṭafī quoted by the Khaṭīb al-Baghdādī, *Taʾrīkh*, I, 68 = Paris, 3–4.

ʿIjlī in this year. Al-Hayṣam was routed, and Aḥmad auctioned off al-ʿIjlī's wealth and estates.

On the fourth of Shaʿbān this year (January 18, 883), Isḥāq b. Kundāj brought al-Muʿtamid back to Sāmarrā. The latter settled at al-Jawsaq (the palace) overlooking al-Ḥayr.[119]

On the eighth of Shaʿbān (January 22, 883), Ibn Kundāj was given robes of honor. Two swords with swordbelts were conferred upon him, one for his right side and the other for his left, and he was named Possessor of Two Swords (Dhū al-Sayfayn). Two days later he was given a brocade cloak, two sashes, a diadem and a sword; all these were encrusted with gems. Hārūn b. al-Muwaffaq, Ṣāʿid b. Makhlad and the officers escorted him to his residence and lunched with him.

In Shaʿbān of this year (February 13–March 13, 883) Abū Aḥmad's troops burned down the profligate's fortress and plundered everything in it.

The Reason for This and How Abū Aḥmad's Troops Reached It[120]

Muḥammad b. al-Ḥasan reported: When Abū Aḥmad recovered from the wounds which he had received, he resumed fighting the profligate without letup. The abominable one had repaired some of the breaches that had been made in the wall, so that al-Muwaffaq ordered that the area of the breaches be demolished along with the adjoining wall. It happened late one afternoon. The battle had been fought near the Munkā Canal. The profligates were concentrated in this area and were busy fighting [2041]
them, as they believed it to be the only active battleground. Al-Muwaffaq set out with sappers he had prepared earlier, and nearing the Munkā Canal, he charged the profligates there. When the fighting became intense, he instructed the oarsmen and captains to move quickly until they reached the canal

119. That is, al-Muʿtaṣim's palace. The ruins of this immense structure were investigated by Viollet and Sarre and Herzfeld. A concise account of the palace is found in Creswell, *Shorter Early Muslim Architecture*, 260 ff.

120. See Popovic, *Révolte*, 152 ff.

known as the Juwayy Kūr. This was a canal that branched off from the Tigris below the canal known as Nahr Abū al-Khasīb. They did this, and upon arriving there they found the Juwway Kūr free of regular troops and foot soldiers. Al-Muwaffaq drew nearer and sent out the sappers to demolish the section of the wall next to this canal; then he brought up his regular troops, and penetrated his way up the canal, killing many people. They reached some of the profligate fortresses; whereupon, they plundered them, and then set them to the torch, rescuing scores of women who had been (held) there. The government force seized some of the rebels' horses and transported them to the western side of the Tigris. At sunset al-Muwaffaq withdrew safely with the booty. He then returned the next morning in order to resume the battle and demolish the wall. They pushed the demolition of the wall until they reached the residence known as Dār Ankalāy, which was contiguous to the residence of the abominable one. When all of the abominable one's ruses had failed to hinder the demolition of the wall and prevent al-Muwaffaq's troops from penetrating his city, he did not know how to deal with this situation that had gotten out of hand. ʿAlī b. Abān al-Muhallabī advised him to let water flow onto the swampy ground on which al-Muwaffaq's troops passed, so as to deny it to them. He also suggested that the rebel dig trenches in a number of places, which would impede
[2042] their entrance into the city. If the government forces risked crossing the trench and were defeated, they would find it difficult to return to their vessels.

They did all of this in different sections of their city and along the parade ground which the abominable one had turned into a major road. These trenches now extended near his residence. Now that God had enabled him to succeed in demolishing the wall of the profligate's city, al-Muwaffaq was inclined to fill in the trenches, canals, and places where obstructions had been set up, so as to make them passable for (his) cavalry and infantry. That was what he wanted. But the profligates defended themselves and the fight lasted a long time and without respite, both sides sustaining heavy losses in dead and wounded. One day the number of injured reached almost two thousand; this was because the factions were close to each other during combat, and because the trenches prevented each side from dislodging the other from its position. When al-Muwaffaq saw this, he decided to burn down the abominable one's residence and to attack it from the Tigris. A great many Zanj fighting men, who had been prepared by the abominable one, resisted these moves from his residence. They cast stones and shot (arrows and other projectiles) from bows, slings, ballistas, and catapults from the walls and upper reaches of the fortress. In addition lead was melted down and poured upon the government troops. They did all this whenever the barges neared the fortress. As we have described, it was impossible for the attackers to set the abominable one's residence aflame.

Al-Muwaffaq now ordered that wooden screens be prepared for barges. These screens were covered with buffalo skins [2043]
spread over with canvas, and varnished with kinds of chemical substances which would protect them from fire. A number of barges were shielded with screens prepared in this manner. Al-Muwaffaq manned each of these vessels with a force of the bravest lancers and archers from among his pages, and he attached to them a team of fire-hurlers. They were assigned the task of setting the profligate's residence on fire, that is, the leader of the Zanj.

On Friday, the seventeenth of Shaʿbān, 269 (February 28, 883), Muḥammad b. Simʿān, the scribe and wazīr of the abominable one, asked al-Muwaffaq for a guarantee of safe-conduct. The reason for this, as reported by Muḥammad b. al-Ḥasan, was because Muḥammad b. Simʿān was one of those who hated the rebel and loathed his company as he knew he was an imposter.

Muḥammad b. al-Ḥasan reported: This was why I was friendly with Ibn Simʿān. Together we would devise plans for escape, but to no avail. But when the siege took its toll of the abominable one, and his men deserted him, weakening his position, Ibn Simʿān devised a scheme to flee, and informed me about it, saying, "I am willing to leave without child or family, and will save only myself." Then he asked me, "Would you like to do the same?" I replied, "You are right in your decision, for you will leave behind only one small child. The perfidious one will not be able either to assail the child or expose you to

shame through it. But as for myself, I have womenfolk, and I cannot afford to expose them to the rebel's cruelty. So do as you have decided and pass on word about me; that is, about my intention to break away from the rebel and my disgust at being associated with him. If God redeems me and my children, indeed, I shall follow you promptly; but should our fates be con-
[2044] joined, we shall be together and bear it."

Muḥammad b. Simʿān now sent a representative of his called al-ʿIrāqī, who arrived at al-Muwaffaq's camp and secured for his master the safeguards he sought. Al-Muwaffaq prepared barges which reached Ibn Simʿān in the lagoon on the day reported above, and the latter thus arrived at al-Muwaffaq's camp. The day after Muḥammad b. Simʿān sought safe conduct, which was Saturday, the eighteenth of Shaʿbān, 269 (March 1, 883), al-Muwaffaq resumed the conflict against the abominable one, dressed in the finest battle garb and (utilizing the best) equipment. He took with him the barges that had been given screens, as described above, and then went with the rest of his barges and galleys manned by his mawlās and pages. He also took ferries carrying infantry. Al-Muwaffaq ordered his son, Abū al-ʿAbbās to set off for the residence of Muḥammad b. Yaḥyā, that is, the man known as al-Karnabāʾī. This place was opposite the residence of the perfidious one on the eastern side of the canal known as the Abū al-Khaṣīb—it overlooked the canal and the Tigris. He sent him forward to set fire to it and to the adjacent residences belonging to the perfidious one's commanders. In such fashion he would preoccupy the commanders, thus preventing them from assisting the rebel and providing him with support.

Al-Muwaffaq ordered the men in the barges which had screens to move to the structures and balconies of the abominable one which extended over the Tigris. This they did, bringing their barges close to the walls of the fortress. They engaged the rebels in the fiercest of battles, and showered them with fire. Although the rebels fought back tenaciously, God granted victory over them and they were pushed back from these balconies and structures which they were defending. Al-Muwaffaq's pages set all this on fire, while the men in the barges remained unharmed from the arrows, stones, molten lead and other projectiles. This was due to the screens which they had fastened to their vessels. In such fashion, they were able to capture the abominable one's residence. Then, al-Muwaffaq ordered all the people of the barges to withdraw; he removed the pages and replaced them with others, while he stayed, expecting the tide to rise. When this occurred, the barges with screens returned to the abominable one's fortress, and in accordance with al-Muwaffaq's orders, they set fire to those elements of the profligate's fortress which faced out onto the Tigris. The fire in these structures raged on, reaching the coverings with which the abominable one shielded his quarters, and the curtains of his doors. The flames became more intense, making it impossible for him and his men to remove anything in his residences, such as his money, stores, moveable furniture and other items. Fleeing, they left all this behind. Al-Muwaffaq's pages and their men stormed the abominable one's fortress and looted everything which the fire had not reached; this included gold, silver, pearls, jewels and other items. A number of women whom the abominable one had had enslaved were rescued. Al-Muwaffaq's pages also reached the other residences of the abominable one and his son Ankalāy, and set them all on fire. Overjoyed with what God had granted them on this day, the troops kept on fighting the profligates in their city, and before the gate of the abominable one's fortress which was near the review ground. The government forces struck a heavy blow against the rebels, killing, wounding and capturing them. [2045]

In the same manner, Abū al-ʿAbbās attacked the residence of al-Karnabāʾī and the contiguous area, burning, demolishing and plundering. The former cut a massive and strong iron chain which the abominable one had fastened across the Abū al-Khaṣīb Canal in order to make it inaccessible to barges. He took this chain and carried it off in some of his vessels. At the time of evening prayer al-Muwaffaq withdrew with the army, completely victorious. On that day the profligate himself suffered losses in wealth, children, and captive Muslim women. The Muslims had hitherto suffered grief because of him, as well as dispossession, loss of kith and kin, affliction, captivity, [2046] break-up of family, and hardship to women and children. His son, the one called Ankalāy was gravely wounded in the stomach that day, and only narrowly escaped death.

On the morrow of that day, which was the eighteenth of Shaʿbān, 269 (Saturday, March 2, 883), Nuṣayr drowned.

How Nuṣayr Drowned

Muḥammad b. al-Ḥasan reported: On the morrow of that day, al-Muwaffaq rose early to fight against the abominable one. He instructed Nuṣayr, the one called Abū Ḥamzah to set out for the bridge which the perfidious one had constructed of teak wood on the Abū al-Khaṣīb Canal. This was beyond the two bridges which Nuṣayr had seized. Al-Muwaffaq also instructed Zīrak to go with his troops to the area of al-Jubbāʾī's residence to fight the rebels there, and to send another group of commanders to the vicinity of Ankalāy's residence to do the same. As soon as the tide rose, Nuṣayr quickly sailed forth with a number of his barges into the Abū al-Khaṣīb Canal, but the tide
[2047] carried them and forced them against the bridge. At the same time, without being ordered, a number of al-Muwaffaq's barges staffed with mawlās and pages also entered the canal, and these were also carried by the tide and forced against Nuṣayr's vessels. They came so close to each other that the captains and oarsmen were helpless to cope with what had happened.

The Zanj perceived this, and gathered to attack the barges, surrounding them on both sides of the canal. Panicked with fear, the oarsmen jumped into the water, and abandoned their vessels to the Zanj, who seized them. The Zanj killed some of the fighting men, but most of them drowned. Nuṣayr fought back from his barge until, in fear of being captured, he jumped into the water and subsequently drowned.

Al-Muwaffaq began his day in combat with the profligates, pillaging and burning their residences, and he continued to hold the upper hand until the day was over. Among those defending the fortress of the perfidious one were Sulaymān b. Jāmiʿ and his troops. The battle between Sulaymān's men and those of al-Muwaffaq continued without respite as the latter held fast to his position. Sulaymān continued to offer resistance until ambushers drawn from al-Muwaffaq's black pages emerged to his rear; whereupon, Sulaymān was routed. The pages pursued him killing some of his men and capturing others. In this fight Sulaymān was hit in the thigh, an injury which forced him down in a place consumed by fire where the coals were still smoldering. Parts of his body were thus burned, but he was protected by a group of his men as he was about to be captured. Victorious and unharmed al-Muwaffaq withdrew, while the profligates became weaker and more fearful as they saw the end was in sight.

Abū Aḥmad happened to fall ill with arthritis which lasted all through the end of Shaʿbān, Ramaḍān (March 14–April 12, [2048]
883) and part of Shawwāl (April 13–May 11, 883). As a result he had to abstain from fighting the profligate. But as soon as he recovered, he gave the order to prepare everything necessary to encounter the profligates, and all his men prepared for that task.

In this year, ʿĪsā b. al-Shaykh b. al-Salīl passed away.

In this year, al-Muʿtamid cursed Ibn Ṭūlūn from the Dār al-ʿĀmmah[121] and gave instructions that the same be done from the pulpits. On Friday, Jaʿfar al-Mufawwaḍ went to the Friday Mosque and cursed Ibn Ṭūlūn. All the provinces held by Ibn Ṭūlūn were given to Isḥāq b. Kundāj, who was appointed governor of all the regions extending from Bāb al-Shammāsiyyah[122] to Ifrīqiyyah. He was also made responsible for the security of the Caliph's personal force (*shurṭat al-khāṣṣah*).

In Ramadān (March 14–April 12, 883), Aḥmad b. Ṭūlūn sent a message to the people of Syria urging them to assist his deputy. An express messenger seeking Ibn Ṭūlūn with dispatches from his deputy Jawwāb was apprehended. Jawwāb was also seized and imprisoned, and his money, slaves and animals were seized.

In Shawwāl (April 13–May 11, 883), a skirmish took place

121. That is, that chamber where the Caliph gave public audiences.

122. Al-Shammāsiyyah was, at the time, a staging ground for the ʿAbbāsid armies just north of the settled areas in East Baghdad. The expression would seem to be a metaphor for ʿAbbāsid rule extending from the capital westward. For al-Shammāsiyyah, see Lassner, *Topography*, index, 322.

between Ibn Abī al-Sāj and the tribesmen, in which the former was routed. Later he attacked them by night, killing some of them and taking others captive. He then sent the heads of the dead and also the captives to Baghdad. They arrived in Shawwāl of 269 (April 13–May 11, 883).

On the eighteenth of Shawwāl this year (Tuesday, April 30, 883), Jaʿfar al-Mufawwaḍ appointed Ṣāʿid b. Makhlad governor of Shahrazūr,[123] Darābādh,[124] al-Sāmaghān,[125] Ḥulwān, Māsabadhān,[126] Mihrijānqadhaq and the Euphrates districts. He also as-
[2049] signed to him Mūsā b. Bughā's commanders except for Aḥmad b. Mūsā, Kayghalagh, Isḥāq b. Kundājīq and Asātakīn. On Saturday the twenty-second of Shawwāl (May 11, 883), Ṣāʿid, in turn, delegated the government of the provinces which he received from al-Mufawwaḍ to Lu'lu'. He also sent a message to Ibn Abī al-Sāj confirming him as governor of the provinces he was ruling on behalf of Hārūn b. al-Muwaffaq, namely, al-Anbār, the Euphrates Road, and Raḥbat Ṭawq b. Mālik. Ibn Abī al-Sāj had departed there in the month of Ramaḍān (March 14–April 12, 883). As soon as all these lands were added to Ṣāʿid's domains, Ṣāʿid confirmed Ibn Abī al-Sāj in his territory.

Toward the end of Shawwāl (April 13–May 11, 883), Ibn Abī al-Sāj entered Raḥbat Ṭawq b. Mālik after its inhabitants came out against him. He overwhelmed them, and Aḥmad b. Mālik b. Ṭawq fled from there to Damascus. Thereupon, Ibn Abī al-Sāj went to Qarqīsiyyā and entered the city. It had been evacuated by Ibn Ṣafwān al-ʿUqaylī.

On Tuesday, the tenth of Shawwāl (Monday night, April 15, 883), a battle took place in the profligate's city between Abū Aḥmad and the Zanj. In this engagement Abū Aḥmad obtained his desired objective.

The Reason for This Battle and What Transpired

According to Muḥammad b. al-Ḥasan: While al-Muwaffaq was preoccupied by his sickness, the abominable one, the en-

123. See Yāqūt, *Muʿjam*, III, 340.
124. Ibid., 364.
125. Ibid., 340.
126. Op. cit., IV, 392.

emy of God, restored the bridge into which Nuṣayr's barges had run. He added those elements to the bridge which he thought strengthened it. Beyond it he erected interlocking teakwood stakes and overlaid them with iron. In front of this he put a barricade of stones to narrow the entrance for the [2050] barges and to cause a whirling current in the canal known as Abū al-Khaṣīb so that people would dread entering it.

Al-Muwaffaq recruited two officers from among his pages—they commanded four thousand men—and instructed them to go to the Abū al-Khaṣīb Canal; one of them was to travel along the eastern side of the canal and the other along the western side. They were to march to the bridge which the rebel had restored, and to the dam which he had erected in front of it. Having done this, they were then to combat the troops of the abominable one in the area of the bridge and dislodge them from it. He assigned carpenters and sappers to them in order to dismantle the bridge and the stakes that had been put in front of it. At his command, boats were also made ready and filled with reeds doused in naphtha. These would enter this canal—the one called Abū al-Khaṣīb—and when the tide rose, they would be put to the torch, setting the bridge on fire.

On that day al-Muwaffaq rode out with the army until he reached the mouth of the Abū al-Khaṣīb Canal. He ordered that the fighting men be sent ashore at a number of places above and below the abominable one's camp in order to divert the rebel troops from assisting those defending the bridge. The two officers and their troops advanced and were met by the men of the perifidious one, a force of Zanj troops and others. They were led by his son Ankalāy, ʿAlī b. Abān al-Muhallabī, and Sulaymān b. Jāmiʿ. The two forces then engaged in fighting. The battle was protracted, with the profligates fighting violently in defense of their bridge. They understood that dismantling this bridge could bring calamity upon them, and that the two pontoon bridges which the abominable one had established beyond it on the Abū al-Khaṣīb Canal would now be- [2051] come a target easy to reach. The number of killed and wounded grew for both factions and the battle lasted until the time of the afternoon prayer. Then al-Muwaffaq's pages dislodged the rebels from the bridge and crossed over it. The carpenters and workers cut the bridge loose, and they dismantled it as well as the aforementioned stakes. The profligate had constructed the bridge and stakes so solidly that it was impossible for the workers and carpenters to dismantle them quickly. Because of this, al-Muwaffaq commanded that the vessels bearing the naphtha-doused reeds enter the canal and be set on fire, whereupon, they would float with the current. This was done, and the ships reached the bridge, setting it aflame. The carpenters were now able to carry out their plan of dismantling the stakes, thereby opening the canal to the men on the barges. The force on the vessels then entered the canal. This raised the spirits of the pages and, driving the rebel's troops from their positions, they chased them until the latter reached the first pontoon bridge behind the bridge. A great many of the rebels were killed and a group of them sought guarantees of safe-conduct from al-Muwaffaq. He immediately ordered that they be given robes of honor and placed in positions where their comrades could observe them. Their compatriots would thus become eager for similar treatment.

The pages reached the first pontoon bridge—it was near sunset. Al-Muwaffaq disliked having his men deep within the Abū al-Khaṣīb Canal with the advancing darkness, lest the rebels seize the opportunity. Therefore, he ordered the troops to withdraw safely to al-Muwaffaqiyyah. Al-Muwaffaq now dispatched letters to the districts to be read from the pulpits about the victory and conquest that God had granted to him. He ordered that those of his pages who had distinguished themselves
[2052] be rewarded according to their gallantry, their sacrifice and the manner in which they carried out orders, so as to inspire great effort in the fight against their enemies. This was carried out. Al-Muwaffaq now crossed over to the mouth of the Abū al-Khaṣīb Canal, together with some of his mawlās and pages. They crossed in barges, galleys, and skiffs. The abominable one had already obstructed the passage with two stone barriers in order to make the entrance narrow and the current rapid, so that if the barges entered the canal, they would founder about and find their way back difficult. Al-Muwaffaq ordered these two barriers removed, and his men worked at this from sunrise to sunset.

The workers then withdrew and returned the next morning to finish dismantling what had remained. They discovered, however, that during the night the rebels had restored what had been removed. At this, al-Muwaffaq ordered two ballistas installed on two vessels stationed in front of the Abū al-Khaṣīb Canal; the ballistas had been prepared for these boats in advance. Their anchors were dropped so as to hold them steady. He assigned a team of barge troops to the vessels and charged them with removing these two barriers. The troops of the two ballistas were instructed to fire at any of the profligate's men who drew near to restore parts of the barriers, whether by day or night. The rebels kept their distance, and, after that, the men in charge of removing the stones pressed on until they had accomplished what they intended to do. The route in and out of the canal thus became more accessible for the barges.

In this year, the rebel moved from the western side of the Abū al-Khaṣīb Canal to its eastern side, and provisions were cut off from all directions.

The Rebel's Situation and That of His Men When He Transferred From the West

It is reported that when al-Muwaffaq laid waste the residences of the leader of the Zanj and set them to the torch, the latter took refuge by fortifying himself in the residences further along the Abū al-Khaṣīb Canal. The rebel camped at the residence of Aḥmad b. Mūsā, who was known as al-Qalūṣ, where he gathered around him his extended family and children. His markets were now transferred to a nearby marketplace, that is the one called Sūq al-Ḥusayn.

His position, nevertheless, became extremely weak, and it became clear to the people that his cause was doomed. They were afraid of bringing provisions to him, and he was thus cut off from all supplies. The price of a *raṭl*[127] of corn bread in his camp now reached ten dirhams. As a result, the rebels ate barley and then different kinds of grain. This continued until, fi-

127. One *raṭl* = 12 *ūqiyah.* The Iraqi *raṭl* was 406.25 gr. See Hinz, *Islamische Masse und Gewischte,* 27 ff.; also, see above, nn. 101, 109.

nally, they started to practice cannibalism.[128] If one of them was isolated with a woman, child, or man, he would slaughter that person and devour the victim. The stronger Zanj then assailed the weaker ones, and when they isolated a weak person, they killed him and ate his flesh. Then they ate the flesh of their children. Following that, they dug up corpses, sold the shrouds, and ate the flesh. The only punishment imposed by the abominable one on the perpetrators of such deeds was imprisonment, but once their imprisonment became prolonged, they were released.

It is reported that when the profligate's residence was demolished and set to the torch, and after everything in it was plundered, he was driven, like a homeless outcast, from the western
[2054] side of the Abū al-Khaṣīb Canal to the eastern side. Abū Aḥmad now decided to lay waste the east bank, thereby replicating the conditions which had faced the abominable one on the opposite bank— that is, the western side from which he had been driven. Al-Muwaffaq instructed his son Abū al-ʿAbbās to take up positions in barges with a group of his men in the Abū al-Khaṣīb Canal. He also told him to select a team of his troops and pages and land them in the section where the residence of al-Karnabāʾī was located on the eastern side of the canal. Sappers were to be landed with them in order to demolish any houses or dwellings of the rebel's companions which they might come upon.

Al-Muwaffaq positioned himself at the fortress named after al-Hamdānī, who was entrusted with the defense of this sector. He was commander of the abominable one's troops and one of his earliest companions. On the instruction of al-Muwaffaq, a team of his officers and mawlās set off for the residence of al-Hamdānī—they had sappers with them. The place had been fortified with a great body of Zanj and other troops of the abominable one. Protecting it were ballistas, catapults, and Nāwukiyyah bows. A fight began in which many were killed and wounded. Finally the troops of al-Muwaffaq dislodged the profligates, putting them to the sword; a great many of the enemy were killed. Abū al-ʿAbbās's troops meted out the same to

128. Lit. "chase after people."

any rebel coming within their reach. Then al-Muwaffaq's troops and those of Abū al-ʿAbbās joined forces in concerted action against the profligates who fled to the residence of al-Hamdānī. It had been fortified with ballistas, and surrounded on all sides with white flags of the rebel, his name inscribed upon them. Now, it was impossible for the troops of al-Muwaffaq to surmount the walls of this house because they were high and thus inaccessible. They applied long ladders but still they could not reach the top. Then, some of al-Muwaffaq's pages hurled grappling hooks which were attached to long ropes. They were especially prepared for a place such as this. [2055]
They fastened the hooks to the banners of the profligate and they pulled. At that, the banners tumbled from the top of the wall, and into the hands of al-Muwaffaq's men. The defenders of that residence were now certain that Abū Aḥmad's troops were on the wall. Seized with fear, they fled, surrendering the residence and everything around it. The naphtha-hurlers ascended (the wall) and set fire to the catapults, the ballistas, and the belongings of al-Hamdānī's residence. They also burned down the surrounding residences of the rebels. On that day, many captive Muslim women were wrested from them, and al-Muwaffaq ordered them transported by barge, galley and ferry to the city of al-Muwaffaqiyyah, and treated with kindness. The battle continued without respite from daylight until after afternoon prayers. A group of the profligate's troops and a party of his special pages, who were his personal attendants and guards, asked for safe-conduct. Al-Muwaffaq granted this to all of them, and ordered that they be treated kindly, given robes of honor and presents and alloted military pay. Al-Muwaffaq returned and ordered that the profligate's flags be hung upside down in the middle of the barges so that they could be seen by his men. A group of those who had asked for safe-conduct guided al-Muwaffaq to an immense marketplace which the abominable one had behind the residence of al-Hamdānī adjacent to the first bridge spanning the Abū al-Khaṣīb Canal. The abominable one had named the market al-Mubārakah. They told al-Muwaffaq that if he succeeded in burning it down, no other market would be left to the rebels, and the merchants, who were the source of their subsistence, would leave them.

The rebels would thus feel deserted and compelled to leave seeking guarantees of safe-conduct.

[2056] Al-Muwaffaq was resolved to go with troops to this market and its surroundings from three directions. He ordered Abū al-ʿAbbās to set off for the side of this market contiguous to the first bridge; he ordered his mawlā Rāshid to go to the market where it was adjacent to the residence of al-Hamdānī; and he ordered an officer of his black pages to go to the market sector adjacent to the Abū Shākir Canal. Each of these detachments did as ordered.

The Zanj became aware of the government troops marching against them and set out to encounter them. The battle was engaged, and the fighting grew heavy. The rebel reinforced his men. Al-Muhallabī, Ankalāy and Sulaymān b. Jāmiʿ and their troops had been fully prepared, and with the arrival of the reinforcements, they fought fiercely in defense of their sector. At the very beginning of their attack, al-Muwaffaq's men reached a point on the perimeter of this market, and set it to the torch. It burned, and the flames spread to most of the market. The two factions fought while the flames enveloped them—the booth coverings above, which had already caught fire, fell on the heads of the fighting men, often burning them. This situation lasted until sundown and the onset of night. Then they stopped fighting and al-Muwaffaq and his men returned to their vessels, and the profligates returned to their tyrant. This was after the market had gone up in flames. Its inhabitants, as well as those merchants with the perfidious one's army and the rabble from the market, fled and reached the upper parts of his city. They had with them money and goods of theirs which they had saved. They had already carried off the bulk of their merchandise and goods from this market, fearing that they would suffer that which befell them on the day God granted al-
[2057] Muwaffaq victory at the residence of al-Hamadānī, and made it possible for him to burn down everything he set to the torch around it.

Then, after this battle, the abominable one dug trenches on the east bank and made obstacle courses of the roads, just as he had done on the west bank. He dug a broad trench from the edge of the Juwayy Kūr to the Gharbī Canal. His main concern was fortifying the section from al-Karnabā'ī's residence to the Juwway Kūr Canal, since this sector contained the main residences and dwellings of his men. As a result, gardens and (other) vacated places surrounded by walls and trenches stretched all the way from the Juwway Kūr to the Gharbī. Whenever the battle broke out in this sector, the Zanj rushed from their positions to defend it, preventing the enemy from advancing. Because of this, al-Muwaffaq decided to demolish the rest of the wall up to the Gharbī Canal, which he accomplished after a long drawn out battle.

The profligate was on the eastern side of the Gharbī in a camp in which there were contingents of Zanj and others. They were entrenched behind a protective wall and moats. These troops were the most courageous and valiant of the abominable one's men; they were defending the area adjacent the wall along the Gharbī Canal. During the battle at the Juwayy Kūr and the adjacent areas, they attacked al-Muwaffaq's troops from the rear. Al-Muwaffaq therefore gave orders to set out for this place, take on its defenders, demolish its walls, and dislodge those who were entrenched there. He forwarded instructions to Abū al-ʿAbbās and a number of commanders drawn from his pages and mawlās to prepare themselves for this task, and they did as ordered. Al-Muwaffaq advanced with troops he had prepared to the Gharbī Canal, whereupon he ordered the barges arrayed from the limits of the canal known as Nahr Juwayy Kūr to the place called al- [2058]
Dabbāsīn. The fighting men landed on both sides of the Gharbī Canal, and ladders were put aqainst the wall—the Zanj had a number of ballistas arrayed there—and a fight broke out which lasted from daylight to the afternoon. A number of breaches were made in the wall and the ballistas on it were set aflame, but the parties then desisted from further fighting, neither of them having gained an advantage over the other except that the troops of al-Muwaffaq had succeeded in making those breaches and setting fire to the ballistas. Both parties were severely stricken with suffering and pain from their wounds. Al-Muwaffaq and all his troops then returned to al-Muwaffaqiyyah, where he ordered the wounded treated and rewarded, everyone according to their injury. This was the policy he had

pursued in all of his battles from the beginning of his campaign against the profligate until God saw the latter dead.

After this battle, al-Muwaffaq remained where he was for a while. Then, he saw fit to return to this place and deal with it rather than with any other sector, because he perceived how well fortified it was, and he noted the courage and perseverance of the defenders. He realized that he would be unable to gain mastery over the area between the Gharbī and Juwway Kūr canals without first dislodging these troops. So he prepared what he needed in the way of equipment for demolition, and he increased the number of sappers. Then, he selected the fighting men, the archers, lancers, and expert black swordsmen, and set off for this place just as he had the first time. He landed the footmen in places he considered suitable and sent a number of barges into the canal. The battle commenced and raged on as the profligates displayed great persistence, and al-Muwaffaq's troops did likewise against them. The profligates now asked for
[2059] reinforcements from their tyrant, and al-Muhallabī and Sulaymān b. Jāmiʿ came with their armies. This strengthened the enemy's resolve, and they charged al-Muwaffaq's troops. Sulaymān attacked from an ambush in the vicinity of the Juwayy Kūr, pushing al-Muwaffaq's force back to their ships and killing many of the men. Al-Muwaffaq withdrew without seeing his plans through. It had become clear that he should fight the profligates at a number of places, thereby splitting their troops and relieving the pressure they exerted on those coming to this difficult place. In such fashion, he would achieve his objective there.

He decided to renew the assault against the enemy, and instructed Abū al-ʿAbbās and some other commanders of his to make the crossing, choosing the best of their men. He entrusted his mawlā Masrūr with the canal known as Nahr Munkā, and instructed him to lead his men to this place and to the adjacent hills and palm grove. Masrūr would, as a result, divert the rebels, making them believe there was an attack intended against them from this direction. He instructed Abū al-ʿAbbās to land his troops along the Juwway Kūr and arrange his barges at these places until he reached the place called al-

Dabbāsīn, which was below the Gharbī Canal. Al-Muwaffaq set out for the Gharbī and ordered the commanders of his pages to set out with their men and start fighting the profligates in their stronghold and fortress. The government troops were not to turn away from them until God granted the government victory, or until they had received new orders from al-Muwaffaq. Then he ordered people to demolish the walls. As they went to (do this), the profligates, emboldened by the two battles which we have reported, rushed forward, but al-Muwaffaq's pages remained steadfast and fought against them gallantly. God bestowed victory upon the government troops, and they dislodged the profligates from their positions. Al-Muwaffaq's men became emboldened and charged the Zanj, putting them to flight. The fleeing enemy vacated their stronghold which fell into the hands of al-Muwaffaq's pages. The latter demolished the stronghold and burned the Zanj residences, looting every- [2060]
thing there. They pursued the fleeing enemy, killing a great many of them, and taking captives. Scores of captive Muslim women held in this stronghold were rescued, and upon al-Muwaffaq's instructions, they were removed and treated kindly. Then, al-Muwaffaq ordered the men to return to their vessels. They did so and retired to their camp in al-Muwaffaqiyyah. He had attained his objective in this sector.

In this year, al-Muwaffaq entered the city of the profligate and set fire to his residences on the eastern side of the Abū al-Khaṣīb Canal.

How He Came to Succeed Therein

It is reported, that after he had demolished the walls of this residence belonging to the rebel, Abū Aḥmad wished to penetrate the city. He, therefore, started to repair the paths on both sides of the Abū al-Khaṣīb and at the profligate's fortress in order to make a road wide enough for the fighting men to go in and out during combat. On his instructions, the gate of the abominable one's fortress, the same which he latter had dismantled from the Ḥiṣn Arwakh in al-Baṣrah, was removed and transferred to

Baghdad (Madīnat al-Salām).[129] Then al-Muwaffaq decided to raze the first bridge which was on the Abū al-Khasīb Canal, since this bridge would hinder his troops assisting one another should fighting break out in the area of their camp. So, upon his instructions, a large vessel was prepared and filled with reeds which had been doused in naphtha. In the middle of the vessel a tall mast was set up, which would prevent the vessel from sailing through when it reached the bridge.[130] He seized the opportunity which presented itself towards the end of day-
[2061] light when the rebels were careless and scattered about. The vessel was advanced by barges which towed it until it reached the canal where it was set ablaze and released after the tide had risen. The Zanj became aware of this as the vessel reached the bridge. They gathered their forces and flocked there in such numbers that they covered the bridge and the entire area. The Zanj now started to blanket the vessel with stones and burnt bricks, and they deposited earth and poured water on it. The bridge had caught fire and was burned slightly, but some of the Zanj plunged into the water and put holes in the vessel, sinking it, and putting out the fire. They now took possession of the vessel which fell into their hands.

When Abū Aḥmad saw what they had done, he decided to contest them for this bridge until he destroyed it. For that purpose he singled out two officers from among his pages, and ordered them to cross over with all their troops, taking sharp-pointed arms, strong breast-plates, special tools, equipment for naptha-hurlers and tools for demolishing the bridge. Al-Muwaffaq ordered one of the officers to the western side of the canal; he placed the other to the eastern side. Al-Muwaffaq, together with his mawlās, servants and pages, embarked on the

129. On the symbolic meaning of transferring gates from one city to another, see Lassner, *Topography*, 136–37.

130. Thus far the references to bridges along the Abū al-Khaṣīb have all been to pontoon bridges (*jisr*) which were easily constructed, dismantled and moved. The reference here may be to a masonry bridge (*qanṭarah*) or more likely, a permanent wooden bridge since it allowed for clearance. This could be one of the stone barriers spoken of earlier, or a structure similar to it. See text, 2052. It is more likely to have been some sort of wooden bridge since the plan was to set it ablaze. See below, n. 133.

barges and galleys, and set off for the mouth of Abū al-Khaṣīb Canal. This happened early Saturday morning, the fourteenth of Shawwāl, 269 (April 27, 883).

The first to reach the bridge was the officer who was directed to the western side of the canal. He charged the profligate's troops who had been entrusted with the bridge. A number of them were killed. The bridge was then set aflame; reeds and other incendiary material had been prepared for this purpose and were dumped on the structure. The abominable one's supporters who had been stationed there now fled. After this, the [2062] government troops which had been sent to the eastern side of the canal arrived at the bridge, and, as instructed, they did their share of burning. The abominable one had ordered his son, Ankalāy, and Sulaymān b. Jāmiʿ to stand with their armies in defense of the bridge in order to prevent its destruction. When the two did as ordered, al-Muwaffaq's troops, which had been positioned to their rear, set off against them and engaged them in heavy fighting until the Zanj were put to flight.

Thus the government troops were able to burn down the bridge, and they did so. They crossed over the bridge and advanced toward the yard where the profligate's barges, galleys and weapons were manufactured, and they burned absolutely everything, except for a few barges and galleys which were in the canal. Ankalāy and Sulaymān b. Jāmiʿ fled, and al-Muwaffaq's pages reached a prison which the abominable one had on the western side of Abū al-Khaṣīb Canal. The Zanj defended it for part of the day until a group of them were chased away. Then the prison fell into the hands of al-Muwaffaq's pages, who released the men and women detained there. After burning the bridge as ordered, al-Muwaffaq's pages on the eastern side penetrated to the place known as Dār Muṣlīḥ. This Muṣlīḥ was one of the earliest of the profligate's commanders. They broke into his residence and plundered it. They seized his children and womenfolk, and then set fire to everything they could reach along the way.

In the middle of the bridge there still remained poles which the abominable one firmly fixed. Al-Muwaffaq thus ordered Abū al-ʿAbbās to dispatch a number of barges to that place, and he did so. Among those sent there was Zīrak with a number of [2063] his troops. Upon their arrival, they sent out people with specially-prepared pickaxes and saws; the poles were cut and then pulled out of the canal. The rest of the bridge collapsed, and al-Muwaffaq's barges entered the canal. The two officers and all their troops moved ahead on both banks of the canal as the rebel's troops fled. At this, al-Muwaffaq and all his men withdrew safely; numerous people were rescued (as a result of all this). A great number of heads of the profligates were brought to al-Muwaffaq, and he meted out rewards and gifts to all those who brought them. Al-Muwaffaq's withdrawal commenced at three o'clock in the morning that day. This was after the profligate and all his Zanj and non-Zanj troops fled to the eastern side of the Abū al-Khaṣīb Canal, thus completely evacuating the western side, which was occupied by al-Muwaffaq's forces. The latter razed everything that hindered their fighting the rebels; that is, the fortresses of the profligate and those of his companions. They widened the narrow passages through Abū al-Khaṣīb, giving rise to increasing apprehension among the tyrant's men. Scores of his officers and troops, whom he had never expected to desert him, now were inclined to seek safe-conduct (from al-Muwaffaq). As their requests for safety were granted, they deserted in droves and were accepted and treated generously. They were granted military allotments, and given presents and robes of honor according to their rank.

After this, al-Muwaffaq devoted his attention to getting his barges and pages into the canal. He gave orders to burn the rebel residences along the banks and their ships in the water. He wished to train his men to penetrate the canal to make traveling the water course easy for them, because he intended
[2064] to burn down the second bridge and advance to the remotest positions of the rebels.

During one of those days in which al-Muwaffaq took the fight to the abominable one, and pressed forward into the Abū al-Khaṣīb Canal—it was a Friday, and al-Muwaffaq was positioned at a certain spot of the canal—one of the rebel troops asked al-Muwaffaq for safe-conduct and came to him with a pulpit which his master had had on the western side of the canal. Al-Muwaffaq ordered this man to turn the pulpit over to him—the latter was accompanied by a judge who had served the abominable one in his city. This was the kind of incident that caused the rebels' support to crumble.

Meanwhile, the abominable one had gathered his remaining vessels, those which were seaworthy and others, and placed them near the second bridge. There, he also concentrated his officers and troops and the most valiant of men. Al-Muwaffaq ordered some of his pages to approach the bridge and set fire to the seaworthy vessels that lay nearby. They were to torch as many vessels as possible and seize as many as they could. The pages assigned to this mission accomplished their task. Their operation intensified the rebel's activity in defending the second bridge. He attended to this personally at the head of all his forces, fearing that some ruse was in the making whereby he would be deprived of the western side of the canals. This would give al-Muwaffaq's troops a foothold there, one that eventually would mean the end of him (that is, the rebel).

After the first bridge had been burned, al-Muwaffaq spent several days transporting one detachment of his pages after another to the western side of the Abū al-Khaṣīb Canal. They burned the rest of the rebel dwelling places as they came closer to the second bridge. A group of Zanj, who had remained behind in their residences on the western side in the vicinity of the second bridge fought back against the government force. Al-Muwaffaq's pages used to come to this sector and establish positions on the major roads and paths taken by the army of the abominable one. When al-Muwaffaq found that his pages [2065]
and troops were familiar with the road and able to find their way along its paths, he decided to burn the second bridge. By that (maneuver) he could wrest the western side of the canal from the abominable one's army and array his combined forces in a single area, without any barrier between the two armies except the Abū al-Khaṣīb Canal.

On Saturday, the twentieth of Shawwāl, 269 (May 11, 883), al-Muwaffaq instructed Abū al-ʿAbbās to proceed with his troops and pages to the western bank. He sent orders for the latter to move out with his force at the site of a building which the rebel had named the Friday Mosque, and to take the route leading to the place which the abominable one had established as a prayer-platform for his festivals. When Abū al-ʿAbbās

reached the platform, he was to turn toward the hill (*jabal*) named after Abū ʿAmr, the brother of al-Muhallabī. Al-Muwaffaq attached to his command officers from among his pages drawn from the cavalry and infantry; together they came to about ten thousand men. He ordered Abū al-ʿAbbās to position the vanguard under Zīrak at the open expanse of the platform in order to forestall an attack from an ambush that the rebels might have prepared in these places. Al-Muwaffaq also ordered a group of officers from among his mounted pages to spread out among the hills there, between the hill named after Abū ʿAmr and the other one named after Abū Muqātil al-Zanjī. They were to do this until they all converged from this range of hills on the place of the second bridge along the Abū al-Khaṣīb. He forwarded instructions to anther group of officers from the pages assigned to Abū al-ʿAbbās, to go out with their troops between the profligate's residence and that of his son Ankalāy. They were to travel along the bank of the Abū al-Kaṣīb Canal and the adjacent territory, with the aim of joining the forward
[2066] groups of pages coming from the hills. Their common cause was the bridge. Al-Muwaffaq ordered them to take along tools, such as iron-bars, pickaxes, saws, and a detachment of naptha-hurlers so that they might demolish and burn everything that they could.

He ordered his mawlā Rāshid to set off for the eastern bank of the Abū al-Khaṣīb Canal with similar equipment, and then head for the bridge, taking on its defenders. Abū Aḥmad entered the Abū al-Khaṣīb Canal with the barges, having already set aside some vessels specially manned with his most valiant pages from among the bowmen and lancers. In addition to the men, he set aside tools necessary to demolish the bridge. Now he sent the force ahead along the canal.

Fighting between the opposing forces broke out on both banks of the canal, and the battle raged. On the western side, against Abū al-ʿAbbās and his men, were Ankalāy, son of the profligate, and his troops. The latter was supported by Sulaymān b. Jāmiʿ with his troops. On the eastern side, facing Rāshīd and his force, were the rebel, that is, the leader of the Zanj, and al-Muhallabī with the rest of their army. The battle this day lasted three hours past daytime. Then the profligates were routed and ran without looking about, the swords taking their toll of them. The number of profligate heads taken was so great it could not be counted. Whenever a head was brought before al-Muwaffaq, he ordered it dumped into the Abū al-Khaṣīb Canal so that the warriors would stop busying themselves counting the heads and would instead press on in the pursuit of their enemies.[131] Then he ordered the ship commanders assigned to the Abū al-Khaṣīb to approach the bridge and set it aflame, [2067] while turning aside the defenders with arrows. They did so and set the bridge to the torch. At the time, Ankalāy and Sulaymān, wounded and routed, arrived at the bridge, intending to cross to the eastern side of the Abū al-Khaṣīb Canal, but flames blocked their way. They and the guard which they had with them then threw themselves in the water. A great many of them were drowned, but Ankalāy and Sulaymān escaped, narrowly evading death.

Hordes of men gathered on both sides of the bridge, and it was demolished after a ship filled with blazing reeds was rammed into it, assisting the effort to demolish and burn it. At this, the entire government force scattered about the districts of the abominable one's city on both sides of the canal. They burned down a great number of residences, fortresses and markets belonging to the enemy, and rescued countless captive women and small children. Al-Muwaffaq ordered the fighting men to transport them in their ships and deliver them to al-Muwaffaqiyyah.

After his fortress and dwellings were burned down, the rebel lived in the residences named after Aḥmad b. Mūsā al-Qalūṣ and Muḥammad b. Ibrāhīm, that is, Abū ʿĪsā. His son Ankalāy was accommodated in the residence named after Mālik, the nephew of al-Qalūṣ. Now, a detachment of al-Muwaffaq's pages went to the locations where the abominable one resided, and entered them. They set fire to several places and looted everything which the profligate had salvaged from the first con- [2068] flagration. The abominable one fled, but on that day his treasures were not uncovered. Many ʿAlid ladies, who had been held

131. They, no doubt, busied themselves seeking heads so as to collect bonuses.

captive in a place close to his residence, were rescued, and al-Muwaffaq ordered that they be transported to his camp and treated with kindness and consideration. A group, consisting of al-Muwaffaq's pages and some of those who had deserted the rebels and were now assigned to Abū al-ʿAbbās, set off for a prison which the profligate had set up on the eastern side of the Abū al-Khaṣīb Canal. They captured it and released a great many imprisoned soldiers who had fought against the profligate and his troops, as well as other detainees. The prisoners were all taken out in their chains and manacles and brought before al-Muwaffaq, who ordered that their shackles be removed and that the prisoners be transported to al-Muwaffaqiyyah. On that day, all barges, seaworthy vessels, and other boats, large and small, including *ḥarrāqah*s and *zallālah*s, were moved from the canal into the Tigris. These ships, and everything taken from the camp of the abominable one and packed in the vessels, were auctioned off by al-Muwaffaq to his troops and pages. It was a rich and precious booty.

In this year, al-Muʿtamid visited Wāsiṭ; he arrived there in Dhū al-Qaʿdah (May 12–June 10, 883) and was accommodated in the residence of Zīrak.

In this year, Ankalāy, the son of the profligate, sought a guarantee of safe-conduct from Abū Aḥmad al-Muwaffaq. As regards the pardon, Ankalāy sent him a messenger requesting
[2069] special consideration. Al-Muwaffaq agreed to everything and returned his messenger. In the wake of this event, it was plain for al-Muwaffaq to see why Ankalāy was distracted from war. But the profligate, Ankalāy's father, knew of his son's intention. He reportedly upbraided him until he ultimately caused him to give up seeking safe-conduct. Thereafter, Ankalāy returned to the fight against al-Muwaffaq's forces with added determination, taking part personally in the fighting.

In this year, Sulaymān b. Mūsā al-Shaʿrānī—he was a commander in the profligate's army—sent someone to Abū Aḥmad to seek a guarantee of safety on his behalf. Abū Aḥmad refused to grant the request because of al-Shaʿrānī's past behavior and his spilling of blood. Then word reached him that a group of the abominable one's companions were frightened by this rebuff to al-Shaʿrānī. Abū Aḥmad now let him know that he would grant him safe-conduct in order to appease the profligate's other companions. Al-Muwaffaq gave orders to send vessels to the place at which al-Shaʿrānī had promised to appear and indeed, al-Shaʿrānī, his brother, and a group of his officers came out to the spot and were carried away on board barges. The abominable one had empowered al-Shaʿrānī to defend the lower part of the Abū al-Khaṣīb Canal.

Abū al-ʿAbbās delivered him to al-Muwaffaq; whereupon, the latter treated al-Shaʿrānī benevolently, granting him safety, as promised, and ordering that he and his companions be given gifts and robes of honor. They were to be paraded on mounts that were saddled and fully equipped, and they were to be entertained sumptuously. Al-Shaʿrānī and his men were assigned to Abū al-ʿAbbās, who included them in the ranks of his troops. Then, Abū al-ʿAbbās ordered that al-Shaʿrānī be placed on a barge, to appear in full view before the troops of the abominable one. This would make them more confident in the promise of safe-conduct. And, indeed, not long after al-Shaʿrānī's barges were removed from their position in the Abū al-Khaṣīb Canal, scores of Zanj officers and others sought guarantees of safe-conduct. They were all brought before Abū Aḥmad, who presented them with gifts and bestowed upon them the same robes and presents as had been granted to those who had preceded them.

With the defection of al-Shaʿrānī, the abominable one's grip over the lower part of the camp was loosened and his cause was [2070] undermined and weakened. The latter now charged Shibl b. Sālim with defending the sector formerly assigned to al-Shaʿrānī, and sent him down to the lower part of Abū al-Khaṣīb Canal. But before the day was over—that is, the day on which al-Muwaffaq displayed the barge with al-Shaʿrānī in full view of the abominable one's men—a messenger arrived from Shibl b. Sālim requesting al-Muwaffaq for safe-conduct. He also asked that barges be positioned near the residence of Ibn Simʿān in order that Shibl and the officers and men accompanying him might set off for them by night. The messenger was sent back with word that the request was accepted, and the barges were positioned at the designated place. Late in the night, Shibl, his household and children, and a group of his officers and men,

went to the ships. However, his men had to display their arms, for the abominable one, having learned of Shibl's intention, sent out a group of Zanj to prevent them from reaching the barges. Fighting back, Shibl and his men killed a number of the Zanj, and arrived at the vessels safely. When dawn reddened the sky, the barges had brought them to the fortress of al-Muwaffaq at al-Muwaffaqiyyah. On al-Muwaffaq's order, Shibl was given costly gifts, clothed with many robes of honor and paraded on several horses equipped with saddles and bridles. This Shibl had been one of the abominable one's close associates, among the earliest of his companions, and someone who had displayed great courage and fortitude on the rebel's behalf. Shibl's men were rewarded as well; they were given robes of honor, and along with their master they were granted military allotments and quarters. All of them were assigned to an officer from al-Muwaffaq's pages. Shibl and his men were transported in barges positioned where they could be observed by the abominable one and his supporters. This impressed the profligate and his leading men as they saw their commanders
[2071] eager to seize the opportunity and request safe-conduct.

Shibl's advice and sagacity induced al-Muwaffaq to entrust him with carrying out some tactics against the abominable one. Al-Muwaffaq thus ordered Shibl with a team of valiant Zanj deserters, who were especially assigned to him, to carry out a night attack on the abominable one's camp. He singled out Shibl and these men for the task because of their daring and their familiarity with the roads of the camp. Shibl left to carry out this (assignment), setting out for a place which he knew well; and then at dawn he took it by surprise. Here, he came upon a great body of Zanj including many officers and their guards whom the abominable one had arrayed to defend the residence known as Dār Abī ʿĪsā. This was the place where the abominable one was quartered at the time. Shibl took them by surprise, killing a great many of them. He also took a group of Zanj officers captive and seized many of their weapons, while withdrawing safely with all his men. They came to al-Muwaffaq, who rewarded them handsomely, gave them robes of honor, and promoted a number of them to a higher rank. This attack of Shibl's men upon the troops of the perfidious one drove deep terror into the hearts of the latter; they feared sleeping and kept vigil in turns every night. They were filled with terror to such a degree that the camp was continuously laden with uneasiness as anxiety overwhelmed them. The commotion and shouts of the nightwatch was heard as far away as al-Muwaffaqiyyah.

Following this, al-Muwaffaq continued to send patrols out against the abominable ones, harassing them day and night on both sides of the Abū al-Khaṣīb Canal. The rebels were thus [2072]
kept awake at night and thwarted in their search for food. Meanwhile, his troops were getting familiar with the roads and experienced in penetrating the abominable one's city, and then rushing (to the attack). These persistent raids kept the rebels' camp in a continual state of terror. When al-Muwaffaq felt that his troops had obtained all the training they needed, he decided to cross the canal and fight the profligate on the eastern side of the Abū al-Khaṣīb. He convoked a general assembly and called for the presence of the rebel officers who had gone over to his side, as well as the leaders of their cavalry and infantry from among the Zanj and white troops. They were brought to him and stood where they could hear al-Muwaffaq's speech. Then he addressed them enlightening them of their former waywardness, their foolishness and their violation of what is sacred, as well as the apostasy with which the profligate had indoctrinated them. All this, he said, had made their blood licit to him, but he had pardoned them of their sins, forgiven their transgressions, and granted them safety. He further recalled that he had been kind to those who had taken refuge with him, bestowing upon them gifts, granting them military allotments, and assigning them among his leading men and loyal troops. He said that these favors which he bestowed upon them obligated them to obey and follow him. They were not to undertake anything which might be inconsistent with loyalty to God, and the call to loyalty to their ruler obliged them to fight zealously in the holy war against the enemy of God, that is, the traitor and his accomplices. Since, more than anyone else, they were well acquainted with the roads of the abominable one's camp, the danger spots on the thoroughfares of his city, and the places of refuge he had prepared for his flight, it was incumbent [2073]

upon them to provide him with good advice and to do their utmost to invade and penetrate (the city of) the abominable one and to reach him in his strongholds, until God helped them overcome him and his supporters. If they did this, their lot would be reward and bounty. Anyone who did not live up to his obligation would be inviting the authorities to lower his position, reduce his status, and depose him from his rank.

Together, they raised their voices, hailing al-Muwaffaq, acclaiming his bounty and proclaiming their true intentions to heed and obey him. They declared their intention to fight his foes zealously as well as their readiness to shed their blood and sacrifice their lives in any task he might set for them. Whatever task he summoned them for only strengthened their intention and showed them that he had confidence in them and that he accorded them a place in the ranks of his leading men. They requested him to single out some area of the battle where they could fight, in order to show the sincerity of their intentions and their hatred to the foe, and to demonstrate that they had wholeheartedly abandoned the errors of their earlier foolishness. Al-Muwaffaq approved their request and let them know of his satisfaction with the loyalty they had manifested to him. They left encouraged by the response given to them—that is, by the kind words and fine promises.

In Dhū al-Qaʿdah of this year (May 12–June 10, 883), al-Muwaffaq entered the profligate's city on the east side of the Abū al-Khaṣīb Canal. He razed his residence and plundered everything in it.

[2074] *The Account of This Battle.*

It is mentioned that when he decided to attack the profligate in his city on the eastern side of the Abū al-Khaṣīb Canal, Abū Aḥmad gave the order to gather the vessels and ferries from the Tigris, and The Great Swamp and the surrounding areas. He did this in order to add them to the vessels he had in his camp, since the latter were not sufficient for his numerous troops. A count was taken which showed that there were about ten thousand sailors receiving their monthly allotments from the treasury. This number included men from the barges, galleys, and boats (*raqqiyyah*) which usually transported the cavalry. It did not include the vessels for the people of the camp in which provisions were carried, or which they sailed for their personal needs; nor did it include the galleys and small boats (*jāribiyyah* and *zawraq*) that were attached to each commander and his personal entourage. These had a permanent crew of sailors.

When the vessels and ferries were fully assembled, and their number proved satisfactory, al-Muwaffaq sent word to Abū al-ʿAbbās and the commanders from among his mawlās and pages to be ready and able to meet their foe. He gave instructions to assign a number of vessels and ferries to transport the cavalry and infantry. He also ordered Abū al-ʿAbbās to proceed with his army to the western side of the Abū al-Khaṣīb Canal; then he assigned him some commanders from among his pages with about eight thousand of their troops. Al-Muwaffaq instructed him to go to the rear of the profligate's camp until he passed the residence known as Dār al-Muhallabī. The abominable one had already fortified this place and had settled a great many of his men near there in order to secure the rear of his camp and to make access to it difficult for any attacking forces. Abū Aḥmad then ordered Abū al-ʿAbbās to cross with his men to [2075]
the western side of the Abū al-Khaṣīb Canal, and to reach this area from the rear. In addition, Abū Aḥmad instructed Rāshid, his mawlā, to emerge from the eastern side of the Abū al-Khaṣīb with a great number of cavalry and infantry, that is, about twenty thousand men. Some of them were to attack at the corner of the residence known as Dār al-Karnabāʾī, the scribe of al-Muhallabī. It was on the point of the Abū al-Khaṣīb Canal, on the east bank. He instructed them to march along the bank of the canal until they reached the residence where the abominable one resided; this was the residence known as Dār Abī ʿĪsā. He further ordered a detachment of his pages to emerge at the mouth of the canal known as the Abū Shākir—it was below the Abū al-Khaṣīb Canal—while another group was assigned to come out with their men at the mouth of the canal known as Nahr Juwayy Kūr.

All these columns were instructed to move out with the infantry preceding the cavalry, and with all their forces marching towards the residence of the traitor. If God should deliver him into their hands together with its occupants from among his men, and the members of his household and his children, so much the better; if not, they should set off for the residence of al-Muhallabī to be joined there by those who were ordered to cross (the river) with Abū al-ʿAbbās, thereby forming a single command against the profligates.

Abū al-ʿAbbās, Rāshid and the other commanders drawn from the mawlās and pages did as ordered; they all appeared and set off on their vessels. This took place on the evening of Monday, the seventh of Dhū Qaʿdah, 269 (Sunday, May 10, 883). The horsemen rode out one after the other while the infantry marched. From the noon service on Monday until the end of the late evening service of Tuesday, the ships sailed
[2076] along the Tigris until they reached a place below the camp. Abū Aḥmad had ordered that this place be repaired, cleaned, and cleared of rubble and weeds. He filled in its streamlets and canals, so that it would become level and spacious as the outer perimeter was extended. Then he established a tower there and a square for mustering the infantry and cavalry; these he positioned in front of the profligate's fortress. His aim in doing so was to counter the assurances which the abominable one had made to his troops, namely, that he, that is, al-Muwaffaq, would move from his position hurriedly. He wanted both factions to know that he was there to stay until God passed the final judgment between him and his enemy. The government force spent Tuesday night in that place in front of the profligate's camp. The army consisted of some fifty thousand men, including horsemen and infantry. They were handsomely outfitted and sported the finest equipment. The army began to call out the *takbīr* and *tahlīl*.[132] They started to recite the Qur'ān and their prayers, and lit fires as well. The abominable one observed the multitude, their equipment and supplies, and it was sufficient to dazzle him and his men.

On Monday evening, al-Muwaffaq sent out the barges. There were one hundred fifty of them, each manned with bowmen and lancers from among his most valiant pages and mawlās. He arrayed them in front of the traitor's camp, from one end to the

132. That is, the formulas recited at the time of prayer.

other, so that they would serve as a battle line for the army behind him; they assumed positions near the bank and cast their anchors. He singled out a number of them which he selected for himself, and assigned to them some special officers from among his pages, so that they would accompany him when he attacked in the Abū al-Khaṣīb Canal. Then he selected ten thousand cavalry and infantry and instructed them to march along the banks of the canal, emulating his route, taking his positions, and following his orders in the course of the battle.

Early Tuesday morning al-Muwaffaq set out to fight the profligate, that is, the leader of the Zanj. He sent each of the commanders to his point of destination, as the army marched out against the profligate and his men. They subsequently encountered the abominable one and his army. The engagement began and both sides sustained heavy losses in dead and wounded. The profligates furiously defended the part of the city to which they were now limited, showing no regard for their own lives. But al-Muwaffaq's forces persevered and gallantly fought back. God granted them victory, and the profligates fled, as the government force inflicted heavy losses upon them and captured a great many of their warriors and brave men. The captives were brought before al-Muwaffaq, who ordered them beheaded on the spot. [2077]

Al-Muwaffaq set out for the traitor's residence with a body of his troops, and arrived there. The traitorr had taken refuge there, concentrating his most valiant men to defend it. But when this proved fruitless, he surrendered it, and his men dispersed. Al-Muwaffaq's pages entered it, and there, left behind, was what remained of the abominable one's money and valuables. They carried off all this and seized his women, his male and female children; their number exceeded a hundred persons. The profligate escaped and fled to the residence of al-Muhallabī, forsaking family and wealth. His house and the rest of his goods and valuables were subsequently set on fire. The rebel's women and children were brought before al-Muwaffaq, and he ordered them transported to al-Muwaffaqiyyah, placed under supervision, and accorded fair treatment.

A group of Abū al-ʿAbbās's officers crossed the Abū al-Khaṣīb

Canal, setting out for an assigned place at the residence of al-Muhallabī. Without waiting for their troops to join them, they
[2078] arrived at al-Muhallabī's residence. Now, most of the Zanj had fled there after their escape from the abominable one's residence. The troops of Abū al-ʿAbbās entered the residence and busied themselves with looting, grabbing everything that al-Muhallabī had amassed. They also seized Muslim women and the children al-Muhallabī had had by them. Everyone took something and left with it for his vessel in the Abū al-Khaṣīb Canal. Meanwhile, the Zanj noticed how few al-Muwaffaq's men were, and how they were preoccupied with looting; so they attacked them from a number of places where they had hidden in ambush, and they dislodged them from their positions. The government troops were routed and the Zanj chased them as far as the Abū al-Khaṣīb Canal. The latter killed a small number of the government horsemen and infantry, and recovered some of the women and valuables which al-Muwaffaq's men had taken.

A detachment of al-Muwaffaq's pages and troops which set off for the residence of the abominable one along the eastern side of the Abū al-Khaṣīb Canal took to plundering and carrying the booty to their vessels. This emboldened the Zanj who attacked, routing the government troops; they followed on their heels until (they reached) the place known as the Sheep Market (Sūq al-Ghanam) of the Zanj camp. A group of officers from the pages now stood fast with their bravest and most valiant men and repelled the Zanj commanders, giving the rest of the troops a chance to recover and return to their positions. The battle between them lasted until late afternoon, when Abū Aḥmad ordered his pages and their forces to charge the profligates with all their might. They did so, and the Zanj were routed. Al-Muwaffaq's swords found them until they reached the residence of the abominable one. As a result, al-Muwaffaq decided to withdraw his pages and troops, although they held the initiative. He ordered his men to return, and they withdrew
[2079] calmly and quietly. Al-Muwaffaq and the men with him on barges positioned themselves in the canal and protected them, until they embarked on their vessels and brought their horses

aboard. The Zanj, having suffered the effects of the last battle, refrained from pursuing them.

Al-Muwaffaq, together with Abū al-ʿAbbās, the rest of his officers and all his army, left, having plundered the wealth of the profligate and having rescued many Muslim women who had been abducted by the latter. That day, the evacuation of the women began, as they were taken by droves to the mouth of the Abū al-Khaṣīb Canal. They were then transported by vessels to al-Muwaffaqiyyah until the end of the war.

That very day, al-Muwaffaq forwarded orders to Abū al-ʿAbbās to send one of his officers with five barges along the Abū al-Khaṣīb Canal to the lower part of the abominable one's camp. They were to burn an enormous threshing floor which the abominable one used to provision his Zanj troops and others. This was done, and the officer set most of the threshing floor on fire; this action proved to be one of the most significant factors in weakening the profligate and his troops, since they had no other reliable source of food.

On that day, Abū Aḥmad ordered that dispatches should be sent to the regions concerning his victories over the abominable one and his troops. The dispatches were to be read aloud in public, and this was done.

On Wednesday, the second of Dhū al-Ḥijjah, 269 (Tuesday night, May 12, 883), Ṣāʿid b. Makhlad, al-Muwaffaq's scribe, arrived at the latter's camp, having come to him from Sāmarrā. Arriving with Ṣāʿid was an enormous army which, it was said, included some ten thousand cavalry and infantry. Al-Muwaffaq ordered Ṣāʿid to give his troops a rest, to have them put their weapons in order and straighten out their affairs, and then make ready to fight against the abominable one. Ṣāʿid remained several days after arriving in order to carry out these or- [2080]
ders. His force was busy at this when a dispatch arrived from Lu'lu', Ibn Ṭūlūn's commander—it was carried by one of his officers. In this dispatch, Lu'lu' asked for permission to come to al-Muwaffaq and participate in the fight against the profligate. Al-Muwaffaq agreed to this and granted Lu'lu' permission to come. Anticipating Lu'lu''s arrival, al-Muwaffaq delayed resuming the battle against the rebel as he had decided earlier.

Lu'lu' was stationed in al-Raqqah with an enormous army consisting of men from Farghānah, Turks, troops from Bilād al-Rūm, Berbers, blacks and others, all the choicest troops of Ibn Ṭūlūn.

When Abū Aḥmad's letter with permission to come reached Lu'lu', the latter left Diyār Muḍar and came to Baghdad (Madīnat al-Salām) with his men. He remained there for some time; and then departed for Abū Aḥmad, reaching the latter in his camp on Thursday, the second of al-Muḥarram, 270 (July 12, 883). Abū Aḥmad held an audience for him which was attended by the former's son Abū al-ʿAbbās, Ṣāʿid, and the officers according to their rank. Lu'luʿ, in fine attire, was brought to him, whereupon, Abū al-ʿ Abbās ordered Lu'luʿ accommodated in a camp quarter which was especially prepared for him opposite the Abū al-Khaṣīb Canal. After Lu'lu' and his men settled there, Abū al-ʿAbbās ordered him to come, together with his officers and men, to al-Muwaffaq's quarters. He was to appear early next morning in order to salute al-Muwaffaq. Friday morning, on the third of al-Muḥarram (July 13, 883), Lu'lu' and his men appeared in great numbers. He arrived in al-Muwaffaq's presence and saluted him. Al-Muwaffaq drew him near and made generous promises to him and his companions, and ordered that Lu'lu' and one hundred fifty of his officers be given robes of honor, and be paraded with numerous horses bearing saddles and harnesses set in gold and silver. In front of Lu'lu' were one hundred pages who were required to carry different kinds of garments and purses of money. Al-Muwaffaq also ordered that Lu'lu''s officers be presented with gifts and gar-
[2081] ments, each according to his rank. He further bestowed upon Lu'lu' great estates and, in the most auspicious of circumstances, he sent him off to his camp in front of the Abū al-Khaṣīb Canal where lodging and fodder had been prepared for him and his men.

Abū al-ʿAbbās requested Lu'lu' to present him with the roster of his troops indicating the sums of their allotments according to rank, and when these registers were presented, he doubled everyone's allowance. At the same time, he assigned salaries to them and paid them according to the place inscribed on the roster. Then, Abū al-ʿAbbās instructed Lu'lu' to make ready and prepare to cross to the western side of the Tigris to fight against the profligate and his men.

After he had lost his control over the Abū al-Khaṣīb Canal, and his masonry and pontoon bridges there had been cut, the abominable one constructed a dam which extended from both banks of the canal. In the middle of the dam he constructed a narrow opening, so that the current through it would become swift and hinder the barges from entering during the ebbtide and from exiting during the rising tide. Abū Aḥmad saw that without the destruction of this dam he would be unable to do battle, and he made efforts to raze it; but the profligates intensified their defense. Indeed, they began to strengthen the dam day and night. It was in the middle of their territory and it was thus easy to supply them (that is, the defenders), but difficult to supply those who tried to destroy the dam.

Abū Aḥmad decided to employ the troops of Lu'lu'. One detachment after another would be sent to fight, so that they would get training in fighting the Zanj, and to position themselves on the paths and thoroughfares of the enemy city. He thus ordered Lu'lu', to be present with a detachment of his troops in order to participate in the fight for this dam. He also ordered that the sappers be brought along to demolish it. Al-Muwaffaq saw Lu'lu''s bravery in advancing, and the courage [2082] and perseverance of his men, as they disregarded the pain and wounds, and he rejoiced. He was also gladdened when he saw their small force bravely and steadfastly facing the large numbers of the Zanj army. However, seized by apprehension and concern for them, he ordered Lu'lu' to call off his troops. Al-Muwaffaq then bestowed gifts upon them, treated them generously and sent them back to their camp.

Al-Muwaffaq continued to press the attack against the dam, combatting the defense troops of the abominable one with the help of Lu'lu''s men and others. All the while, the sappers worked at demolishing it. The troops fought the rebel and his factions from a number of directions, burning their dwelling places, killing their fighting men, and causing their leaders to seek safe conduct, one batch after another.

Some grounds in the vicinity of the Gharbī Canal were still held by the abominable one and his men. They had the use of

fields and meadows, and two bridges spanning the canal by which they could cross over to these grounds. Abū al-ʿAbbās discovered this and was inclined to march there, so he asked al-Muwaffaq for permission. The latter granted him this, and gave him instructions to select men who were among the bravest of his troops and pages. Abū al-ʿAbbās did as instructed, and turned towards the Gharbī Canal. He positioned Zīrak and a body of his troops as ambushers on the western side of the canal, and he ordered his page Rashīq to set off with a large body of his bravest and choicest men to the canal known as Nahr al-ʿUmaysiyyīn, so as to emerge behind the Zanj and catch them unawares. They would then attack the enemy on these grounds. He ordered Zīrak to attack the Zanj head-on when he
[2083] perceived them fleeing before Rashīq.

Abū al-ʿAbbās positioned himself, with a number of barges whose fighting men he had already selected, at the mouth of the Gharbī Canal. He had with him a sufficient number of his white and black pages. When Rashīq emerged to meet the rebels on the eastern side of the canal, he frightened them; whereupon, they moved forward seeking to cross to the western side in order to flee to their camp. Perceiving this, Abū al-ʿAbbās broke into the canal with the barges; landing his infantry on the banks, he overtook the Zanj and put them to the sword. Many of them were killed in the canal and on its banks, while others were taken prisoner and still others fled. Zīrak and his troops now met them, and they killed all but the few who escaped. Abū al-ʿAbbās's troops seized arms that weighed upon them so heavily that they could not carry them; they dropped most of them. Abū al-ʿAbbās now cut the two bridges and ordered that the posts and the wood be dumped into the Tigris.[133] He then returned to al-Muwaffaq with the captives and the heads of the slain which were paraded about the camp. The profligates were thus deprived of the cultivated fields along the Gharbī Canal, fields which provided them with foodstuffs.

In Dhū al-Ḥijjah of this year (June 11-July 10, 883), the household of the Zanj leader and his children were brought to Baghdad.

---

133. This would seem to indicate a wooden bridge. See above, n. 130.

In this year, Ṣāʿid was named Dhū al-Wizāratayn.[134]

In Dhū al-Ḥijjah of this year, a skirmish occurred involving two officers of Ibn Ṭūlūn and their troops; one of them was named Muḥammad b. al-Sarrāj, the other was called al-Ghanawī. Ibn Ṭūlūn had sent both of them to Mecca, and they arrived there on Wednesday, the twenty-eighth of Dhū al-Qaʿdah (June 8, 883), with a force of four hundred seventy horsemen and two thousand infantry. They gave the Jazzārīn and Ḥannātīn two dinārs each and the headmen (*ra'īs*) were given seven. At the time, Hārūn b. Muḥammad, the governor of Mecca was in Bustān b. ʿĀmir.[135] [2084]

On the third of Dhū al-Ḥijjah (Wednesday, June 13, 883), Jaʿfar b. al-Bāghamardī arrived in Mecca with a force of about two hundred riders. Hārūn met himwith one hundred twenty horsemen, two hundred blacks, thirty cavalrymen from the troops of ʿAmr b. al-Layth, and two hundred infantry from those who had arrived from Iraq. Jaʿfar was strengthened by their presence. Then, assisted by the pilgrims who came from Khurāsān, Jaʿfar's force met the troops of Ibn Ṭūlūn and killed about two hundred of them in the hollow of the city. The rest fled to the hills, with Jaʿfar's men taking their animals and money as booty. Jaʿfar lifted his sword and seized al-Ghanawī's tent—it is said there were two hundred thousand dīnārs in it. He granted a pardon to the Egyptians, the Ḥannātīn and the Jazzārīn. In the holy mosques a letter was read cursing Ibn Ṭūlūn. The people as well as the possessions of the merchants were now safe.

Leading the pilgrimage this year was Hārūn b. Muḥammad b. Isḥāq al- Hāshimī.

Although Isḥāq b. Kundāj was appointed governor of the entire Maghrib, he did not leave Sāmarrā before the year ended.

---

134. That is, "the Master of Two Wazīrates." The reference was to his serving two masters, the Caliph and Abū Aḥmad.

135. Bustān b. ʿĀmir was also referred to as Bustān b. Maʿmar. See Yāqūt, *Muʿjam*, I, 611.

The Events of the Year

270

(July 11, 883–June 28, 884)

In al-Muḥarram of this year (July 11–August 9, 883) a battle which sapped the power of the leader of the Zanj took place between him and Abū Aḥmad. In Ṣafar (August 10–September 7, 883), the rebel was slain, Sulaymān b. Jāmiʿ and Ibrāhīm b. Jaʿfar al-Hamdānī were captured and the entire affair of the profligate came to an end.

The Two Battles[136]

We have already mentioned the dam which the abominable one constructed and, with regard to this, about Abū Aḥmad and his troops. It is mentioned that Abū Aḥmad pressed the fight for this dam without respite until he reached his objective, thus easing the entrance of the barges into the Abū al-Khaṣīb Canal both at the ebb and high tide. From the place where he was positioned, it became easy for Abū Aḥmad to do as he wished. This included keeping prices low, making food-

136. See Popovic, *Révolte*, 152 ff.

stuffs available, and allowing for the delivery of tribute from the provinces. He also succeeded in instilling zeal among his fighting men, in order that they might carry on the holy war against the abominable one and his supporters. Among the volunteers joining him was Aḥmad b. Dīnār, the governor of Īdhaj and the surrounding territories from the districts of al-Ahwāz; he came with a great force of cavalry and infantry. Aḥmad himself, as well as his troops, took part in the fight until the abominable one was killed. Aḥmad was, in turn, followed by people from al-Baḥrayn, reportedly a large throng of about two thousand men, led by one of the ʿAbd al-Qays tribe.

Abū Aḥmad held an audience for them, and he was visited by their leader and notables, whom he ordered given robes of honor. He reviewed all their men and gave instructions to provide lodging for them. Following them, about one thousand in- [2086] dividuals from the districts of Fārs arrived under the leadership of an elderly volunteer whose patronymic was Abū Salamah. Al-Muwaffaq held an audience for them as well. This old man and his leading companions arrived, and Abū Aḥmad gave them robes of honor and made provision for their lodging. They were then followed by successive groups of volunteers from the provinces.

After al-Muwaffaq succeeded in taking care of the dam, as mentioned above, he decided to meet the abominable one in battle. He gave instructions to make ready the ships and ferries, and to prepare the military equipment necessary for fighting on land and water. He selected cavalry and infantry upon whose courage and valor he could rely, because the places where he would do battle were narrow, difficult and marked by numerous defensive trenches and canals. The number of cavalrymen selected was about two thousand, the infantry were fifty thousand or more. This number did not include the volunteers who crossed over, nor the people of the camp who were not listed on the military roll. He left a large army behind in al-Muwaffaqiyyah, mostly horsemen whom his ships could not carry.

Al-Muwaffaq then sent orders to Abū al-ʿAbbās to set out with his troops, pages and whatever cavalry and infantry and barges he had attached to his command. They were to set out

for the place which Abū al-ʿAbbās had reached on Tuesday, the tenth of Dhū al-Qaʿdah, 269 (May 22, 883). This was the place on the east bank in front of al-Muhallabī's residence. He also ordered Ṣāʿid b. Makhlad to attack on the east bank along the canal known as the Abū Shākir. In turn, al-Muwaffaq arrayed his mawlās and pages from the mouth of the Abū al-Khaṣīb Canal to the Gharbī. The sector from the residence of al-Karnabāʾī to the Abū Shākir Canal was occupied by Rāshid and Luʾluʾ, the mawlās of al-Muwaffaq. They had with them
[2087] a force of some twenty thousand horsemen and infantry in closed ranks. In the sector from the Abū Shākir to the canal known as Nahr Juwayy Kūr he placed a group of officers from his mawlās and pages, and he did the same in the sector between the Juwayy Kūr and the Gharbī Canal. Al-Muwaffaq commanded Shibl to set out with his troops and the forces which had been added to his command. They were to make for the Gharbī from which they would emerge facing the rear of al-Muhallabī's residence. At the outbreak of fighting, they were to attack from behind it. He ordered the entire government force to march out against the rebel at the same pace. The marching sign was the waving of a black banner which he hung on a place high atop the residence of al-Karnabāʾī at the mouth of Abū al-Khaṣīb Canal. Another sign was the blowing of a distant trumpet. The crossing took place on Monday, the twenty-seventh of al-Muḥarram, 270 (Monday night, August 4, 883).

One commander based on the canal known as Nahr Juwayy Kūr started to march before the banner appeared, and he drew near the residence of al-Muhallabī. He and his men were subsequently met by the Zanj who pushed them back to their positions, killing many of them. Because the rest of al-Muwaffaq's force was so large, and because the distance between contingents was so vast, they did not notice what had happened to those who had rushed into the fight. As the officers and their men left for their assigned places, and the cavalry and infantry took up their positions, al-Muwaffaq ordered the flag waved and the trumpet sounded. He himself entered the canal on a barge while the people marched out in successive waves. Encouraged by their success against those who had rushed toward them prematurely, the Zanj who had banded together encountered the troops. The government army met them and struck [2088] with firm, well-calculated blows. After a few skirmishes in which both parties lost many fighting men, they dislodged the Zanj from their positions. Abū Aḥmad's men persevered and God granted them victory over the profligates. The rebels fled, and al-Muwaffaq's troops pursued them, killing some and capturing others. Abū Aḥmad's men surrounded the rebels from all directions. God destroyed countless multitudes of them on that day; and a similar number were drowned in the canal known as Nahr Juwayy Kūr. The troops of al-Muwaffaq took possession of the profligate's city and rescued all the prisoners who were there: men, women and children. They seized the entire households, including children, of ʿAlī b. Abān al-Muhallabī and his brothers al-Khalīl and Muḥammad, as well as the household and children of Sulaymān b. Jāmiʿ. All the captives were then transported to al-Muwaffaqiyyah.

The profligate and his companions, among them his son Ankalāy, al-Muhallabī, Sulaymān b. Jāmiʿ, Zanj commanders and others, fled, setting off for a place which the abominable one had seen fit to prepare as a refuge for himself and his men should they lose control of his city. The place was on the canal known as Nahr al-Sufyānī. The abominable one fled, and Abū Aḥmad's troops triumphed as they did; but the troops remained at the residence of al-Muhallabī, which protruded into the Abū al-Khaṣīb Canal. The government forces busied themselves with looting what was in the residence and with setting the residence and the contiguous areas on fire. They broke into groups seeking plunder. All that remained to the abominable one and his men had been assembled in this residence.

Abū Aḥmad advanced with his barges for the canal known as Nahr al-Sufyānī. With him were Lu'lu' and his cavalry and [2089] infantry. Abū Aḥmad became separated from the rest of the army, so they thought that he had withdrawn; thus they returned to their ships with their loot.

Meanwhile, al-Muwaffaq and the men accompanying him reached the camp of the profligate and his troops—they were fleeing. Lu'lu' and his force pursued them, crossing the canal known as Nahr al-Sufyānī. Lu'lu' rushed into the water on his mount, and was followed by his men. Then the rebel went on to the canal known as Nahr al-Qarīrī; but Lu'lu' and his force reached him. The government troops attacked the rebel and his cohort and drove them off. The enemy fled, pursued by Lu'lu' and his men, until he crossed the canal known as Nahr al-Qarīrī. Then Lu'lu' and his force crossed behind them, forcing the enemy to retreat to the canal known as Nahr al-Masāwān. The rebels crossed the waterway and took refuge in the mountains behind it. Lu'lu' and his men were the only government contingent taking part in this action. Their zeal in pursuing the profligate and his supporters brought them to the place which we have described, at the end of daylight. Then, al-Muwaffaq gave the order to withdraw and Lu'lu' withdrew, lauded for his action. Al-Muwaffaq took him along in the barges and again, was generous and bountiful to him. In recognition of what Lu'lu' had done in fighting the profligates, Abū Aḥmad also promoted him to a higher rank.

Accompanied by the troops of Lu'lu', al-Muwaffaq returned with his barges to the Abū al-Khaṣīb Canal. When he came face to face with al-Muhallabī's residence, he found none of his troops; he thus understood that they had withdrawn. Al-Muwaffaq ordered Lu'lu' to move out with his men to his camp, while he himself, seized with anger at his (missing) troops, turned toward his fortress.

Now, Abū Aḥmad was sure of victory, for he saw its signs,
[2090] and all the people rejoiced at what God had granted—namely, the rout of the profligate and his men. They rejoiced as well at God's having made it possible to expel the enemy from their city, and seize everything in it, and distribute what had been taken as booty—that is the money, treasures and weapons. Finally there was the rescue of all the captives held by the rebels. But Abū Aḥmad was angry at his men because they disobeyed orders and abandoned the positions in which he had placed them. He ordered that the commanders of his mawlās and pages and the leading men among them be gathered together. When they were assembled for him, he scolded them for what they had done, judging them weak and castigating them in harsh language. Then they made excuses; they supposed that he had returned, and they had not known about his advance

against the profligate, nor about his having pressed so far into the rebel's camp. Had they known this, they would have rushed toward him. They did not leave their places until they had taken a solemn oath and covenant that, when sent against the abominable one, none of them would withdraw before God had delivered him into their hands; and should they fail, they would not budge from their positions until God had passed judgment between them and him. They requested of al-Muwaffaq that, after they had left al-Muwaffaqiyyah to fight, he order the ships transporting them to return and, thus, eliminate any temptation to those who might seek to leave the battle against the profligate.

Abū Aḥmad accepted their apologies for their wrongdoing and again took them into his favor. Then he ordered them to prepare for crossing and to forewarn their troops just as they themselves had been forewarned. Abū Aḥmad spent Tuesday, Wednesday, Thursday and Friday preparing whatever he would need. When this was completed, he sent word to his entourage and the officers of his pages and mawlās, instructing them as to their tasks when crossing (into combat). Friday evening he sent word to Abū al-ʿAbbās and the officers of his pages and mawlās to set out for places which he, that is, Abū Aḥmad, had specified. [2091]

Al-Muwaffaq instructed Abū al-ʿAbbās and his troops to set a course for a place known as ʿAskar Rayḥān, which lay between the canal known as Nahr al-Sufyānī and the spot where the rebel sought refuge. He and his army were to follow the route along the canal known as Nahr al-Mughīrah, so that they would exit where the canal intersects the Abū al-Khaṣīb and reach ʿAskar Rayḥān from this direction. He forwarded instructions to an officer of his black pages to reach the Nahr al-Amīr and cross at its center. At the same time, he ordered the rest of his officers and pages to pass the night on the eastern side of the Tigris, opposite the profligate's camp, and be prepared to attack him in the early morning.

During Friday night, al-Muwaffaq made the rounds among the officers and men in his barge. He divided amongst them key positions and locations which he had arranged for them in the profligate's camp. According to the assigned plan, they were to march towards these places in the morning. Early Saturday morning, on the second of Ṣafar, 270 (August 11, 883), al-Muwaffaq reached the Abū al-Khaṣīb Canal in his barge. He remained there until all his men had crossed (the waterway) and disembarked from their vessels, and the cavalry and infantry had assumed their positions. Then, after giving instructions for the vessels and ferries to return to the eastern side, he gave the troops the go-ahead to march against the profligate. He himself preceded them until he reached the spot where he estimated the profligates would make a stand in an attempt to repel the government army. Meanwhile, on Monday, after the army had withdrawn, the traitor and his men returned to the city and stayed there, hoping to prolong their defense and repel the attack.

[2092] Al-Muwaffaq found that the fastest of his cavalry and infantry among the pages had preceded the main force of the army and had attacked the rebel and his companions, dislodging them from their positions. The enemy force fled and dispersed without paying attention to one another, and the government army pursued them, killing and capturing whomever they managed to catch. The profligate, with a group of his fighting men, was cut off from (the rest) of his officers and troops—among them was al-Muhallabī. Ankalāy, the rebel's son, had abandoned him, as had Sulaymān b. Jāmiʿ. Moving against each of the contingents which we have named was a large force of al-Muwaffaq's mawlās, and cavalry and infantry drawn from his pages. Abū al-ʿAbbās's troops, assigned by al-Muwaffaq to the place known as ʿAskar Rayḥān, met the rebel's fleeing men and put them to the sword. The officer assigned to the Amīr Canal also arrived there, and having blocked the rebels' path he attacked them. Encountering Sulaymān b. Jāmiʿ, he took the fight to him, killing many of his men and seizing Sulaymān. He made Sulaymān a captive and delivered him to al-Muwaffaq without conditions. The people were glad to learn of Sulaymān's capture, and there were many cries of "God is Great!" and great clamor. They felt certain of victory, since Sulaymān was known to be the most able of the rebel's companions. After him, Ibrāhīm b. Jaʿfar al-Hamdānī, one of the field commanders of the rebel's army, was taken captive; then Nādir al-Aswad, the one known as al-Ḥaffār, one of the earliest companions of the rebel, was captured.

Upon al-Muwaffaq's order, precautionary measures were taken, and the captives were transferred in barges to Abū al-ʿAbbās.

Following this, those Zanj who had separated from the main body, together with the profligate, assaulted the government force, dislodging them from their positions and causing them to lose the initiative. Al-Muwaffaq noticed the loss of initiative, but he pressed on with the search for the abominable one, [2093]
advancing quickly in the Abū al-Khaṣīb Canal. This bolstered his mawlās and pages, who hastened to pursue (the enemy) with him. As al-Muwaffaq reached the Abū al-Khaṣīb Canal, a herald arrived with the good news of the rebel's death; before long another herald arrived carrying a hand, and claimed that this was the hand of the rebel. This seemed to lend credence to the report of the rebel's demise. Finally a page from Lu'lu''s troops arrived, galloping on a horse and carrying the head of the abominable one. Al-Muwaffaq had the head brought closer, and then showed it to a group of former enemy officers who were in his presence. They identified it, and al-Muwaffaq prostrated himself in adoration to God for both the hardships and bounties He had conferred upon him. Abū al-ʿAbbās, the mawlās and the officers of al-Muwaffaq's pages then prostrated themselves, offering much thanks to God, and praising and exalting Him. Al-Muwaffaq ordered the head of the rebel raised on a spear and displayed in front of him. The people saw it and thus knew that the news of the rebel's death was true. At this, they raised their voices in praise to God.

It is reported that al-Muwaffaq's troops surrounded the abominable one after all his field commanders had abandoned him save al-Muhallabī; the latter now turned away from him and fled, thus betraying the rebel. The rebel then set off for the canal known as Nahr al-Amīr and plunged into the water, seeking safety. Even before that, Ankalāy, the son of the abominable one, had split off from his father and fled in the direction of the canal known as Nahr al-Dīnārī, where he entrenched himself in the swampy terrain.

Al-Muwaffaq retired, with the head of the abominable one

displayed on a spear mounted in front of him on a barge. The vessel moved along the Abū al-Khaṣīb Canal, with the people on both sides of the waterway observing it. When he reached the Tigris, he took his course along the river and gave the order to return the vessels, with which he had crossed to the western side of the Tigris at daylight, to the eastern side of the river.
[2094] They were returned to ferry the troops (back) across the river.

Then al-Muwaffaq continued his trip, with the abominable one's head on the spear before him, while Sulaymān b. Jāmiʿ and al-Hamdānī were mounted for display. When he arrived at his fortress in al-Muwaffaqiyyah, he ordered Abū al-ʿAbbās to sail the barge, keeping the rebel's head and Sulaymān b. Jāmiʿ and al-Hamdānī in place, and to take his course to the Jaṭṭā Canal where the camp of al-Muwaffaq began. He was to do this so that all the people of the camp could have a look at them. Abū al-ʿAbbās did this, and then returned to his father, Abū Aḥmad, whereupon the latter imprisoned Sulaymān b. Jāmiʿ and al-Hamdānī and ordered that the rebel's head be properly prepared and cleaned.

It is reported that the Zanj who had remained with the abominable one, preferring his company, were continuously arriving (at al-Muwaffaq's camp), and that about one thousand of them arrived that day. Al-Muwaffaq saw fit to grant them safe-conduct because of their numbers and bravery. Otherwise, there might remain among them a group that could become an annoyance to Islām and the Believers. During the rest of Saturday, Sunday and Monday, about five thousand Zanj officers and troops surrendered. Those who had been killed in battle, drowned and captured were so numerous that their numbers cannot be ascertained. A group of about one thousand Zanj, who had been cut off, made for the hinterland. Most of them died of thirst, and those who survived fell into the hands of the tribesmen who enslaved them.

Word reached al-Muwaffaq that al-Muhallabī, Ankalāy, and the bravest Zanj officers and men who followed them, were staying at certain places. So he sent out his most courageous pages to pursue and harass them. When the besieged were certain that there was no escape for them, they surrendered. Al-Muwaffaq seized them and their followers without exception;

there were almost as many of them as those who had gone to al-Muwaffaq and asked him for guarantees of safety immediately after the death of the abominable one. Al-Muwaffaq then ordered that al-Muhallabī and Ankalāy be imprisoned and closely guarded. This was done. Among those fleeing from the camp of the abominable one on Saturday, without any guarantee, was Qarṭās, who had shot an arrow at al-Muwaffaq. He had succeeded in fleeing to Rāmhurmuz, but a man who happened to have seen him in the abominable one's camp recognized him and pointed him out to the governor of the city, who seized him and had him bound. Abū al-ʿAbbās asked his father to let him slay Qarṭās; the latter was thus handed over to Abū al-ʿAbbās who put him to death. [2095]

In this year, Darmawayh al-Zanjī asked Abū Aḥmad for a guarantee of safe-conduct. This Darmawayh was, reportedly, one of the most courageous and heroic of the Zanj. Long before his death, the rebel had sent Darmawayh to the lower part of the Fahrāj Canal. The waterway was west of the Tigris near al-Baṣrah. He took up his position there in a rugged place close to The Great Swamp, which was full of palms, thickets and bushes. Using fast skiffs and galleys they had taken for their own use, Darmawayh and the men stationed with him there would intercept travellers. If pursued by the barges, they would enter the narrow canals and take refuge in the thickets. If some of these canals proved too narrow, even for them, they would disembark, carry their vessels over their backs, and seek refuge in inaccessible spots. All the while, they would raid the villages of The Great Swamp and of the neighboring territory, killing and looting whatever they could get their hands on.

Darmawayh and his men carried out these actions until the rebel was killed. At the time, they were in the place which we have described, and they knew nothing of what befell their master. Following the death of the abominable one, the territory around his retreat was conquered, and the people, feeling safe, spread out in search of business, travelling along the Tigris and transporting merchandise. Darmawayh now attacked them, murdering and looting, causing people to be shocked (and frightened). A band of villains and profligates were inclined to do the same as Darmawayh. They made up [2096] their minds to go to him, stay with him and lead the same kind of life.

Al-Muwaffaq now decided to send out a troop of his black pages and others, who were expert in fighting among the thickets and the narrow canals. For this purpose he equipped them with small boats and different kinds of weapons. But while he was completing preparations, a messenger from Darmawayh arrived asking al-Muwaffaq to grant safe-conduct to Darmawayh and his men. Al-Muwaffaq decided to grant him safety in order to put an end to the evil suffered by the populace, because of the rebel and the factions supporting him.

It is reported that the reason for Darmawayh's request for safe-conduct was that among the people he had attacked, there were some who had been on their way from al-Muwaffaq's camp to their homes in Baghdad (Madīnat al-Salām)—among them were women. Darmawayh killed the men, plundered their possessions, and seized the accompanying women. When the latter fell into his hands, he interrogated them, and they told him of the profligate's death and that al-Muhallabī, Ankalāy, Sulaymān b. Jāmiʿ and other field commanders and officers of the profligate's troops had been seized. They also indicated that most of the Zanj had gone to al-Muwaffaq seeking safe-conduct, and that he had received them and treated them kindly. This news confounded Darmawayh, and he saw no way out but to commend himself to the mercy of al-Muwaffaq and ask him to pardon his crimes. So he sent word (to al-Muwaffaq) concerning this, and his request was accepted. When the guarantee arrived, Darmawayh and all his followers went to the
[2097] camp of al-Muwaffaq. This was a fine unit that arrived; fully equiped, it had not suffered from the harm and misery of the siege which had been so hard on the rest of the abominable one's troops. The former unit had benefited from the influx of money and provisions taken from others.

It is reported that after he was accorded protection, and he and his people were well treated, Darmawayh gave up all the money and property they had and openly returned it to the owners. This manifested his repentant return to God, and al-Muwaffaq gave him, his leading men, and his officers robes of honor, and bestowed presents upon them. Then, he assigned all of them to one of his pages who was an officer.

Al-Muwaffaq ordered that letters be written to the centers of the Muslim world announcing to the people of al-Baṣrah, al-Ubullah, and the Tigris districts, and to the people of al-Ahwāz and its districts, and the people of Wāsiṭ and the surrounding areas—regions penetrated by the Zanj—that the rebel was dead and they could return to their native lands. These orders were carried out and the populace hastened to do as instructed. They came to the city of al-Muwaffaqiyyah from every direction. After that, al-Muwaffaq remained in al-Muwaffaqiyyah so that the populace would feel more secure and at ease. He appointed al-ʿAbbās b. Tarkas, one of his mawlā officers, as governor of al-Baṣrah, al-Ubullah and the districts of the Tigris—he had praised him for his behavior and was aware of the fine manner in which al-ʿAbbās acquitted himself. Al-Muwaffaq ordered him to move to al-Baṣrah and establish his residence there. He also appointed Muḥammad b. Ḥammād over the judiciary of al-Baṣrah, al-Ubullah, and the districts of al-Ahwāz and Wāsiṭ.

Then, al-Muwaffaq sent his son Abū al-ʿAbbās to Baghdad (Madīnat al-Salām) with the head of the abominable one, the leader of the Zanj. He was to show it to the people, so that they might rejoice. Abū al-ʿAbbās and his men carried out this order, and on Saturday, the eighteenth of Jumādā I, 270 (November 30, 883), he and his troops reached Baghdad and entered the [2098] city sporting the finest raiment. Upon Abū al-ʿAbbās's command, the head of the abominable one was brought forth on a spear in front of him, and the populace gathered to view this procession.

The leader of the Zanj began his revolt on Wednesday, the twenty-sixth of Ramaḍān, 255 (August 6, 870). He was killed on Saturday, the second of Ṣafar, 270 (August 11, 883). From the inception of his revolt until the day he was killed, fourteen years, four months and six days passed. His entry into al-Ahwāz took place on the seventeenth of Ramaḍān, 256 (Friday, Aug. 18, 870); his entry into al-Baṣrah, at which time the massacre of its population and the burning of the city took place, was on the sixteenth of Shawwāl, 257 (Thursday, September 6, 871).

The contest between al-Muwaffaq and the rebel became the subject of many poets. Among the works dealing with the subject is the following poem written by Yaḥyā b. Muḥammad al-Aslamī:

> I say the harbinger of good tidings brought word of a battle
> which steadied all that had been shaken in Islam.
>
> May God bestow the highest reward upon the best of men
> who was so noble to people made homeless and robbed.
>
> When no one appeared to uphold God's cause
> He alone restored the faith, which had begun crumbling away.
>
> [2099] He strengthened the Empire when its glory was on the wane
> and followed this up by wreaking his vengeance on the foe.
>
> He rebuilt devastated and ruined habitations,
> so that collapsing roofs might be restored.
>
> And cities, despoiled and destroyed repeatedly
> and turned into desert-land and wastes, be rebuilt.
>
> This battle will bring a consolation to our weeping eyes;
> it will bring healing to the hearts of the believers.
>
> The Book of God is read in every mosque;
> the appeals of the Ṭālibīs[137] are rejected as comptemptible.
>
> He forsook comfort and friends and pleasures
> to emerge victorious in the cause of Islam.

These verses are from a lengthy ode. He has also written the following lines on the same subject:

137. That is, ʿAlids.

Where are the stars of the heretic, the apostate,
indeed he was not one of skill and shrewdness;

Good fortune by the hand of a Prince, whose words are deeds,
visited calamity upon him.

The abominable one fell in battle and was left an easy prey
to lions of the bush that swooped down on the field;

From the cup of perdition he tasted a drink,
a beverage most loathsome to the palate of men.

On the same subject, Yaḥyā b. Khālid said:

O son of the caliphs of the stock of Hāshim, [2100]
of those who heap upon people their bounties

And repel the foe assailing the home,
of those whose days are marked with battles,

You are a ruler who restored the Faith after it was trampled down,
Who released captives from shackles and bonds;

You are the protector in time of misfortune
and unto you the needy [man] turns with his plea.

You extinguished the flames of impiety after they rose high,
O, you, who abundantly metes out both hope and death;

How excellent you are, O offspring of caliphs,
in decisions so wise, with armor so resplendent!

You have destroyed the infidel's hosts. To the ground they
fell looking death in the eyes. With a resolute mind

You have showered upon them decisive blows,
making their hearts swell with horror.

When the accursed rebel exceeded all bounds
you swooped down upon him with the whirling sword and spear.

And you cast him to the ground. Crows fly around him
picking the joints and limbs of his body.

He plunged into the depth of the scorching hell,
[2101] under the weight of chains wearing him away;

This he earned so justly by his numerous crimes
and by the wicked deeds of his own hands.

By saving it from the plotter you delighted all Islām,
and rid it of infanticide.

The attack of al-Muwaffaq was dealt in Iraq
but this heroic assault terrified those in the west.

Similarly, the verses of Yaḥyā b. Khālid b. Marwān:

Give me a clear answer, O waste habitation
whose yards are still flooded by the heavy rain;

Tell me about the people, where have they gone,
will they return, will the traveller be back?

But what answer could the ruined home give me,
where no sign remained of the dwellers?

The songs of the people of those homes made me weep
and plunged me into grief; endurance betrayed me.

As if the camel's shriek came to them with a warning
about fatal days with doom in their wake,

[2102] Swiftly and viciously the vicissitudes of fate broke loose upon them,
and utmost evil it was, what fate had wrought.

But better times had arrived, and the plant is ripening;
under the auspices of the prince, the world has changed.

To their homes returned all those who had fled,
and not even a foothold for Satan remained.

By the sword of the heir-apparent Islām has regained its strength;
true faith has triumphed, and heresy has been uprooted.

Verily, he led the believers in holy war,
himself safe and sound and victorious.

This is also a lengthy ode. Yaḥyā b. Muḥammad:

Off with you, I have had enough of you!
do not blame one who is above blame.

Do not blame one for leaving. I am a man
bent upon exploit, travel and travail.

Where shall I sojourn when I loath the land
as if I were in a nuptial chamber with an evil-eyed bride.

Desire is not aroused if it finds not
man awake at the side of his sweetheart.

None passes a night safely who did not know fear at night, [2103]
fear of the neighbor's nightly terror.

The meter is also ṭawīl.

In Rabīʿ I of this year (September 8–October 7, 883), a report reached Baghdad (Madīnat al-Salām) that the Byzantines camped at Bāb Qalamyah, some six *mīl* (twelve km) from Ṭarsūs;[138] they were a force of some hundred thousand men led by Andrayās the head patrikios. Four others accompanied him. Yāzamān al-Khādim set out against them by night and attacked

138. See Yāqūt, *Muʿjam*, IV, 167.

them, killing the head patrikios and those of Cappadocia and Anatolikon. The patrikios of Qurrah, though gravely wounded, escaped. Seven of their crosses, made of gold and silver, were seized, among them the great cross made of gold and beset with gems. Seized as well were fifteen thousand horses and mules, about as many saddles, sabres ornamented with gold and silver, many vessels (*āniyah*), about ten thousand brocade standards, heaps of brocade, silk fabrics with ornaments, and sable-fur wrappers. The attack upon Andrayās took place on Tuesday, the seventh of Rabīʿ I (September 11, 883). The Byzantines were besieged by night and a great many of them were killed. Some people assert that seventy thousand of them were slain.

[2104] In this year, Hārūn, the son of Abū Aḥmad al-Muwaffaq passed away. This happened in Baghdad (Madīnat al-Salām) on Thursday, the second of Jumādā I (November 7, 883).

On the sixth of Shaʿbān this year (Saturday, February 8, 884), a report reached Baghdad that Aḥmad b. Ṭūlūn had died. Some said that his death occurred on Monday, the eighteenth of Dhū al-Qaʿdah (May 18, 884).

In this year, al-Ḥasan b. Zayd al-ʿAlawī died in Ṭabaristān, either in Rajab (January 4–February 2, 884) or in Shaʿbān (February 3-March 2, 884).

In the middle of Shaʿbān, al-Muʿtamid entered Baghdad. He exited from the city (al-Madīnah) and camped opposite Qaṭrabbul.[139] He had set his troops in order, with Muḥammad b. Ṭāhir marching in front of him carrying a spear. Following that, he moved on to Sāmarrā.

In this year, towards the end of Rajab (January 4–February 2, 884), Yāzamān ransomed the inhabitants of Sātīdamā.

On Sunday, the twentieth of Shaʿbān, 270 (February 22, 884), the troops of Abū al-ʿAbbās b. al-Muwaffaq mutinied in Baghdad. Their action was directed against Ṣāʿid b. Makhlad, who was then al-Muwaffaq's wazīr. They demanded their allotments; whereupon, Ṣāʿid's men came out to repel them. Abū

139. One of the four ancient districts of the Baghdad area, the others being Kalwādhā, Bādurāyā, and Nahr Būq. Qaṭrabbul represented the northwest section of the greater urban area. See Le Strange, *Baghdad*, index, 369 s.v. Ḳaṭrabbul. Also, see below, n. 156.

al-ʿAbbās's infantry went to the plaza at the bridge while Ṣāʿid's men were inside the gates of Sūq Yaḥyā.[140] They became locked in battle, and both sides bore losses in dead and wounded; then night intervened. When Abū al-ʿAbbās's men began their morning's activities Ṣāʿid provided them with pay, and they became reconciled with him.

In Shawwāl of this year (April 2—30, 884) a battle occurred between Isḥāq b. Kundāj and Ibn Daʿbāsh. Ibn Daʿbāsh was governor of al-Raqqah and its administrative districts. He also ruled the border region and major towns on behalf of Aḥmad b. Ṭūlūn while Ibn Kundāj was governor of Mosul on behalf of the central authorities. [2105]

In this year, the waters of the ʿĪsā Canal in western Baghdad broke through the dam at al-Yasīriyyah. The waters engulfed the Tanner's Market (al-Dabbāghīn) and that of the teakworkers (*aṣḥāb al-sāj*) which were situated in al-Karkh. About seven thousand houses were reportedly demolished.[141]

In this year, the Byzantine emperor, who was known as Ibn al-Ṣaqlabī, was killed.[142]

Leading the pilgrimage this year was Hārūn b. Muḥammad b. Isḥāq al-Hāshimī b. ʿĪsā b. Mūsā b. Muḥammad b. ʿAlī b. ʿAbdallāh b. al-ʿAbbās.

---

140. The reference here is to the area in the general vicinity of the Main Bridge which linked West Baghdad in the area of the Khuld Palace with the eastern neighborhoods of al-Ruṣāfah and the upper part of al-Mukharrim. Sūq Yaḥyā was situated in the Bāb al-Ṭāq area just below the bridge. See Lassner, *Topography*, index, s.v. and 203 (Le Strange, *Baghdad*, Map V).

141. Al-Karkh was the great market suburb (*rabaḍ*) of southwest Baghdad. It was framed by the ʿĪsā and Ṣarāt canals. Al-Yāsiriyyah marks the western limits of this area. See Lassner, *Topography*, index, s.v.; Le Strange, *Baghdad*, Maps IV, VI. For the Tanner's Yard see Le Strange, op. cit., 156.

142. The reference is to Vasil, who actually died August 29, 886, that is, 273 A.H. He is referred to previously as Ibn al-Ṣaqlabiyyah.

The Events of the Year 271

(June 29, 884–July 28, 885)

It began on Monday,the twenty-ninth of Ḥazīrān, in the year 1195 of the Alexandrine calendar.

The Major Events of the Year

Among these events, in the beginning of Ṣafar (July 29—August 26, 884), a report arrived (at Baghdad) indicating that Muḥammad and ʿAlī, the sons of al-Ḥusayn b. Jaʿfar b. Mūsā b. Jaʿfar b. Muḥammad b. ʿAlī b. Ḥusayn, had entered al-Madīnah. The report stated that they had killed many townspeople, demanded money from the populace, and took it from a certain group of the local inhabitants. The dispatch went on to state that the people of the city did not hold Friday services nor did they congregate (for devotion) in the Mosque of the Prophet for four weeks. Abū al-ʿAbbās b. al-Faḍl al-ʿAlawī commented:

[2106] Desolate lies the abode of the Prophet;
O Muslims, I lament over its devastation!

O eye, weep over the station of Gabriel, and the sepulchre,
and shed tears over the auspicious pulpit!

And cry over the place of worship which the Prophet had
founded in piety,
but which is empty of worshippers.

Cry over Ṭaybah upon which God had invoked His blessing
by sending thereto the seal of the prophets.

May God destroy the band which has laid it waste
obeying a master corrupt and accursed.

On the twenty-fifth of Shawwāl, 271 (Thursday, April 21, 885), pilgrims from Khurāsān who were staying in Baghdad were brought to al-Muʿtamid, who announced in their presence that ʿAmr b. al-Layth was dismissed from the office to which he had been assigned. He then cursed ʿAmr. At the same time, the Caliph informed them that he had bestowed the governorship of Khurāsān upon Muḥammad b. Ṭāhir. Al-Muʿtamid also ordered that ʿAmr b. al-Layth was to be cursed from all the pulpits. This order was subsequently carried out.

On the twenty-first of Shaʿbān (Thursday, February 11, 885), Ṣāʿid b. Makhlad left Abū Aḥmad's camp in Wāsiṭ bound for Fārs to fight against ʿAmr b. al-Layth.

On the tenth of Ramaḍān, 271 (Monday, March 1, 885), Aḥmad b. Muḥammad al-Ṭāʾī[143] was appointed governor of al-Madīnah and the Mecca road.

In this year, a battle took place between Abū al-ʿAbbās b. al-Muwaffaq and Khumarawayh b. Aḥmad b. Ṭūlūn at al-Ṭawāḥīn.[144] Abū al-ʿAbbās routed Khumarawayh and the latter fled from him on a donkey to Egypt. The troops of Abū al-ʿAbbās took to plundering, and Abū al-ʿAbbās himself [2107]
occupied the tent of Khumarawayh, not thinking that anyone remained to harm him. However, Khumarawayh left ambushers behind to lay in wait for Abū al-ʿAbbās, among them Saʿd al-Aʿsar with a group of his officers and men. Abū al-ʿAbbās's men had already laid down their arms and settled in their quar-

143. See Ṭabarī, below, 2039.
144. A village between Ramlah and Damascus. See Le Strange, *Palestine*, 544.

ters when Khumarawayh's ambushers attacked, and the government troops were routed. The government forces scattered and Abū al-ʿAbbās withdrew toward Ṭarsūs with very few of his men. Everything was lost, the weapons, shields, valuables and money which were in the camps of both Abū al-ʿAbbās and Khumarawayh; all of it was looted. According to what has been said, this battle took place on Friday, the tenth of Shawwāl (Wednesday, March 31, 885).

In this year, Yūsuf b. Abī al-Sāj, who was governor of Mecca, attacked one of al-Ṭāʾī's pages, the one called Badr—the latter was in charge of the pilgrims—and put him in chains. A detachment from the garrison, assisted by the pilgrims, fought against Ibn Abī al-Sāj until they rescued al-Ṭāʾī's page and captured Ibn Abī al-Sāj. The latter was bound and taken to Baghdad (Madīnat al-Salām). The battle between them took place at the gates of the holy mosque.

In this year the mob ravaged the Ancient Monastery (Dayr al-ʿAtīq) which was behind the ʿĪsā Canal, stripping it of all its valuables and removing the gates and woodwork, etc. They also demolished part of the walls and the roof.[145] Al-Ḥusayn b. Ismāʿīl, the prefect of police in Baghdad on behalf of Muḥammad b. Ṭāhir, arrived and prevented them from demolishing what still remained. For several days he and the mob returned
[2108] to the place so that the government troops and the mob almost engaged in fighting. Then, several days later, everything the mob had destroyed was rebuilt. The restoration work was reportedly carried out under the auspices of ʿAbdūn b. Makhlad, the brother of Ṣāʿid b. Makhlad.

Leading the pilgrimage this year was Hārūn b. Muḥammad b. Isḥāq b. ʿĪsā b. Mūsā al-ʿAbbāsī.

145. There were several monasteries in the Baghdad area, but I have not succeeded in identifying this particular one. Perhaps the reference is to the Monastery of the Virgins which was situated near the ʿĪsā Canal. See Lassner, *Topography*, 259, n. 60; also Le Strange, *Baghdad*, Map IV, ref. no. 30. The reason for the hostility to the Christians seems to be their impertinence in riding animals. See Ibn al-Jawzī, *Muntaẓam*, V, 84–85, *sub anno* 272.

The Events of the Year 272

(June 18, 885–May 7, 886)

It began on Friday, the eighteenth of Ḥazīrān, in the year 1196 of the Alexandrine calendar.

Among the events of this year, the populace of Ṭarsūs ousted Abū al-ʿAbbās b. al-Muwaffaq because of a dispute between him and Yāzamān. He left the city in the middle of al-Muḥarram (June 18–July 17, 885), setting out for Baghdad.

On Tuesday, the seventeenth of Ṣafar, 272 (August 3, 885), Sulaymān b. Wahb died in al-Muwaffaq's prison.

On Thursday, the eighth of Rabīʿ II, 272 (September 23, 885), a mob gathered and demolished the repairs which were made to the monastery.

In this year, a heretic established his rule over the road to Khurāsān. He arrived in Daskarat al-Malik,[146] killing and plundering.

---

146. This is not the large village in the area of the Nahr al-Malik, west of Baghdad, but rather the Daskarat al-Malik on the road to Khurāsān near Shahrābān. The Sassanian emperor Hurmuz b. Sābūr b. Ardashīr b. Bābak stayed there frequently and it was subsequently named after him; that is, "the Daskarah of the Ruler [al-Malik]." See Yāqūt, *Muʿjam*, II, 575.

In this year, a report reached Baghdad (Madīnat al-Salām)
[2109] that Ḥamdān b. Ḥamdūn and Hārūn al-Shārī entered the city of Mosul. Al-Shārī led the people in the services in the Friday Mosque.

On the twentieth of Jumādā II, 272 (Thursday, December 2, 885), Abū al-ʿAbbās b. al-Muwaffaq arrived in Baghdad, returning from his battle with Ibn Ṭūlūn at al-Ṭawāḥīn.

In this year, a tunnel was dug from inside the Maṭbaq Prison,[147] and al-Dhawā'ibī al-ʿAlawī together with two others were brought out. Horses had been made ready for them and remained there all night so that they might come out and make their escape on them, but warning was received and the gates to Abū Jaʿfar al-Manṣūr's city were locked. Al-Dhawā'ibī and the others who fled with him were thus apprehended. Muḥammad b. Ṭāhir wrote about this incident to al-Muwaffaq, who was stationed at the time in Wāsiṭ. The latter ordered him to have al-Dhawā'ibī's hands and feet severed in parts. This was carried out in the police headquarters at the bridge (*majlis al-jisr*)[148] on the western side of the river. While this took place, Muḥammad b. Ṭāhir sat on his mount (nearby). On Monday, the third of Jumādā II (November 16, 885), al-Dhawā'ibī's wounds were cauterized.

In Rajab of this year (December 12, 885–January 10, 886), Ṣāʿid b. Makhlad arrived in Wāsiṭ en route from Fārs. On the instructions of al-Muwaffaq, all the commanders went out to welcome him on his arrival. They dismounted and kissed his hand.

In Wāsiṭ, on Monday, the ninth of Rajab (December 21, 885), al-Muwaffaq, seized Ṣāʿid b. Makhlad and his retinue and expropriated everything they had in their houses. Ṣāʿid's two sons in Baghdad, Abū ʿĪsā and Abū Ṣāliḥ, his brother ʿAbdūn, and his staff in Sāmarrā were taken into custody. All this occurred on
[2110] one day, the same day on which Ṣāʿid was seized. Thereupon,

---

147. This fortress-like structure was situated in the street of that name between the Kūfah and Baṣrah gates of al-Manṣūr's famous Round City at Baghdad. See Yaʿqūbī, *Buldān*, 240. For a similar occurance in which the iron gates of the Round City were locked to keep escaping prisoners from leaving the structure, see Khaṭīb, *Ta'rīkh*, I, 75-76 = Paris, 14.

148. See above, n. 112.

al-Muwaffaq appointed Ismāʿīl b. Bulbul as secretary, limiting him to this function alone.

News arrived (at Baghdad) that in Jumādā II (November 13–December 11, 885), an earthquake shook Egypt destroying houses and the Friday Mosque, and that a thousand dead were counted in one day.

In the middle of Ramaḍān 272 (February 9–March 10, 886), prices rose in Baghdad. The reason for this was that the people of Sāmarrā reportedly prevented vessels with flour from reaching Madīnat al-Salām. Moreover, al-Ṭā'ī did not let the owners of estates thresh the crops and distribute them in anticipation of the rise in prices. In turn, the people of Baghdad prevented olive oil, soap, dates and other foods from being shipped to Sāmarrā.[149]

In this year the rise in prices caused the mob to become disquieted and they rallied to attack al-Ṭā'ī. In the middle of Shawwāl (March 11–April 8, 886), they went from the Friday Mosque to his house, which lay between the Baṣrah and the Kūfah gates, approaching it from the direction of al-Karkh.[150] Al-Ṭā'ī placed his troops on the roofs, and they greeted the mob with arrows. He also positioned his men, armed with swords and lances, at the gate and in the courtyard of his house. Some of the mob were killed and many were wounded, but they did not stop fighting until nightfall. When night came, they withdrew only to reappear early the next morning. Then Muḥammad b. Ṭāhir rode (to the scene) and calmed the people, and had them withdraw.

On Tuesday, the eighteenth of Shawwāl 272 (March 28, 886), Ismāʿīl b. Burayh al-Hāshimī passed away; and three days later, ʿUbaydallāh b. Abdallāh al-Hāshimī followed suit.

In this year, the Zanj rioted in Wāsiṭ shouting, "Ankalāy, O Manṣūr."[151] At the time Ankalāy, al-Muhallabī, Sulaymān b. [2111]

149. The economic rivalry between Baghdad and Sāmarrā is a subject that is worthy of attention.

150. This residence seems to have been in the section known as Bayn al-Sūrayn. See Lassner, *Topography*, 275.

151. On the name Manṣūr (he who is aided by God to win victories) in battle cries, see Lewis, "Regnal Titles", 16 ff.

Jāmiʿ, al-Shaʿrānī, al Hamdānī, and other leaders of the Zanj were imprisoned in the house of Muḥammad b. ʿAbdallāh b. Ṭāhir in the Dār al-Baṭṭīkh at Baghdad (Madīnat al-Salām).[152] One of the pages of al-Muwaffaq, Fatḥ al-Saʿīdī by name, was in charge of them. Al-Muwaffaq wrote to Fatḥ, ordering him to send off the heads of the six to him. Fatḥ went to the prisoners and sent them out one by one to a page of his who beheaded them. He then removed the lid of the sewer which was in the house and dumped the (decapitated) bodies in it. Then he covered the sewer with its lid and the heads were sent off to al-Muwaffaq.

In this year, a letter from al-Muwaffaq reached Muḥammad b. Ṭāhir concerning the bodies of these six who were slain. He ordered the latter to hang them for display in the vicinity of the Main Bridge (al-Jisr). Accordingly, the bodies were taken out of the sewer; they had already become swollen, foul-smelling, and parts of their skin had fallen off. They were carried on litters, each litter being carried by two men. Three of the bodies were hung on the west side and three on the east.[153] This took place on the twenty-second of Shawwāl 272 (April 1, 886); Muḥammad b. Ṭāhir rode out to the spot, and the bodies were hung in his presence.

In this year, quiet was restored to the city of the Messenger of God, and it flourished as people gradually returned to it.

In this year, the summer expedition (against the Byzantines) was conducted by Yāzamān.

Leading the pilgrimage this year was Hārūn b. Muḥammad b. Isḥāq b. Mūsā al-Hāshimī.

---

152. The Dār al-Baṭṭīkh (Melon Market) was a fruit market situated at the juncture of Nahr ʿĪsā and Nahr Ṭābaq. See Lassner, *Topography*, 249, n. 10; Le Strange, *Baghdad*, Map IV, ref no. 42.

153. That is, at the approaches to the Main Bridge on both sides of the river.

The Events of the Year

[2112]

273
(June 8, 886–May 27, 887)

On the sixteenth of Rabīʿ I (Sunday, August. 22, 886), a battle occurred between Aḥmad b. ʿAbd al-ʿAzīz b. Abī Dulaf and ʿAmr b. al-Layth al-Ṣaffār.

Also, on Tuesday, the ninth of Jumādā I (October 12, 886), a battle took place in al-Raqqah between Isḥāq b. Kundāj and Muḥammad b. Abī al-Sāj; Isḥāq was routed in this battle.

In this year, messengers from Yāzamān returned from Ṭarsūs with a report that three sons of the Byzantine emperor had rebelled against their father and killed him. They had placed one of themselves on the throne.

On the twenty-second of Dhū al-Qaʿdah, 273 (Friday, April 21, 887), Abū Aḥmad had Lu'lu' bound. The latter had come to him with a guarantee of safe conduct from Ibn Ṭūlūn, and Abū Aḥmad seized his wealth. The money seized reportedly amounted to four hundred thousand dīnārs. It is said, that Lu'lu', exclaimed, "Apart from my being wealthy, I do not know of any other sin I might have committed for which I should deserve what has been done to me."

On the fourteenth of Dhū al-Ḥijjah, 273 (Monday, May 12, 887), another battle between Muḥammad b. Abī al-Sāj and Isḥāq b. Kundāj took place. This time Ibn Kundāj was defeated.

Leading the pilgrimage this year was Hārūn b. Muḥammad b. Isḥāq b. ʿĪsā b. Mūsā b. ʿAlī b. ʿAbdallāh b. ʿAbbās.

The
Events of the Year

[2113]

274
(May 28, 887–May 15, 888)

Among the events taking place, Abū Aḥmad departed for Kirmān to do combat with ʿAmr b. al-Layth. This took place on the eighteenth of Rabīʿ I (Friday, August 4, 887).

In Ramaḍān 274 (January 19–February 17, 888), Yāzamān set out on a border raid and reached Maskanayn, where he took captives and booty. He and the Muslims returned safely.

In this year, Ṣiddīq al-Farghānī entered Dūr Sāmarrā[154] and plundered the possessions of the merchants, causing much damage among the populace. This Ṣiddīq was formerly a road guard, but then he turned into an armed brigand of the highway.

Leading the pilgrimage this year was Hārūn b. Muḥammad al-Hāshimī.

---

154. The upper limits of the city. See Yāqūt, *Muʿjam*, II, 618.

The Events of the Year

275

(May 16, 888–May 5, 889)

Among the events taking place, al-Ṭā'ī sent an army to Sāmarrā because of what Ṣiddīq had done there, and because he had freed his brother from prison—the latter had been Ṣiddīq's prisoner. Al-Ṭā'ī's action took place during al-Muḥarram of this year (May 16–June 14, 888). Later, al-Ṭā'ī (himself) went to Sāmarrā and began corresponding with Ṣiddīq, making promises to him, arousing his ambition and offering him assurances. Ṣiddīq thus decided to go to al-Ṭā'ī under a guarantee of safeconduct. However, Hāshim, one of Ṣiddīq's servants—he he was reportedly a courageous man—cautioned his master against such a move. But Ṣiddīq did not accept his advice, and together with his men, he entered Sāmarrā; whereupon al-Ṭā'ī seized him and those of his men who entered the city. Al-Ṭā'ī
[2114] then cut off one of his hands and feet. Hāshim and a group of others were similarly treated and then imprisoned. Subsequently, they were carried on litters to Baghdad (Madīnat al-Salām); their severed hands and feet had already been displayed before the the populace. They were then imprisoned (at Baghdad).

In this year, Yāzamān carried out a sea raid and wrested four vessels from the Byzantines.

In this year, al-ʿAbdī became a vagabond and caused trouble in the vicinity of Sāmarrā. He went to Karkh Sāmarrā[155] and looted the habitations of the Ḥashanaj clan. Al-Ṭāʾī then set out against him and overtook him at al-Ḥadīthah. They clashed and al-Ṭāʾī routed al-ʿAbdī, seizing most of his men. The former then went to the Tigris and embarked on his flyer (*ṭayyār*) with the intention of crossing the river. But al-ʿAbdī's men overtook him and seized the anchor of the vessel, whereupon al-Ṭāʾī jumped into the Tigris and swam across the river. As he came out of the river, he shook the water from his beard and exclaimed: "What does al-ʿAbdī think. Don't I swim better than a fish?" Following that, al-Ṭāʾī camped on the eastern bank, while al-ʿAbdī was opposite him on the western side.

Concerning al-Ṭāʾī's withdrawal, Alī b. Muḥammad b. Manṣūr b. Naṣr b. Bassām said:

Al-Ṭāʿī came, would that he had not come;
his deeds were evil, certainly, not good.

What with his soft verbiage
he is like a young girl masticating a tough sweetmeat.

In this year, Abū Aḥmad ordered al-Ṭāʾī bound and put in prison. This was carried out on the fourteenth of Ramaḍān (Monday, January 21, 889), thus putting an end to al-Ṭāʾī's career. He had been governor of al-Kūfah and its territories, and [2115] had been responsible for securing the Khurāsān Road. He had also been governor of Sāmarrā, in charge of security in Baghdad and the tax-collector of Bādurāyā,[156] Qaṭrabbul, Maskin,[157] and some of the domains belonging to the notables.

In this year, Abū Aḥmad put his son Abū al-ʿAbbās in jail, but the latter's troops rioted and took up arms. His pages took to their mounts and, as a result, all of Baghdad was in an uproar. Because of this, Abū Aḥmad (set out for the city) and rode

155. See Le Strange, *Lands*, 52, 54, 55.
156. See Lassner, *Topography*, 256, n. 46; and n. 139 above.
157. For the district of Maskin near Baghdad, see Yāqūt, *Muʿjam*, IV, 520.

until reaching the Ruṣāfah Gate. He reportedly spoke to the troops and pages of Abū al-ʿAbbās as follows, "What is the matter with you, are you really more anxious about my son than I am? He is my offspring and it is incumbent upon me to set him straight." At this, the people put away their arms and withdrew. This happened on Tuesday, the sixth of Shawwāl 275, (February 12, 889).

Leading the pilgrimage this year was Hārūn b. Muḥammad al-Hāshimī.

The Events of the Year 276

(May 6, 889–April 24, 890)

Among the events taking place ʿAmr b. al-Layth was charged with the security at Baghdad (Madīnat al-Salām) and his name was inscribed on the flags, poles and shields of the police headquarters at the bridge. This took place in al-Muḥarram (May 6–June 4, 889).[158]

On the fourteenth of Rabīʿ I, 276 (Thursday, July 4, 889), Abū Aḥmad left Baghdad (Madīnat al-Salām) bound for al-Jabal. The reason for this was, they say, that al-Mādharāʾī, the secretary of Adhkūtakīn, wrote to Abū Aḥmad that his master had an immense fortune there, and that should he come (to al-Jabal), it would pass into his hands. But when Abū Aḥmad arrived there he found none of the wealth which had been reported to him. [2116]
When he did not find this wealth, Abū Aḥmad departed to al-Karaj, and from there he went to Iṣbahān seeking Aḥmad b. ʿAbd al-ʿAzīz b. Abī Dulaf; whereupon, the latter together with his troops and family departed from the city, leaving his house

158. These references to ʿAmr were later removed in Shawwāl. See Ibn al-Jawzī, *Muntaẓam*, V, 99–100; and text above, 2117.

and its furnishings to accommodate Abū Aḥmad upon his arrival.

Before Abū Aḥmad left his tent at Bāb Khurāsān,[159] Muḥammad b. Abī al-Sāj arrived, having fled from Ibn Ṭūlūn. This was after several engagements between them, the last of which had enfeebled Ibn Abī al-Sāj to the point that he could no longer put up a fight, as his force was too small relative to the numerous troops of Ibn Ṭūlūn. Ibn Abī al-Sāj reached Abū Aḥmad and joined him; and the latter bestowed robes of honor upon him, and took him along to al-Jabal.

In the month Rabīʿ II 276 (August 3-August 31, 890), ʿUbaydallāh b. ʿAbdallāh b. Ṭāhir was put in command of security at Baghdad on behalf of ʿAmr b. al-Layth.

In this year, a report arrived at Baghdad that at Nahr al-Ṣilah,[160] (the interior of) a hill bearing the name Tall Banī Shaqīq became exposed, disclosing seven graves with seven perfectly preserved bodies. The shrouds covering them were new and soft, with fringes giving off the smell of musk. One of the corpses was that of a youngster with luxuriant hair, his forehead, ears, cheeks, nose, lips, chin and the places of the eyelashes were free from any blemish. His lips were moistened, as if he had just drunk water, and (his eyes), as if he had just been made up with kohl. There was (the indication of) a blow on his waist. His shroud was put back on him. One of our colleagues told me that he pulled the hair on some of the bodies and found
[2117] that it had strong roots as if it were on a living person. It is said that the exposed area of the hill above the graves revealed the likes of a stone basin of whetstone color, which bore an inscription nobody could decipher.

In this year, orders were issued to remove the poles, flags and shields bearing the name of ʿAmr b. al-Layth from the headquarters of the police. Moreover, no mention was to be made of

159. The reference here is not to the Khurāsān Gate of the Round City, but to the gate of that name which was situated at the outer limits of East Baghdad. See Lassner, *Topography*, index, 319.

160. The Ṣilah Canal was situated in Wāsiṭ. See Yāqūt, *Muʿjam*, IV, 841.

his name. These orders were issued on the eleventh of Shawwāl (Friday, February 6, 890).

Leading the pilgrimage this year was Hārūn b. Muḥammad b. Isḥāq al-Hāshimī, who was also governor of Mecca, al-Madīnah and al-Ṭā'if.

The Events of the Year

277

(April 25, 890–April 14, 891)

Among the events taking place, in Ṭarsūs, Yāzamān called upon the people to swear allegiance to Khumarawayh b. Aḥmad b. Ṭūlūn. It is reported that the reason for this was that Khumarawayh had sent him 30,000 dīnārs, five hundred garments, one hundred fifty horses, one hundred fifty rain cloaks and weapons. When all this arrived, Yāzamān called for allegiance to Khumarawayh. Then Khumarawayh sent him fifty thousand (more) dīnārs.

In the beginning of Rabīʿ II (July 23–August 20), there was enmity between Waṣīf, the eunuch (*khādim*) of Ibn Abī al-Sāj, and the Berbers who were the troops of Abū al-Ṣaqr. They fought, and four of the eunuch' pages were killed, as were
[2118] seven of the Berbers. The battle between them took place between the Damascus Gate and the thoroughfare of Bāb al-Kūfah.[161] Then Abū al-Ṣaqr rode over to them and spoke to them, whereupon they dispersed. Two days later they resumed hostilities and, again, Abū al-Ṣaqr rode over and calmed them.

161. That is, on the west side of Baghdad.

In this year, Yūsuf b. Yaʿqūb was put in charge of the court of appeals (*maẓālim*).[162] He gave the order to announce, "Whosoever has an appeal against the prince al-Nāṣr li-Dīn Allāh[163] or against any notable, let him come forward." He then sent word to the prefect of police not to release any prisoners except those on whose behalf petitions had been presented to himself (that is, Yūsuf), and whose release he had seen fit to grant.

On the first day of Shaʿbān (Monday, November 8, 890), one of Ibn Ṭūlūn's commanders arrived in Baghdad with a great army consisting of cavalry and infantry.

Leading the pilgrimage this year was Hārūn b. Muḥammad al-Hāshimī.

---

162. He was the judge (*qāḍī*) of the city. See Ṭabarī III/4, 2161.
163. That is, al-Muwaffaq.

The Events of the Year

278

(April 15, 891–April 2, 892)

Among these events was the battle which took place between the troops of Waṣīf al-Khādim, the Berbers, and the troops of Mūsā, the son of Mufliḥ's sister. The battle lasted for four successive days before the parties to the conflict made peace. Some ten of their men had been slain. This took place in the beginning of al-Muḥarram (April 15–May 14, 891).

Then a disturbance broke out on the east side between the populace of al-Naṣrāniyyah[164] and the troops of Yūnus. During the course of the battle a man was killed; afterwards the contestants dispersed.

In this year, Waṣīf, the eunuch of Ibn Abī al Sāj, left for Waṣīt. He did so on the command of Abū al-Ṣaqr, reportedly, so that he might become of service to him, for Abū al Ṣaqr had conferred benefits upon Waṣīf his men, having granted him gifts and bountifully assigned allotments to them. Word had
[2119] reached Abū al-Ṣaqr that Abū Aḥmad was coming. He feared

164. Perhaps this should be read al-Naṣriyyah, referring to the place on the Dujayl Road in West Baghdad. See Lassner, *Topography*, 253, n. 18.

for his life, since he had embezzled all the money from Abū Aḥmad's treasuries in order to present gifts, presents, and robes of honor to the officers, and for other expenditures regarding them. When he had spent what he had from the treasury, he demanded from the landowners the payment of a year's land tax, and, regarding this demand, he arrested many of them. He assigned al-Zaghal to the task of carrying out this measure, and in doing so the latter treated the people ruthlessly. But Abū Aḥmad arrived before al-Zaghal finished extorting the money, and the practice was discontinued. Waṣīf's departure took place on Friday, the seventeenth of al-Muḥarram (Apr. 30, 891).

On the twenty-eighth of al-Muḥarram, 278 (Wednesday, May 12, 891), a star with a fringe appeared; the fringe later became a hanginq lock.

In this year, Abū Aḥmad returned from al-Jabal to Iraq. He was so sorely afflicted with the pain of gout that he was unable to ride. A covered bedstead was arranged for him; he would sit on it, while a servant cooled his feet with cold stuff. The gout became so severe, that the servant took to applying snow. Then his feet were stricken with elephantiasis. Forty men carried his bedstead in two teams, twenty porters in each. At times, his pain became excruciating, and he would order them to put him down. It is said that one day he remarked to those carrying him: "You are annoyed with carrying me, I know; but I wish I were like one of you, bearing a burden on my head, [2120]
tired but in good health." He also said while sick, "This is my most complete military roll; a hundred thousand troops are inscribed. Not one of them awoke worse off than I am."

On Monday, the twenty-seventh of al-Muḥarram (May 11, 891), Abū Aḥmad reached al-Nahrawān, where the populace welcomed him. He set sail along the (Nahrawān) Canal, and then on to the Diyālā and Tigris, until he arrived in al-Zaʿfarāniyyah. On Friday night he travelled to al-Firk. It was on Friday, the second night of Ṣafar (May 16, 891) that he entered his residence. On Thursday, the eighth of Ṣafar (May 23, 891), after Abū al-Ṣaqr left his house, rumors spread of his death. Abū al-Ṣaqr had sent orders to guard Abū al-ʿAbbās and kept him behind several locked doors. He had also taken Ibn al-Fayyāḍ along to Abū al-ʿAbbās's residence and Ibn al-Fayyāḍ stayed nearby. Abū al-Ṣaqr remained at home that day, while excitement grew on account of the news of Abū Aḥmad's death; but the latter had only fainted. On Friday, Abū al-Ṣaqr went to al-Madā'in and brought al-Muʿtamid and his sons to his (Abū al-Ṣaqr's) residence. Thereafter, he stayed home and did not go to Abū Aḥmad's residence.

Perceiving Abū Aḥmad's condition, those of his pages who were in sympathy with his son Abū al-ʿAbbās, as well as the leaders of Abū al-Abbās's pages, who were present, broke the locks of the doors behind which Abū al-ʿAbbās was confined.

The page who had been in the same room with Abū al-ʿAbbās reportedly said: Upon hearing the sounds of locks being broken Abū al-ʿAbbās remarked, "They can only be coming to take my life." He seized a sword at his disposal, unsheathed it, [2121] and sat so as to be ready to rise, while keeping the sword in his lap. Then he said to me, "Step aside. By God, they will not reach me as long as there is any life left in me." As the door opened, the first to enter was Waṣīf Mūshkīr, who had been the page of Abū al-ʿAbbās. When Abū al-ʿAbbās saw him, he dropped the sword, since he knew that they had come to him only with good intentions. They took him out and sat him before his father, who had just fainted. When Abū Aḥmad opened his eyes and came to, his glance fell upon his son, whereupon he drew Abū al-ʿAbbās close to him and embraced him.

Al-Muʿtamid, his son, the heir apparent, Jaʿfar al-Mufawwaḍ ilā-llāh, and his other sons, ʿAbd al-ʿAzīz, Muḥammad, and Isḥāq, all arrived in Baghdad (Madīnat al-Salām) on the same day that they had been summoned. This was Friday noon, before the Friday service, the ninth of Ṣafar (April 24, 891). They stayed at the residence of Abū al-Ṣaqr. Then word reached Abū al-Ṣaqr that Abū Aḥmad had not died, whereupon he sent Ismāʿīl b. Isḥāq on to verify this report—this was on Saturday. Meanwhile, he assembled the officers and troops, and filled his residence and its surroundings with armed men. He did as well for the area between his residence and the bridge. In addition he cut the two bridges.[165] A group stood at the bridgehead on

165. It may be that Abū al-Ṣaqr's residence was on the East Side where the troops were stationed. The bridge referred to was the Main Bridge of the city

the eastern side (of the river) and fought the troops of Abū al-Ṣaqr, as both sides suffered losses in dead and wounded. Abū Ṭalḥah, the brother of Sharkab, was stationed with his men at Bāb al-Bustān.[166]

Meanwhile, Ismāʿīl returned to Abū al-Ṣaqr, and informed him that Abū Aḥmad was alive. The first of the commanders to turn to Abū Aḥmad was Muḥammad b. Abī al-Sāj, who crossed the ʿĪsā Canal. After that, they started to steal away, some crossing over to Abū Aḥmad's residence; others returned to their homes, and still others left Baghdad. When Abū al-Ṣaqr [2122]
saw this and was certain that Abū Aḥmad was still alive, he and his two sons went to the latter's residence. Abū Aḥmad made no mention of what had happened and did not question him, and Abū al-Ṣaqr remained at Abū Aḥmad's residence. When al-Muʿtamid saw that he alone remained at Abū al-Ṣaqr's home, he embarked on a skiff together with his sons and Buktimur. They were then met by Abū Laylā b. ʿAbd al-ʿAzīz b. Abī Dulaf's flyer. The latter sailed with them to his residence which is the palace of ʿAlī b. Jahshiyār at the head of the bridge. But when al-Muʿtamid told him, "I want to go to my brother," Abū Laylā took him and those accompanying him from that house to Abū Aḥmad's residence.

Meanwhile, Abū al-Ṣaqr's residence was stripped of everything to the extent that the women had to leave barefoot and without veils. The house of his secretary, Muḥammad b. Sulaymān, was also looted and the house of Ibn al-Wāthiqī was plundered and set on fire. Looted as well were the residences of al-Wāthiqī's intimates. The gates of the prisons were broken and their walls were pierced. All the prisoners escaped including all the inmates of the Maṭbaq. The two police headquarters

---

connecting Bāb al-Ṭāq with the West Side near al-Khuld. The city had at different times two or three bridges spanning the Tigris. See Lassner, *Topography*, 280, n.1.

166. If these men were stationed on the East Side (see above, n. 165), the Bāb al-Bustān (Gate of the Garden) referred to here is likely the Bustān al-Ẓāhir. See Lassner, *Topography*, 280, n.2.; 295, n. 48.

167. Note that al-Muwaffaq granted ʿAlī b. Jahshiyār the famous Ṭāq (Archway of) Asmā' which formed part of the Asmā's palace. It was situated between al-Ruṣāfah and al-Mukharrim and gave its name to the larger neighborhood near the bridge; that is, Bāb al-Ṭāq. See Lassner, *Topography*, 261, n.3.

buildings at the (main) bridge were looted and stripped of everything. Even the houses in the vicinity of Abū al-Ṣaqr's residence were robbed.

Abū Aḥmad gave robes of honor to his son Abū al-ʿAbbās and to Abū al-Ṣaqr. They rode together wearing the robes of honor from Sūq al-Thalāthā' to Bāb al-Ṭāq;[168] then they proceeded to Abū al-ʿAbbās's residence which was the Palace of Ṣāʿid,[169] and from there Abū al-Ṣaqr set sail for his home, which had been so thoroughly plundered that they had to bring him a mat from al-Shāh's residence to sit on.

Abū al-ʿAbbās entrusted his page Badr with the security (of the city). He also appointed Muḥammad b. Ghānim b. al-Shāh
[2123] as his deputy on the east side and ʿĪsā al-Nūsharī on the west side. This took place on the fourteenth of Ṣafar (Wednesday, April 28, 891).

On Wednesday, the nineteenth of Ṣafar, 278 (June 2, 891), Abū Aḥmad al-Muwaffaq passed away. He was buried Thursday night near the tomb of his mother in al-Ruṣāfah.[170] That same day, Abū al-ʿAbbās received people who came to express their condolences.

In this year, the officers and pages took the oath of allegiance to Abū al-ʿAbbās as heir apparent following al-Mufawwaḍ (in the line of succession). He was given honorific title al-Muʿtaḍid bi-llāh. That was on Thursday (the day his father was buried). Pay was distributed among the troops, and on Friday, the sermon mentioned the names of al-Muʿtamid, al-Mufawwaḍ and Abū al-ʿAbbās al-Muʿtaḍid in that order. This took place on the twenty-first of Ṣafar (June 4, 891).

---

168. Presumably along the Main Thoroughfare (Shāriʿ al-Aʿẓam) that ran from Sūq al-Thalāthā' in the south to Bāb al-Ṭāq in the north. That thoroughfare was frequently used for processions. See for example Khaṭīb, *Ta'rīkh*, I, 100 ff. = Paris, 49 ff.; Miskawayh, *Tajārib*, I, 53–55, Ibn al-Jawzī, *Muntaẓam*, VI, 143–44; Ibu al-Athīr, *Kamil*, VIII, 79; Ṣabī', *Rusūm*, 11 *ff.; Ibn al-Zubayr, Dhakhā'ir*, 131–139; the secondary literature is listed in Lassner, *Topography*, 268, n. 10.

169. The reference is to a palace that was to the north of the bridge in the area of al-Shammāsiyyah. It was used as a guest house for important visitors. See Lassner, *Topography*, 268, n.12.

170. That is , he was buried in the Tombs of the Caliphs. See Le Strange, *Baghdad*, 193–95.

On Monday, the twenty-third of Ṣafar (June 6, 891), Abū al-Ṣaqr and his intimates were seized and their houses plundered. A search was made for the Banū al-Furāt,[171] who had been in charge of the Dīwān al–Sawād; they subsequently went into hiding. On Tuesday, the twenty-fourth of Ṣafar (June 7, 891), ʿUbaydallāh b. Sulaymān b. Wahb was granted robes of honor and entrusted with the wazīrate.[172]

In this year, Muḥammad b. Abī al-Sāj sent a message to Wāsiṭ, ordering his page, Waṣīf, to return to Baghdad (Madīnat al-Salām). Waṣīf went to al-Ahwāz and refused to return to Baghdad. Instead, he plundered al-Ṭīb and caused mayhem in al-Sūs.[173]

In this year, Abū Aḥmad b. Muḥammad b. al-Furāt was seized, and subsequently imprisoned. He was also required to give up his wealth. Al-Zaghal was seized along with him, and he too was imprisoned and required to give up his wealth.

In this year, dispatches arrived (at Baghdad) that Alī b. al-Layth, the brother of al-Ṣaffār had been killed. He had been slain by Rāfiʿ b. Harthamah, who had deserted al-Ṣaffār and joined ʿAlī.

In this year despatches arrived (at Baghdad) from Egypt that [2124]
the Nile's level had dropped and that prices had risen.

The Origins of the Qarmaṭians[174]

In 278 (891/852), reports arrived (at Baghdad) of a revolutionary group in the Kūfah area (Sawād al-Kūfah) known as the Qarmaṭians. Their movement began with the arrival there of a man from the province of Khuzistān. Settling in a place known as al-Nahrayn, he led an ascetic life and displayed his piety to all. He earned his living by weaving baskets from palm leaves, and spent much of his time praying. He continued this way for some time. If anyone joined him, he would discourse with him

171. For this wazīrial family, see Sourdel, *Vizirat ʿAbbāside*, II, index, 762–63.

172. Ibid., 785.

173. See Le Strange, *Lands*, 240, 246, 247 (al-Sūs), 241, 247 (Ṭīb).

174. See *EI*², s.v. Ḳarmaṭī (includes extensive bibliography).

upon religious affairs, inculcate him with contempt for this world, and teach him that it was incumbent upon everyone to pray fifty times each day and night. He did this until news spread about his activity in this place. Then he disclosed that he was urging allegiance to an Imām from the house of the Messenger.[175] He went on in this manner attracting people to his side and spreading his message which won over their hearts. He stayed at a greengrocer's in the village. Nearby there was a palm-grove, which was acquired by a group of merchants. The latter built an enclosure in which they stored the fruits they gathered from the grove. They came to the greengrocer and asked him to find them a man who could guard what they had gathered. The greengrocer pointed this man out
[2125] to them, and said, "If this man consents to guard your dates, he is just the man you want." So the merchants discussed the matter with him, and he agreed to act as guard for a certain remuneration. He acted as guard for them, spending most of his day at prayers and fasting. For breakfast, he would take a *raṭl*[176] of dates, and after eating he would collect the stones. When the merchants had loaded all their dates, they went to the greengrocer to settle their account with this hired-hand of theirs, and they paid him what he had earned. Then, the latter reckoned what he owed the greengrocer for his dates, and deducted from that sum the worth of the stones which he returned to the latter.

When the merchants heard what was going on between the man and the greengrocer concerning the date stones, they attacked him, and striking him, they said, "Was it not enough for you to eat our dates, but that now you even sell their stones?" The greengrocer then said to them, "Leave him alone; this man would not even touch your dates." And he told them his story. The merchants now regretted having struck him, and asked him to forgive them. This he did, and, as a result, when they

175. The expression "house of the Messenger [*ahl bayt al-Rasūl*]" here refers to the family of ʿAlī b. Abī Ṭālib. For an analysis of the term *ahl al-bayt* and the various interpretations of it by ʿAlids and ʿAbbāsids, see Sharon, "ʿAbbāsid Daʿwa," 9, n. 23.

176. See above, n. 127, also nn. 101, 109.

came across his asceticism, the people of the village esteemed him even more.

Afterwards, he fell sick and lay abandoned on the road. Now there was a man in that village who drove oxen. He had extremely red eyes; his eyes were so red that the people of the village came to call him Karmītah, on account of the redness of his eyes—Karmītah in Aramaic[177] means "red-eyed." The greengrocer asked this Karmītah to take the sick man to his home and ask his family to watch over him and take care of him. Karmītah did this, and the man stayed with him until he recovered.

Thereupon he would receive townspeople in his home, in- [2126]
vite them to join him in his cause, and describe his creed to them. The people of this region responded and he took a dīnār from everyone who joined his religious group—they thought that he took it for the Imām. In this fashion, he continued to summon the people of those villages, and they responded favorably to him. Then he selected twelve agents (*naqīb*) from among them, and he instructed them to summon people to their faith. He said to the agents, "You are like the apostles of Jesus, the son of Mary."[178]

The farmers of that region neglected their work because of the fifty prayers he prescribed for them, and which he had declared incumbent upon them. Al-Hayṣam happened to have estates in this area. When he noticed that his farmers had become remiss in the tilling of the soil, he inquired about it and was informed that a man had appeared and revealed religious practices (*madhhab min al-dīn*) to them. He taught them that God made it incumbent upon them to pray fifty times during the day and night, and that this had kept them from their work. Al-Hayṣam then sent for the man; he was seized and brought before him. Al-Hayṣam asked him about his activities, and the

177. Lit. "Nabatean."

178. The ʿAbbāsid propaganda also utilized twelve agents who were designated as *naqībs*. The model was Muḥammad, who sent twelve agents to pave the way for his journey to al-Madīnah. It is interesting that the Qarmaṭians should have traced this back to Christian sources. The ʿAbbāsids relying on the Qur'ān found a prototype in the twelve leaders of the Banū Isrāʾīl. A study of the term *naqīb* in ʿAbbāsid propaganda is being readied by J. Lassner.

man told him his story; whereupon, al-Hayṣam swore to kill him. At the latter's command, the man was imprisoned in a house behind locked doors, and the key was placed under al-Hayṣam's pillow. Al-Hayṣam had been drinking when one of the maid-servants who had been in the house and heard the man's story was moved to pity for him. When al-Hayṣam fell asleep, she took the key from under his pillow, opened the door and led the man out. Then she locked the door and put the key back in its place. When al-Hayṣam awoke, he called for the key, opened the door and found that the man was not there. When news about this spread among the people of that region,
[2127] they were excited and said, "He has been taken to heaven."

Later on, he appeared in another place, and met some of his friends and others. They asked him about his experience and he replied, "No one can work evil upon me and thus control me." This lifted him still higher in their eyes. Fearing for his safety, he left for the vicinity of Damascus, and nothing was heard of him. People called him by the name of the owner of the oxen in whose house he had been, Karmītah. Later they found it easier to pronounce it as Qarmaṭ.[179]

This story was reported by one of our colleagues—someone who was in the presence of Muḥammad b. Dāwūd b. al-Jarrāḥ. The latter had summoned some Qarmaṭians from prison and interrogated them about Zikrawayh—this was after he had slain the latter—and about Qarmaṭ and his story. These men pointed to one of the group, an old man, and said, "This man is Zikrawayh's brother-in-law, and he knows his story best, so ask him whatever you wish." Ibn al-Jarrāḥ asked him, whereupon, the man told him this story.

According to Muḥammad b. Dāwūd: Qarmaṭ was a man from the Kūfah area, who used to cart the crops of the villages of al-Kūfah with oxen; his name was Ḥamdān, and they nicknamed him Qarmaṭ.

Subsequently, word of the Qarmaṭians and their belief spread, and their numbers increased in the Kūfah area. When al-Ṭā'ī, that is, Aḥmad b. Muḥammad, learned about them, he

179. This etymology does not seem likely. See Madelung's comments on the origins of the name Qarmaṭ in *EI*², s.v. Ḳarmaṭī.

taxed everyone of them a dīnār a year, and in this way he collected an enormous fortune. Some Kūfans went to the authorities and brought the matter of the Qarmaṭians to their attention, saying that the latter had invented a new religion which was different from Islām, and that they thought of putting Muḥammad's people to the sword, all except those who did homage to their religion. They added that al-Ṭā'ī was concealing thc Qarmaṭian cause from the authorities, that he neither paid attention nor listened to them (that is, the Kūfans). [2128]
The Kūfans left, but one of them remained at Baghdad (Madīnat al-Salām) for a long time, making his appeal and asserting that he could not possibly return to his city for fear of al-Ṭā'ī.

Among the stories about these Qarmaṭians and their beliefs is the following. They had brought a book which contained this text, "In the name of God, the Compassionate, the Merciful!" Thus says al-Faraj b. ʿUthmān—he was from the village called Naṣrānah[180] which preached the religion of Christ, who is Jesus, who is the Logos, who is the Messiah (Mahdī), who is Aḥmad b. Muḥammad b. al Ḥanafiyyah, who is Gabriel.[181] He mentioned that Christ appeared before him in human form, and told him, "You are the preacher, and you are the proof; you are the she-camel, and you are the ass; you are the Holy Spirit, and you are John the Baptist (Yaḥyā b. Zakariyyā')." He also informed al-Faraj that the prayer consists of four prostrations, two before the sunrise and two after sunset. He added that the call to every prayer is, "Allāh is great, Allāh is great, Allāh is great, Allāh is great. I testify that there is no God but Allāh"—to be said twice—"I testify that Adam is the Messenger of God; I testify that Noah is the Messenger of God; I testify that Abraham is the Messenger of God; I testify that Moses is the Messenger of God; I testify that Jesus is the Messenger of God; I testify that Muḥammad is the Messenger of God; I testify that Aḥmad b. Muḥammad b. al-Ḥanafiyyah is the Messenger of God." He

180. I have not succeeded in identifying this place. Naṣrānaḥ may be a play on words; the word *naṣrānī* means Christian.

181. This statement may be a lingering echo of the doctrine of the transmigration of souls which was popular among the proto-Shīʿite groups of the eighth century. See Watt, *Islamic Thought*, 53, 57, 153.

further let him know that the *istiftāḥ*[182] is to be read with every prostration, as it was revealed to Aḥmad b. Muḥammad b. al-Ḥanafiyyah; and that the orientation of prayer (*qiblah*) is toward Jerusalem, and that the pilgrimage is to Jerusalem.

[2129] He added that Monday is the day of congregational prayers and no work is to be done on it, and that the *sūrah* reads:

> Praise God for His Logos. May He be exalted in His name, bestowed upon His saints through His saints. Say, "The new moons were given to the people." Their exoteric meaning allows people to calculate the years and months and days, but the esoteric meaning indicates that they are my Saints, who have taught my worshipers my path. Beware of me, O people of superior mind. I am the one who would not be called to account for his deeds. I am the knowing, I am the wise, and I am the one who will test my worshipers and try my creatures. He who bears patiently my test, trial and experience, I shall place in Paradise, and I will grant him my everlasting grace. But he who deserts my cause and speaks against my messengers will be flung into eternal pain and humiliation. I shall fulfill my purpose and reveal my cause through the tongues of my apostles. I am the one who is not surpassed by any powerful one, but I depose him; nor by any glorious one, but I render him contemptible. But I am not one of those who persist in their cause and persevere in their ignorance and say, "I shall continue to cleave to it, and believe it." For those are the unbelievers.

And when he would prostrate himself he would say, "Praise be to my Lord, the Lord of Glory, who is above all description by the wicked.' " This is to be said twice. And when he prostrated himself fully, he said, "God is most high, God is most high, God is most powerful, God is most powerful."

Among his precepts were these: that two fasts were to be observed during the year, on Mihrajān and Nawrūz;[183] that nabīdh

---

182. The reciting of the opening *sūrah* (fātiḥah) of the Qur'ān.
183. That is, the Persian festivals marking the fall and the new year.

was prohibited and wine permitted;[184] that ablution, in the sense of washing away legal impurity, was invalid and only ablution for prayer was left in force; that anyone who rose to fight against him was to be punished by death, but that those who opposed him without fighting were to have a poll-tax imposed upon them; that animals with tusks and talons were forbidden food.

The arrival of Qarmaṭ in the neighborhood of al-Kūfah took place before the leader of the Zanj was killed. That is, one of our colleagues (heard this from) Zikrawayh's brother-in law: I went to the leader of the Zanj. Arriving before him I said, "I subscribe to a certain religious practice, and have one hundred thousand swords at my command. Let us discuss this matter. If we agree about the practice, I will join you with all my men; if not, I will withdraw." I then said to him, "Grant me safe-conduct." He did this. I held a discussion with him until noon, but then it finally became clear to me that he was opposed to my ideas. When he rose to go to perform the prayer I slipped out, and, leaving his city, I went to the area of al-Kūfah. [2130]

On the twenty-fourth of Jumādā II, 278 (Sunday, October 3, 891), Aḥmad al-ʿUjayfī came to the city of Ṭarsūs, together with Yāzamān; he carried out the summer expedition (against the Byzantines), reaching Salandū. During this raid Yāzamān died. The cause of his death was a fragment from a ballista stone that hit him in the ribs when he was standing at the fortress of Salandū. The army withdrew, although they were on the verge of taking it. Yāzamān expired on the road the next day, that is, Tuesday, the fourteenth of Rajab (October 23, 891). He was brought to Ṭarsūs on the shoulders of the troops and buried there.

Leading the pilgrimage this year was Hārūn b. Muḥammad al-Hāshimī.

184. This reverses Muslim practices which allow the drinking of certain slightly fermented beverages (*nabīdh*) but prohibit wine.

The Events of the Year

[2131]

279

(April 3, 892–March 22, 893)

Among the events taking place, the authorities decreed in Baghdad (Madīnat al-Salām) that no popular preachers, astrologers, or fortune-tellers should sit (and practice their trade) in the streets or in the Friday Mosque. Moreover, the booksellers were sworn not to trade in books of theology, polemics or philosophy.

On the twenty-eighth of al-Muḥarram, 279 (Sunday, April 30, 892), Jaʿfar al-Mufawwaḍ was stripped of his right to the throne. That same day, al-Muʿtaḍid was acknowledged as the heir apparent to succeed al-Muʿtamid. Letters about the deposition of Jaʿfar and the appointment of al-Muʿtaḍid were composed and sent to the provinces, and in the Friday sermon al-Muʿtaḍid was named as heir apparent. On behalf of al-Muʿtaḍid, letters were written to the governors and prefects to the effect that the Commander of the Faithful had named him heir to the throne and had transferred to him all the rights which al-Muwaffaq had had, to issue orders and prohibitions and to effect appointments and dismissals.

On the fifth of Rabīʿ II, 279 (Wednesday, May 8, 892), Jarādah, the secretary of Abū al-Ṣaqr, was seized. Al-Muwaffaq had sent Jarādah to Rāfi b. Harthamah, and he returned to Baghdad (Madīnat al-Salām) a few days before he was seized.

On the twenty fourth of Jumādā I, 279 (Tuesday, August 22, 892), Abū Ṭalḥah Manṣūr b. Muṣlim left Shahrazūr—it had been assigned to him. Both he and his secretary, ʿAqāmah, were seized and placed in prison.

On Saturday, the twenty first of Jumādā I, 279 (August 19, [2132]
892), a fierce battle broke in Ṭarsūs between Muḥammad b. Mūsā and Maknūn, the page of al-Muwaffaq's mawlā, Rāghib. The reason for this is as follows. Ṭughj b. Juff came upon Rāghib in Aleppo, and told him that Khumarawayh b. Aḥmad would like to see him. Moreover, on behalf of Khumarawayh, he promised Rāghib his heart's desire. At this, the latter left Aleppo for Egypt with five of his pages, while he dispatched his eunuch Maknūn, together with his available forces, funds, and weapons to Ṭarsūs. Ṭughj, meanwhile, had written to Muḥammad b. Mūsā al-Aʿraj, informing him that he had sent Rāghib away, and that everything Rāghib had in the way of money, arms, and pages was in the hands of Rāghib's servant Maknūn, and that the latter was already en route to Ṭarsūs. It was therefore incumbent upon al-Aʿraj to seize Maknūn and his men the moment they entered the city. And, indeed, no sooner did Maknūn enter Ṭarsūs, than al-Aʿraj attacked him, and seized him and all he had. However, the populace of Ṭarsūs intervened and fell upon al-Aʿraj, seizing the former and turning him over to Maknūn for imprisonment. Having learned that there was a plot against Rāghib, the people of Ṭarsūs wrote to Khumarawayh b. Aḥmad, informing him what al-Aʿraj had done, and that they had taken him into custody. They proposed, "Let Rāghib go free so that he may return to us. Then we will release al-Aʿraj." Khumarawayh then released Rāghib and sent him to Ṭarsūs along with Aḥmad b. Ṭughān who was to serve as governor of the border regions. At the same time, he dismissed al-Aʿraj from this post. When Rāghib reached Ṭarsūs, Muḥammad b. Mūsā al-Aʿraj was released, and Aḥmad b. Ṭughān entered Ṭarsūs, as governor of the city and the border regions, accompanied by Rāghib. They entered Ṭarsūs on Tuesday, the thirteenth of Shaʿbān (November 7, 892).

[2133] On Monday, the nineteenth of Rajab (October 14, 892), al-Muʿtamid passed away. He had spent Sunday drinking to excess on the river bank in the Ḥasanī Palace.[185] Then he had supper and overate. During the night he died. His reign, reportedly, lasted twenty-three years and six days.

185. For the Ḥasanī Palace in Baghdad, see Lassner, *Topography*, index, 321.

Bibliography of Cited Works

Primary Sources

al-Baghdādī, ʿAbd al-Qāhir b. Ṭāhir. *Al-Farq bayn al-firaq.* Edited by M. Badr. Cairo, 1910. Translated and annotated under the title *Moslem Schisms and Sects.* 2 vols. Vol. 1, K. Seelye. New York, 1920. Vol. 2, A. Halkin. Tel-Aviv, 1935.

al-Dhahabī, Muḥammad b. Aḥmad. *Kitāb tadhkirat al-ḥuffāẓ.* 5 vols. Hyderabad, 1915–16.

al-Dīnawarī, Aḥmad b. Dāwūd. *Kitāb al-akhbār al-ṭiwāl.* Edited by V. Guirgass. Leiden, 1888. Indices by I. Kratchkovsky (1912).

Fragmenta Historicorum Arabicorum. Edited by M.J. De Goeje. 2 vols. Leiden, 1869.

Ibn al-Athīr, ʿAlī b. Muḥammad. *Al-Kāmil fī al-taʾrīkh.* Edited by C.J. Tornberg. 12 vols. Leiden, 1851–76.

Ibn Ḥawqal, Abū al-Qāsim al-Nāṣibī. *Kitāb al-masālik wa al-mamālik.* Edited by M.J. De Goeje. Bibliotheca Geographorum Arabicorum No. 2. Leiden, 1851–76.

Ibn Ḥazm, ʿAlī b. Aḥmad. *Kitāb al-faṣl fī al-milal.* Cairo, 1317(1903). Translated and annotated by I. Friedlander under the title "The Heterodoxies of the Shiites." Journal of the American Oriental Society 28 (1907):1–80; 29 (1908):1–83.

Ibn al-Jawzī, ʿAbd al-Raḥmān b. ʿAlī. *Al-Muntaẓam fī taʾrīkh al-mulūk wa al-umam.* Edited by F. Krenkow. Vols. 52–10. Hyderabad, 1938–39.

Ibn Kathīr, Ismāʿīl b. ʿUmar. *Al-Bidāyah wa al-nihāyah.* 14 vols. Cairo, 1932–40.

Ibn Khallikān, Aḥmad b. Muḥammad. *Kitāb wafayāt al-aʿuān wa anbāʾ abnāʾ al-zamān.* Cairo, 1881. Translated and partially annotated by M.G. DeSlane under the title *Ibn Khallikān's Biographical Dictionary.* 4 vols. Paris and London, 1843–71.

Ibn Khayyāṭ, Khalīfah al-ʿUṣfurī. *Taʾrīkh.* Edited by A. al-ʿUmarī. 2 vols. Najaf, 1967.

Ibn Rustah, Aḥmad b. ʿUmar. *Kitāb al-aʿlāq al-nafīsah.* Edited by M.J. De Goeje. Bibliotheca Geographorum Arabicorum no. 7. Leiden.

Ibn Ṭabāṭabā, Muḥammad b. ʿAlī. *Al-Kitāb al-fakhrī fī al-ādāb al-sulṭāniyyah wa al-duwal al-Islāmiyyah.* Edited by H. Derebourg. Paris, 1895; Beirut, 1386(1966). Translated and annotated by E. Amar under the title *Histoire des dynasties musulmanes depuis la mort de Mahomet jusqu'à la chute du Khalifat ʿAbbāside de Baghdadz.* Paris, 1910. Beirut, 1386(1966).

Ibn Ṭahīr al-Baghdādī: see al-Baghdādī, ʿAbd al-Qāhir.

Ibn al-Ṭiqṭaqā: see Ibn Ṭabāṭabā.

al-Iṣṭakhrī, Ibrāhīm B. Muḥammad *Kitāb al-Masālik wa al-mamālik.* Edited by M.J. De Goeje. Bibliotheca Geographorum Arabicorum no. 1. Leiden, 1870, 1892.

———. *Risalāh ilā al-Fatḥ b. Khāqān fī manāqib al-Turk* wa *ʿāmmat jund al-khilāfah.* In *Rasāʾil al-Jaḥiẓ.* Edited by ʿA.M. Hārūn, vol. 1, 1–86. Cairo, 1964–65. A slightly different version in *Tria Opuscula,* edited by G. van Vloten, 1-56. Leiden, 1903.

Kitāb al-ʿuyūn: see *Fragmenta.*

al-Masʿūdī, ʿAlī b. al-Ḥusayn. *Murūj al-dhahab wa maʿādin al-jawāhir.* Edited and translated by C. Barbier de Meynard and P. de Courteille under the title *Les prairies d'or.* 9 vols. Paris, 1861–77. Edited by Y.A. Daghir in 4 vols. Beirut, 1385(1965).

———. *Kitāb al-tanbīh wa al-ishrāf.* Edited by M.J. De Goeje Bibliotheca Geographorum Arabicorum no. 8. Leiden, 1894.

al-Muqaddasī, Muḥammad b. Aḥmad. *Kitāb aḥsan al-taqāsīm fī maʿrifat al-aqālīm.* Edited by M.J. De Goeje. Bibliotheca Geographorum Arabicorum no. 3. Leiden, 1877.

al-Nawbakhtī, al-Ḥasan b. Mūsā. *Firaq al-Shīʿah.* Edited by H. Ritter. Bibliotheca Islamica no. 4. Istanbul, 1931.

Ps. Ibn Qutaybah. *Al-Imāmah wa al-siyāsah.* Edited by T.M. al-Zarīnī. 2 vols. in 1. Cairo(?), n.d.

Qazwīnī, Ḥamdallāh Mustawfī. *Nuzhat al-qulūb* (Persian). Edited by G. LeStrange. London, 1915. Translated by G. LeStrange under the title *The Geographical Part of the "Nuzhat al-Qulūb" of Qazwīnī.* Gibb Memorial Series. London, 1919.

al-Ṣābiʾ Hilāl b. al-Muḥassin. *Kitāb al-wuzarāʾ.* Edited by A. Farrāj. Beirut, 1958.

———. *Rusūm dār al-Khilāfah.* Edited by M. ʿAwad. Cairo, 1963.

al-Shahrastānī, Muḥammad b. ʿAbd al-Karīm. *Kitāb al-milal wa al-niḥal.* Cairo, 1317-1321 (1899-1903).

al-Ṭabarī, Muḥammad b. Jarīr. *Ta'rīkh al-rusul wa al-mulūk* (*Annales*). Edited by M.J. De Goeje *et al.* 13 vols. Leiden, 1879–1901.

al-Ya'qūbī, Aḥmad b. Abī Ya'qūb. *Kitāb al-buldān.* Edited by M.J. De Goeje. Bibliotheca Geographorum Arabicorum no. 7. Leiden, 1892. Translated and annotated by G. Wiet under the title *Les Pays.* Publication de l'Institut d'Études Orientales, No. 1. Cairo, 1937.

———. *Ta'rīkh* (*Historiae*). Edited by M. Th. Houtsma. Leiden, 1883.

Yāqūt, Ya'qūb b. 'Abdallāh. *Irshād al-arīb ilā ma'rifat al-adīb (Mu'jam al-udabā').* Edited by D.S. Marolìouth. Gibb Memorial Series, no. 6. London, 1907–31.

———. *Mu'jam al-buldān.* Edited by F. Wüstenfeld. 6 vols. Leipzig, 1866–73.

Secondary Sources

Ayalon, D. "Preliminary Remarks on the Mamlūk Military Institution in Islam." In *War Technology and Society in the Middle East,* edited by V. Parry and N. Yapp. Oxford, 1975.

———. *The Military Reforms of al-Mu'taṣim: Their Background and Consequences.* Private Circulation. Jerusalem, 1964.

Dozy, R. *Dictionaire détaillé des noms des vêtements chez les arabes.* Amsterdam, 1845.

———. *Supplément aux dictionnaires arabes.* 2 vols. Leyden and Paris, 1881.

Encyclopedia of Islam. Leyden and London, 1913–38. 2nd edition, 1954—.

Faris, N.A. and E. Potter. *Arab Archery.* Princeton, 1945.

Gabrieli, F. "La 'Risāla' di al-Ǧāḥiẓ sui Turchi." *Scritti in onore di G. Furlani,* 477–483. Revista degli Studi Orientali, no. 32. Rome, 1957.

Hassan, Z.M. *Les Tulunides, Étude de l'Egypte Musulmane à la fin du IX*ᵉ *siecle (868–905).* Paris, 1936.

Hellige, W. *Die Regenschaft al-Muwaffaqs.* Berlin, 1936.

Herzfeld, E. *Geschichte der Stadt Sama'ra.* Hamburg, 1948.

Hoenerbach, W. "Zur Heeresverwaltung der 'Abbāsiden. Studie uber Abulfarağ Qudāma: Dīwān al-gaiš." *Der Islam* 29 (1950):257–90.

Kindermann, H. *'Schiff' im Arabischen.* Bonn, 1934.

Lassner, J. *The Topography of Baghdad in the Early Middle Ages: Text and Studies.* Detroit, 1970.

Le Strange, G. *Baghdad During the 'Abbasid Caliphate.* London, 1900.

———. *Lands of the Eastern Caliphate.* Cambridge, 1905.

———. *Palestine Under the Moslems.* London, 1890.

Noeldeke, T. *Orientalische Skizzen.* Berlin, 1892. Translated by J.S. Black under the title *Sketches from Eastern History.* London, 1892.

Pellat, C. "Ǧaḥiẓ a Bagdād et à Sāmarrā." *Revista degli Studi Orientali* 27 (1952):48–67.

Pipes, D. *Slave Soldiers and Islam.* New Haven, 1981.

Popovic, A. *La révolte des esclaves en Iraq au IIIe/IX siecle.* Paris, 1976.

Salmon, G. *L'Introduction topographique à l'histoire de Baghdadh.* Paris, 1904.

Schwarzlose, F. *Die Waffen der Alten Araber.* Leipzig, 1886.

Shaban, M. *Islamic History: A New Interpretation.* 2 vols. Cambridge, 1971, 1976.

Sourdel, D. *Le Vizirat ʿAbbāside de 749 à 936* 2 vols. Damascus, 1959–60.

Wellhausen, J. *Die religios-politischen Oppositionspartien im alten Islam.* Berlin, 1901. Translated by R.C. Ostle and S.M. Walzer under the title *The Religio-Political Factions in Early Islam.* Amsterdam, 1975.

Zambauer, E. *Manual de généalogie et de chronologie pour l'histoire de Islam.* Hanover, 1927.

Index

The index contains all proper names of persons, places, tribal and other groups, as well as topographical data, occurring in the introduction, the text, and the footnotes. However, as far as the footnotes are concerned, only those names that belong to the medieval or earlier periods are listed.

The definite article, the abbreviation b. (for ibn, son) and bt. (for bint, daughter), and everything in parentheses are disregarded for the purposes of alphabetization. Where a name occurs in both the text and the footnotes on the same page, both page and footnote are given, separated by a comma. If it occurs only in the footnote, there is no comma.

A

Abbā 2, 4
ʿAbbāsids 170-71
ʿAbdasī 12, 21-22
ʿAbd al-ʿAzīz b. al-Muʿtamid 166
ʿAbd al-Malik b. Ṣaliḥ al-Hāshimī 78
ʿAbd al-Qays 129
ʿAbdallāh (Village) 14
ʿAbdallāh al-Khujustānī 5, 12, 25, 51, 72, 90
al-ʿAbdī 151
Abdūn b. Makhlad 141, 50
Abraham Messenger of God 7 n. 23, 64, 173
Abruk Bridge 2, 3
Abrūn 1
Abrusān 45, 72
Abū al-ʿAbbās al-ʿAlawī 146
al-ʿAbbās b. at Muwaffaq 12-26, 28-29, 31-32, 34, 38-39, 41-45, 47, 49-50, 62-63, 68, 70-72, 74-77, 87, 94, 102-106, 109, 111-115, 119-124, 126, 130, 133-36, 144-45, 147-50, 157-58, 165-66, 168
Abū Aḥmad, see al-Muwaffaq
Abū Aḥmad b. Muḥammad b. al-Furāt 169
Abū Amr al-Muhallabī 112
Abū al-Asad Canal 56
Abū Ḥamzah, see Nuṣayr
Abū ʿĪsā b. Sāʾid. b. Makhlad 150
Abū Jaʿfar al-Manṣūr, see al-Manṣūr (Caliph)
Abū al-Khaṣīb Canal 33-34, 36, 41-42, 44-45, 47, 49, 54-55, 59, 62, 70, 76, 91, 94-96, 99-103, 107-15, 117-19, 121-25, 128, 132-33, 135-36
Abū Laylā b. ʿAbd al-ʿAzīz 167
Abū al-Maghrāʾ b. Mūsā b. Zarārah 7, 50
Abū al-Mughīrah al-Makhzūmī 64, 79, 81

Abū Muqātil al-Zanjī 112
Abū al-Nidā' 28-29, 56, 85-86
Abū al-Qāsim, see Aḥmad b. Muḥammad b. Ismā'īl
Abū Salamah the Volunteer 129
Abū Sāj 1
Abū Al-Ṣaqr 162, 164-60, 173
Abū Talḥah Manṣūr b. Muslim 167-177
Abū Wathīlah, see Muḥammad b. Hishām al-Kirmānī
Adam 173
'Adī Canal 156
Aghartmish 1-4
Aḥmad b. 'Abdallāh al-Khujustānī 63-64, 78
Aḥmad b. 'Abd al-'Azīz b. Abī Dulaf 2, 5, 29, 72, 76, 153, 155, 159-61,169
Aḥmad b. al-Aṣbagh 72
Aḥmad al-Bardha'i 56
Aḥmad b. Dīnār 120
Aḥmad b. Jayghawayh 88
Aḥmad b. Junayd 70
Aḥmad b. Khāqān 89
Aḥmad b. Mahdī, see al-Jubbā'ī
Aḥmad b. Mālik b. Ṭawk 82, 98
Aḥmad b. Muḥammad b. al-Ḥanafiyyah 173-74
Aḥmad b. Muḥammad b. Ismā'il b. al-Ḥasan b. Zayd 6
Aḥmad b. Muḥammad al-Ṭā'ī 90-91, 147-148, 151, 156-157, 172
Aḥmad b. Mūsā b. Bughā 4-5
Aḥmad b. Mūsā b. Sa'īd al-Baṣrī 35, 68-70, 101, 113
Aḥmad b. Ṭughān al-'Ujaytī 175, 177
Aḥmad b. Ṭulūn 4, 6, 63, 78-79, 81-82, 88-89, 97, 123, 127, 144-45, 150-53, 160, 163
Aḥmad Zaranjī 54
al-Ahwāz 2-4, 7 n. 24, 11, 34-48, 49, 129, 139, 165
'Alī b. Abān al-Mullabi 2-4, 8-11, 24, 34-46, 38, 49, 52, 56, 58-61, 83-84, 92, 98, 104, 106, 112, 119-22, 130-31, 135-37, 151
'Alī b. Abī Ṭālib 170 n. 175
'Alī b. al-Ḥusayn b. Ja'far 146
'Alī b. al-Ḥusayn Kuftimur 78, 90
'Alī b. Jahshiyār 167
'Alī b. al-Layth 169
'Alī b. Muḥammad b. Mansūr b. Naṣr 157
'Alī b. 'Umar al-Nazzāb 69
'Alids 6, 113, 140 n. 137, 170
Aleppo 78,177
Alexandria 66
Āmid 7, 50
'Amīrah 44
'Amir page of Būdhā 40-41
'Amr b. al-Layth 1, 2, 5-6, 12, 51, 63-64, 66, 72, 78, 127, 147, 153, 155, 159, 160-61, 169
Āmul 5
Anatolikon 144
al-Anbār 90, 98

Andrayas 143-44
Ankalāy 8, 59, 62, 83-84, 87
94-96, 98, 104, 109, 112-14, 131, 134-48, 151
Antioch 81
Aqāmah 177
Arbaq 8
Armenia 7
Arzan 7
Asātakīn 1, 98
ʿAskar Mukram 2-3, 37
Rayḥān 133-34
ʿAyn Mushāsh 73

B

Bab al-Baḥr (Ṭarsūs) 81
Bab al-Bustān 167
Bab al-Jihād (Ṭarsūs) 81
Bab Khurāsān (Baghdad) 160
Bab al-Kūfah, see Kūfah Gate (Baghdad)
Bab Qalamyah 143
Bab al-Shammāsiyyah 97
Bab al-Ṭāq 167 nn. 165, 167, 168
Bādhibān 35
Badr page of al-Muʿtaḍid 18, 98, 108, 124, 126, 138-39, 143-52, 156-57, 159-62, 163-64, 166, 169, 173, 176
Badr page of al-Ṭā'īl 148
Bāduraya 144 n. 139, 157
Baghdad 1, 2, 5, 24, 29 n. 56, 38 n. 70, 56, 66, 72 n. 99, 78, 81-82, 88
Bahbūdh b. ʿAbd al-Wahhāb 2-3, 9-10, 36, 44, 48-50, 54, 62, 75-77, 82-83
al-Baḥrayn 129
Bakkār al-Hāshimī 78
Bakr (Tribe) 8
Balad 4 n. 9
Bālis 82
Banū al-Furāt 165
Banū Isrā'īl 171 n. 178
Banū Tamīm 4, 72
Bar Musāwir 20, 22, 25 (Canal) 26-28
Barātiq (Canal) 22, 25-26
Bardūdā 14-18, 25 (Canal) 29-30, 34
Barrtumartā (Bar Tumartā) 16
Basāmī 22
al-Bāsiyēn 36
Basmā 60
al-Baṣrah 15 n. 36, 38 n. 71, 40, 45 n. 78, 47 n. 80, 52 n. 86, 62, 68, 70-72, 107, 137
Baṣrah Gate (Baghdad) 150 n. 147, 151
Bathq Shīrīn 40-41, 56
Bayn al-Surayn 151 n. 130
Bayrūdh 4
Berbers 124, 162, 164
Bilam 8
Bilād al-Rūm 68 n. 94, 124
Blind tigris 33-34, 38-39, 41, 72 n. 109
Border Region 145
Būdan 78
Bughrāj 28-29, 47
Buktimur 5, 7, 46, 167
al-Bushīr 39
Bustān b. ʿĀmir 127
Bustān al-Hādī, see Bustān b. Mūsā
Bustān b. Maʿmar 127 n. 135
Bustān b. Mūsā b. Bughā 14
Bustān b. Mūsā al-Hādī 13

Bustān al-Zāhir 167 n. 166
Byzantine 1-2, 7, 79, 143-44, 145, 152-53, 157

C

Canals, See Nahr
Cappadocia 144
Christianity 173

D

al-Dabbāsīn 105, 107
Dahrshīr 20
Damascus 81-82, 98, 147 n. 144, 172
Dār Abī'Īsā 116, 119
Dār al-'Āmmah 37
Dār Ankalāy 32
Dār Al-Baṭṭīkh 152
Dār al-Karnabā'ī 119
Dār al-Muhallabī 119-22
Dār Musliḥ 109
Darabādh 98
Darmawayh al-Zanjī 137-38
Darustān 35
Daskarat al-Malik 145
Dawlāb 3
Daylam 47, 67
Dayr al-'Atīq 148
Dayr al-'Aqūl 13-14, 24
Dayr Jābīl 47, 83
Dayr al-'Ummāl 20
al-Dhawā'ibī 78, 150
Dīnawar 7
Diyālā 165
Diyār Muḍar 82, 124
Diyār Rabī'ah 1, 6-7
Dubbā 71
Dujayl Canal (al-Ahwāz) 38
Dujayl Road 164 n. 164
al-Dūr (Zanjid) 49
Dūr Sāmarrā 155

E

Egypt 81, 88-89, 147, 151, 169, 177
Euphrates 46, 52, 90, 98

F

al-Faḍl b. al-'Abbās al-'Abbāsī 90
al-Faḍl b. Mūsā b. Bughā 20, 47
Fam al-Ṣilḥ 14
al-Fandam 36
al-Faraj b. 'Uthmān 173
Farghānah 17, 71, 81, 124
Fārs 36, 66, 125, 150
Fārs b. Bughā 89
al-Fatḥ b. Khāqān 81
Fatḥ al-Sa'īdī 152
Fayḍ al-Baṣrah 71
Fazārah 63
al-Firk 13, 24, 165
Furāt al-Baṣrah 38, 47, 68

G

Gabriel 146, 173
al-Ghanawī 137
Great Swamp 52, 56, 69-71, 118, 137
Greeks 79

H

al-Ḥadath 79
al-Ḥadīthah 157
al-Ḥajjājiyyah 19

Ḥamdān, see Qarmaṭ
Ḥamdān b. Ḥamdūn 150
Ḥamdān al-Shārī 50
al-Hamdānī, see Ibrāhīm b. Ja'far
Hamadhān 29
Ḥannātīn 127
Ḥaramayn, see Mecca and al-Madīnah
al-Ḥarūn al-Hāshimī 78-80
Hārūn b. Muḥammad b. Isḥāq al-Hāshimī 11, 64, 127, 152, 154-55
Hārūn b. al-Muwaffaq 34, 38-39, 90-91, 98, 144
Hārūn al-Rashīd 7, n. 19, 33
Hārūn al-Shārī 150
al-Ḥasan b. Muḥammad al-'Uqayqī 5
b. Zayd 5-6, 144
Ḥasanī Palace (Baghdad) 178
Ḥasanids 50
Hashanaj 157
Hāshim servant of Ṣiddīq al-Farghānī 156
Hāshimites 141
al-Ḥawānīt 28-29
al-Ḥayr (Sāmarrā) 91
al-Hayṣam al-'Ijlī 53, 90-91, 171-172
Hirqlah 7
Ḥiṣn Arwakh 107
Homs 4, 78, 82
Ḥulwān 72, 98
Ḥurmūz b. Ṣābūr b. Ardashīr b. Bābāk 129 n. 146
al-Hurth 20
al-Ḥusayn b. Ismā'īl 148
al-Ḥusayn b. Ja'far b. Mūsā 146
al-Ḥusayn b. Ṭāḥir 12
al-Ḥusayn Ḥusaynids 90

I

Ibn 'Abbās al-Kilābī 78
Ibn Abī al-Sāj 2, 6, 7, 53, 78-79, 81, 90, 98, 148, 153-54, 160, 162, 167, 169
Ibn Ankalawayh 56
Ibn Da'bash 145
Ibn al-Fayyāḍ 165
Ibn Kundāj, see Isḥāq b. Kundājīq (Kundāj)
Ibn al-Makhzūmī 7
Ibn Mālik (Zanjd) 78
Ibn Ṣafwan al-'Uqaylī 5, 82, 98
Ibn al-Ṣaqlabī, see Ibn Ṣaqlabiyyah
Ibn Ṣaqlabiyyah 79
Ibn Shabath b. al-Ḥasan 72
Ibn Sim'ān, see Muhammad b. Sim'ān
Ibn Ṭulūn, see Aḥmad b. Ṭulūn
Ibn 'Umar Canal 56
Ibn al-Wāthiqī 167
Ibrāhīm b. Ja'far al-Hamdānī 49, 59, 83, 102-103, 128, 134, 136, 152
Ibrāhīm al-Khalījī 81
Ibrāhīm b. Muḥammad b. Ismā'īl al-Hashīmī (Burayh) 13
Īdhāj 129
Ifrīqiyyah 37
Iraq 63, 127, 142, 165
'Īsā al-Karkhī 4
'Īsā al-Nūsharī 168
'Īsā b. Mūsā al-Sha'rānī 62
'Īsā al-Shaykh 7, 50
'Īsā Shaykh b. Salīl 97
Isḥāq b. Ayyūb 7, 50
Isḥāq b. Ḥammād 13

Isḥāq b. Kundājīq (Kundāj) 4, 7, 50, 89-91, 97-98, 127, 145, 153-54
Isḥāq b. Muḥammad b. Yūsuf al-Jaʿfarī 6
Isḥāq b. Mūsā al-Shaʿrānī 62
Isḥāq b. al-Muʿtamid 166
Ishmael 7 n. 23
Ismāʿīl b. Bulbul 151
Ismaʿil b. Burayh al-Hāshimī 151
Ismaʿil b. Isḥāq 166-67
Iṣṭakhr 66

J

al-Jabal 159-60, 165
Jacobites (Kurds) 4
Jaʿfar al-Baghamardī 127
Jaʿfar b. Ibrāhīm al-Sajjān 65
Jaʿfar b. al-Mufawwaḍ 27, 38, 166, 168, 176
Jaʿfar b. Yaghlaʿuz 46
Jaʿfarawayh 2-3
Jaʿfarids 6, 90
Jaʿfariyyah 39
Jarjarāyā 14, 24
Jannābā 48, 54-55
Jarādah 176-77
Jawsaq Palace 91
Jawwāb 97
Jawwīth Bārūbah 52-53, 71
al-Jazīrah 4, 89
Jazzārīn 127
Jerusalem 174
Jesus, son of Mary 171, 173
John the Baptist 173
Jidda 73, 81
Jubbā 36
al-Jubbāʾī 14, 16-18, 29-31, 40, 49, 86-87, 96
Jūkā 35
Juʿlān 23
Jundīsābūr (Jundaysābūr) 2, 37
Jurjān 5

K

Kaʿbah 6
Kalwādhā 13 n. 32, 144 n. 139
al-Karaj 159
al-Karkh (Baghdad) 145, 151
Karkh Sāmarrā 4 n. 12, 157
Karmītah, see Qarmaṭ
al-Karnabāʾī, see Muḥammad b. Yaḥyā b. Saʿīd
Kārūn Canal, see Dujayl Canal (al-Ahwāz)
Kaskar 12 n. 27, 21 n. 44, 28
Kathīthah 28
Kayghalagh 1, 25, 72, 98
al-Khabīth (the Abominable One), see Zanj (Leader)
Khābūr 4 n. 13
Khafīf 18
Khalaf al-Farghānī 29, 81
al-Khalīl b. Abān 2-3, 9-10, 131
al-Khālil companion of al-Qalūṣ 69
al-Khālil Rīmāl 72
Khatarmīsh 89
Khazars 47
al-Khujustānī, see ʿAbdallāh al-Khujustānī
al-Khuld 145 n. 140, 167 n. 165
Khumarawayh b. Aḥmad b. Ṭulūn 88 n. 116, 147-48, 162, 177

Khurāsān 12, 51, 63, 90, 127, 147, 149, 157
Khusrūsābūr 18
Khussābūr 18 n. 41
Khuzistān 169
Kirmān 155
al-Kūfah 33, 157, 169, 172-73, 175
Kūfah Gate (Baghdad) 150 n. 147, 151, 162
al-Kuḥayl 88
Kumushjūr 20
Kurds 4, 8

L

Lū'lū' 4-5, 21, 78, 82, 89, 123-25, 130-32, 135, 153

M

al-Madā'in 13, 24, 166
Madbad 56
al-Madīnah 2 n. 4, 6, 90, 146-47, 161, 171 n. 178
Madīnat al-Salām, see Baghdad
Madīnat Sulayman b. Mūsā al-Sha'rānī 16, 25
al-Madiyān 16
al-Madhār 27
al-Madharā'ī 159
al-Maghrib 47
Main Bridge (Baghdad) 145 n. 140, 152, 159, 166 n. 165, 168
Main Thoroughfare (Baghdad) 168 n. 168
al-Makhzūmī, see Abū al-Mughīrah
Maknūn 177
Malaṭyah 79
Mālik b. Bishrān 68-70
al-Manīnah 56
al-Manṣūr Abū Ja'far ('Abbāsid Caliph) 15, 150
al-Manṣūrah 28
Mar'ash 79
Māsabadhān 98
Maskanayn 155
Maskīn 157
Masruqān 2
Masrūr al-Balkhī 2, 10, 35, 37, 47, 59, 62, 66, 106
Maṭar b. Jāmbi' 2, 3
Maṭbaq Prison (Baghdad) 159, 167
Mattūth 11
Māyān Rūdhān 49
al-Maymūnah 86
Māzarwān 16, 19-20
Mecca 2, 7, 63, 79, 81, 127, 147-48, 161
Mihrijānqadhaq 98
al-Mīshān 40
Miṣr 86
Monastery of the Virgins (Baghdad) 148 n. 145
Mosque of Ibrāhīm (Mecca) 64
Mosul 1, 2, 7, 89, 145, 159
Mu'ādh b. Muslim 54
al-Mubārak 38 n. 71
al-Mubārakah 103-04
al-Mufawwaḍ, see Ja'far al-Mufawwaḍ
Mufliḥ al-Turk 67
Muhadhhab 51
al-Muhallabī, see 'Alī b. Abān
Muḥammad b. Abān 49, 131
Muḥammad b. 'Abbās al-Kilābī 88

Muḥammad b. ʿAbdallāh b. Ṭāhir 151
Muḥammad b. Abī al-Sāj, see Ibn Abī al-Sāj
Muḥammad b. ʿAlī b. Ḥabīb al-Yashkarī 78
Muḥammad b. Dāwūd b. al-Jarrāḥ 172
Muḥammad b. al-Faḍl b. Sinān al-ʿIjlī 1
Muḥammad Ghānim b. al-Shāh 168
Muḥammad Ḥammād 13, 27, 28, 30, 31, 39, 41, 61, 71, 74, 139
Muḥammad Ḥārith al-ʿAmmī 55-56
Muḥammad al-Ḥasan al-ʿAnbarī 2, 4, 13, 27, 30-31, 39, 41, 70-71, 74, 91, 93, 98
Muḥammad b. Hishām al-Kirmānī 27, 31, 35
Muḥammad b. al-Ḥusayn Jaʿfar 146
Muḥammad b. Ibrāhīm Abū ʿĪsā 39-41, 113, 116
Muḥammad b. Kumushjūr 78
Muḥammad b. al-Layth 66
Muḥammad b. Mūsā b. Bughā 20, 47, 78
Muḥammad b. Mūsā al-Shaʿrānī 62
Muḥammad b. Mūsā b. Ṭulūn al-Aʿraj 177
Muḥammad b. Shuʿayb al-Ishtiyām 13-14, 16, 18-20, 22-24, 28
Muḥammad b. Simʿān 31, 67, 86, 93-94, 115
Muḥammad b. Sulaymān secretary of Abū al-Ṣaqr 167
Muhāmmad b. Ṭāhir 2 n. 13, 12, 51, 144, 147-48, 150-52
Muḥammad b. ʿUbaydallāh b. ʿAbdallāh b. Ṭāhir 81
Muḥammad b. ʿUbaydallāh b. Azarmard al-Kurdī 8-10, 37-38
Muḥammad b. Yaḥyā al-Kirmānī 10
Muḥammad b. Yaḥyā b. Saʿīd al-Karnabāʾī 35-36, 94-95
al-Mukharrim 145 n. 140, 167 n. 167
al-Mukhtārah 43
Muʾnis 18
Munkā 55
Muntāb 19, 41-42
Mūsā Daljawayh 22, 47
Mūsā son of Mufliḥ's sister 164
Mūsā b. Muḥammad al-Jaʿfarī 6
Mūsā client of al-Muwaffaq 67
Mūsā b. Utāmish 4
Musāwir al-Shārī 4
al-Mustaʿīn 2 n. 3
al-Muʿtaḍid, see Abū al-ʿAbbās b. al-Muwaffaq
al-Muʿtamid 51, 88-91, 97, 114, 144, 166-67, 178
al-Muʿtaṣim 91 n. 119
al-Muṭṭawiʿah 63, 76
al-Muwaffaq Abū Aḥmad 5 n. 14, 11, 13, 16, 22-24, 26-39, 41-57, 59-63, 65-71, 73-80, 81-88, 91-126, 129-140, 142, 144, 165-68, 177

al-Muwaffaqiyyah 48, 53, 58, 62, 66-67, 73, 84, 87-88, 100, 103, 105-07, 113, 116-17, 121, 131, 133, 139

N

Nadhīr 18
Nādir al-Aswad 135
Nahr Abān 14-15, 20 n. 43
Nahr ʿAbdallāh 58
Nahr Abī al-Khaṣīb, see Abū al-Khaṣīb Canal
Nahr Abī Shākir 104, 119, 130
Nahr ʿAdī 56
Nahr al-Amīr 15, 17, 19, 62, 70-72, 133-35
Nahr al-Atrāk 46, 58, 60
Nahr Bathq Shirīn 75
Nahr Bayān 49-50
Nahr Būq 144 n. 139
Nahr al-Dayr 56, 75
Nahr al-Dīnārī 68, 135
Nahr Dubays 71
Nahr Dujayl 38
Nahr Fahraj 137
Nahr al-Fayyāḍ 69-70
Nahr al-Gharbī 58-59, 62, 66, 71, 104-107, 125-26, 130
Nahr Ḥālah 47
Nahr ʿĪsā 145, 148, 167
Nahr al-Isḥāqī 73
Nahr Jaṭṭā 45-47, 136
Nahr Juwayy Kūr 66, 92, 104-06, 119, 130
Nahr Mahrūdh 30
Nahr al-Malik 149 n. 146
Nahr Maʿqil 40, 71, 75
Nahr al-Mar'ah 40-41, 56
Nahr al-Masīḥī 71-72
Nahr al-Māsawān 132
Nahr Maṭmah 47
Nahr al-Mubārak 38-39, 41-42, 45
Nahr al-Mughīrah 47, 83, 133
Nahr al-Mundhir 33
Nahr Munkā 59-60, 66, 84-85, 91, 106
Nahr al-Nāfidh 76
Nahr al-Qarīrī 132
Nahr al-Saʿīdī 76
Nahr al-Sidrah 2
Nahr al-Ṣilḥ 14-15
Nahr al-Ṣillah 160
Nahr b. Simʿān 61, 66
Nahr Sindād 17, 25
Nahr Sindādān (Sindād?) 47
Nahr al-Sufyānī 131, 133
Nahr al-Ubullah 71, 75-76
Nahr b. ʿUmar 53
Nahr al-ʿUmaysiyyin 126
Nahr ʿUtbah 68
Nahr al-Yahūdī 45, 63, 69-70, 76
Nahr Yazīd 40-41
al-Nahrawān 165
al-Nahrayn 173
Naṣībīn 1, 6, 50
Naṣr al-Rūmī 54
Naṣr al-Sindī 20
al-Naṣrānah 173
al-Naṣrāniyyah 164
al-Naṣriyyah 164 n. 164
Nile River 169
Noah 173
Nuṣayr Abū Ḥamzah 14-16, 18-19, 22-23, 25, 33-34, 39-41, 44-45, 47-50, 54, 59, 71, 96, 99

P

Palace of ʿAlī b. Jahshiyār 167
Palace of Ṣāʿid 168
Prophet Muḥammad 64, 146-47, 170, 173

Q

al-Qalūṣ, see Aḥmad b. Mūsā al-Baṣrī
Qanṭarat Arbuk 37
Qarmasīn 29
Qarmaṭ 172, see also Karmītah
Qarmaṭians 169-75
Qarqīsiyyā 5, 82, 98
Qarṭās 82, 87, 137
Qaryat al-Jawziyyah 30
Qaṣr ʿĪsā 71
Qaṣr al-Maʾmūn 38, 39
Qaṭrabbul 144, 157
Qayṣar b. Urkhuz 71
al-Qindal 48-49, 71-72, 77
Qinnasrīn 82
Qūmis 63 n. 92
Qumm 78
Qunnā 24
Quraj al-ʿAbbās 39
Qurbub 35
Qurrah 144
Quss Ḥathā 16
Qusyathā 39

R

Rabīʿah 50
Rāfiʿ b. Harthamah 90, 179
al-Rāfiqah 82
Rāhgib mawlā of al-Muwaffaq 177
Raḥbat Ṭawq 90, 98
Rāmhurmuz 7-8, 37, 137
al-Raml 16, 18
Ramlah 147 n. 144
al-Raqqah 5, 82, 124, 145, 152
Raʾs al-ʿAyn 4
al-Rashīd mawlā of al-Mawaffaq 47, 67, 104, 112, 119-20, 130
Rashīq al-Ḥajjājī 18, 59, 62, 71-73, 126
Rawāṭā 22
Rayḥān b. Ṣāliḥ al-Maghribī 62-63, 65
al-Rayy 1, 63
al-Rayyān 69
Riqq (Canal) 22
Round City (Baghdad) 150
al-Rūḥiyyah 70
al-Rūm 47
Rūmī b. Khashanaj 81
Rūmiyat al-Madāʾin 24
Rūmiyyah 24 n. 46
al-Ruṣāfah, see Ruṣāfat Wāsiṭ
al-Ruṣāfah (Baghdad) 145 n. 140, 167 n. 167, 168
Ruṣāfah Gate (Baghdad) 158
Ruṣāfat Wāsiṭ 17

S

Saʿd al-Aʿsar 147
Saʿd al-Aswad 39
Ṣādiq al-Farghānī 81
al-Ṣaffār, see ʿAmr b. al-Layth
Saʿīd b. al-ʿAbbās al-Kilābī 82
Ṣāʿid b. Makhlad 47, 66, 88-89, 91, 98, 123-24, 127, 130, 147, 168
Salamyah 78

Salandū 175
al-Sāmaghān 98
Sāmarrā 1, 5, 45 n. 79, 64, 88-91, 123, 127, 144, 150-51, 156-57
Ṣandal al-Zinjī 50
al-Sarī' 79
Sāriyyah 5
al-Sawād 169
Sayḥān 68
al-Ṣaymarah 29
al-Shāh b. Mīkāl 15, 20
Shahrābādh 4 n. 10
Shahrābān 149 n. 146
Shahrazūr 98, 177
al-Shammāsiyyah 13 n. 32, 97 n. 122, 168 n. 169
al-Sha'rānī, see Sulaymān b. Mūsā
Sharkab 72
Shibāb b. 'Alā' 70-71
Shibl b. Salīm 28, 29, 40-41, 56, 115-16, 130
Shīrāz 66
Shīrzād 25
al-Sīb 24
Ṣiddīq al-Farghānī 155-56
al-Ṣilḥ 24
Ṣilḥ Canal, see Nahr al-Ṣilḥ
Sīmā (Ṣaghrāj) 3, 6
Simnān 63
Sindād Canal, see Nahr Sindād
al-Ṣīniyyah 21, 28
Sīrāf 48
Sulaymān b. 'Abdallāh b. Ṭāhir 2
Sulaymān b. Jāmi' 14-17, 20, 26-30, 32-33, 41, 58-59, 61, 83-84, 86, 96-97, 99, 104, 106, 109, 113, 128, 131, 134, 136, 138, 151
Sulaymān b. Mūsā al-Sha'rānī 14-15, 20, 25-27, 62, 83, 114-115, 151
Sulayman b. Wahb 149
Sumayrā' 80
Sūq al-Ahwāz 37-38
Suq al-Ghanam 122
Suq al-Ḥusayn 101
Suq al-Khamīs 11, 15-16, 20-22, 25-26
Suq al-Thalāthā' 168
Suq Yaḥyā 145
al-Sūs 35-36, 169 n. 173
Syria 6, 79, 81, 97

T

Ṭabaristān 2 n. 3, 5, 47
Ṭaff 69
Tashlib 50
Ṭahīthā 17, 20, 28-30, 32-35, 39, 68
al-Ṭā'ī, see Aḥmad b. Muḥammad
al-Ṭā'if 81, 161
Takīn al-Bukhārī 2
Takshā al-Farghānī 81
Takrīt 88 n. 116
Tall Banī Shaqīq 160
Tall Basmā 1
Ṭalmajūr 1
Tanners Market (Baghdad) 145
Ṭāq Asmā' 167 n. 167
al-Tarmudān 70-71
Ṭarsūs 6, 81-82, 143, 148-49, 153, 162, 175, 177
Tarwiyyah Day 7
al-Tawāḥīn 148, 150
Teak workers (Baghdad) 145
Thābit b. Abī Dulaf 21

Thābit page of al-Muwaffaq 52-53, 60
al-Ṭīb 4 n. 13, 35, 169 n. 173
al-Ṭibā' 64
Tigris 12, 18, 20, 28, 33-34, 36, 38 n. 71, 40, 44, 51-53, 62, 67, 75, 83-85, 92-94, 114, 118, 120, 125-26, 133, 136-37, 139, 157, 165, 167 n. 165
Tombs of the Caliphs (Baghdad) 168 n. 170
Tīnak 89
Ṭughān al-Farghānī 81
Ṭughj b. Juff 177
Turks 47, 124
Tustar 2, 4, 37
Tūz 80

U

'Ubaydallāh b. 'Abdallāh b. Ṭāhir 1, 81, 160
'Ubaydallāh al-Hāshimī 151
'Ubaydallāh b. Muḥammad b. 'Ammār 39
'Ubaydallāh b. Sulaymān b. Wahb 169
al-Ubullah 39-40, 52 n. 86, 139
'Umar b. Sīmā 72
Umm Jabīb bt. al-Rashīd 34
Umm Kaskar 15 n. 37
Umm Wāsiṭ 15 n. 37
al-'Umr 15, 17, 20, 24

V

Vasil, see Ibn al-Ṣaqlabiyyah

W

Wādī, al-Qurā 6
Wādī al-Sūs 35
Waṣīf 'Alamdar 31, 33
Waṣīf al-Ḥijrā'ī 54, 55
Waṣīf al-Khādim 18, 162, 164-65, 169
Waṣīf Mūshkīr 166
Wāsiṭ 11 n. 26, 12 n. 27, 13-15, 20 nn. 42, 43, 24, 26, 32-35, 39, 40 n. 76, 41, 56, 78, 114, 139, 150-51, 169

Y

Yadkūtakīn b. Asātakīn 78
Yaḥyā b. Khālid b. Marwān 141, 142
Yaḥyā b. Muḥammad al-Aslamī 140, 143
Ya'lā b. Juhistār 47
Yaman (Tribe) 50
Yasār (Zanjid) 40
al-Yāsiriyyah 145
Yāzamān al-Khādim 81, 143, 149, 152-53, 155, 157, 162, 175
Yumn 18
Yūnus al-Khādim 164
Yusr 18
Yūsuf b. Abī al-Sāj, see Ibn Abī al-Sāj
Yūsuf b. Ya'qūb 7, 163

Z

al-Za'franiyyah 165
al-Zaghal 165, 169
Zanj 2-4, 6-7, 9-24, 26, 32-

34, 39-45, 49-61, 64, 66-67, 69, 71-72, 74, 76-77, 84-86, 88, 91-123, 125-26, 130-39, 152, 176
Zanj (Leader) 2-4, 6-12, 24-25, 27, 30-31, 33, 35-36, 40-47, 49-58, 60-62, 65-67, 69-71, 73-75, 77-78, 80, 82-83, 86, 88, 91-103, 106-107, 109-121, 123, 125-26, 128, 131-39, 175
Zanzibar 47
Zikrawayh 172
Zīrak 18-20, 25, 31, 34, 39-41, 44-45, 47, 50, 52-53, 56-57, 63, 66, 69, 86, 96, 109, 112, 114, 126
al-Ẓuhr 20